HAITIAN VODOU

ABOUT THE AUTHOR

Mambo Chita Tann ("Mambo T") is a priestess of Haitian Vodou and the head of La Sosyete Fòs Fè Yo Wè ("Strength Makes Them See Society"), a Vodou society based in both Haiti and the Midwestern United States. She has been practicing Vodou for more than a decade and was initiated into the Vodou priesthood in Haiti as a *mambo asogwe* in 2001.

In addition to her work with Vodou, Mambo T serves as the founder and current spiritual head of the Kemetic Orthodox Faith, a modern form of the pre-Christian ancient Egyptian religion. She is also a professional Egyptologist.

Mambo T's first full-length book was published in 1994, and she has authored a number of academic and mainstream articles, papers, and publications about ancient Egypt, Haitian Vodou, and other ancestral practices under her legal name, Tamara L. Siuda. She is a frequent speaker at academic and interfaith conferences and has been interviewed for various books, magazines, and television programs.

TO WRITE TO THE AUTHOR

If you wish to contact the author or would like more information about this book, please write to the author in care of Llewellyn Worldwide, and we will forward your request. Both the author and publisher appreciate hearing from you and learning of your enjoyment of this book and how it has helped you. Llewellyn Worldwide cannot guarantee that every letter written to the author can be answered, but all will be forwarded. Please write to:

Mambo Chita Tann
℅ Llewellyn Worldwide
2143 Wooddale Drive
Woodbury, MN 55125-2989
Please enclose a self-addressed stamped envelope for reply,
or $1.00 to cover costs. If outside the USA, enclose
an international postal reply coupon.

Many of Llewellyn's authors have websites with additional information and resources. For more information, please visit our website at http://www.llewellyn.com.

HAITIAN VODOU

An Introduction to Haiti's
Indigenous Spiritual Tradition

MAMBO CHITA TANN

Llewellyn Publications
Woodbury, Minnesota

FIRST EDITION
Sixth Printing, 2018

Book design by Bob Gaul
Cover art: Altar photo © Allan Spiers, Purple background © Rackermann/iStockphoto
Cover design by Adrienne Zimiga
Editing by Nicole Edman
Interior map and illustrations © Llewellyn Art Department

Llewellyn is a registered trademark of Llewellyn Worldwide Ltd.

Library of Congress Cataloging-in-Publication Data
Tann, Mambo Chita.
  Haitian Vodou : an introduction to Haiti's indigenous spiritual tradition / Mambo Chita Tann.
  — 1st ed. p. cm.
  Includes bibliographical references and index.
  ISBN 978-0-7387-3069-1
  1. Voodooism—Haiti. 2. Haiti—Religious life and customs. 3. Haiti—Religion. I. Title.
  BL2490.T36 2012
  299.6'75097294—dc23
                    2011031511

Llewellyn Worldwide Ltd. does not participate in, endorse, or have any authority or responsibility concerning private business transactions between our authors and the public.

  All mail addressed to the author is forwarded, but the publisher cannot, unless specifically instructed by the author, give out an address or phone number.
  Any Internet references contained in this work are current at publication time, but the publisher cannot guarantee that a specific location will continue to be maintained. Please refer to the publisher's website for links to authors' websites and other sources.

Llewellyn Publications
A Division of Llewellyn Worldwide Ltd.
2143 Wooddale Drive
Woodbury, MN 55125-2989
www.llewellyn.com

Printed in the United States of America

This book is dedicated with love to my godmother Daille and my maman-hounyo Sonia, resting in Ginen, and the people of Haiti, who welcomed me into their lives and culture, and took me in as one of their own.

CONTENTS

PART THREE: Seremoni: Haitian Vodou Ceremonies and Rites of Passage

APPENDICES

Acknowledgments

Aprè Bondye ("after God"), I thank Papa Legba Avadra for showing me why I should write this book and for opening all the doors for me to get it published. To my ancestors and spirits—African, European, and Haudenosaunee—I say thank you, I touch the ground, and I pour water for you.

I owe a great debt to many people for the reality of this book. First, I need to thank the Vodouisants of Jacmel and Cyvadier, Haiti, who welcomed me to their country when I traveled there for the first time in July 2001 for my first initiation into Haitian Vodou. I am deeply grateful for everything I learned about myself and about the Lwa from the various people I got to know or visited or shared ceremonies with during my trips to Jacmel. To all of you, living and dead, I say thank you, I touch the ground, and I pour water for you.

To my family in central Haiti, I owe an even deeper debt of gratitude. Mambo Fifi Ya Sezi, the late *maman-hounyo* Mambo Sonia *(Bondye bene li)*, Houngan Patrick, Houngan François, and all the other people of Sosyete Sipote Ki Di and Sosyete La Fraîcheur. La Fraîcheur Belle Fleur Guinea in Port-Au-Prince permitted my initiation into their lineage and made it a beautiful experience that I will always hold in my heart. I am forever grateful for my godfather, Houngan Benicés, and for my godmother, the late Mambo Daille *(Bondye bene li)*. To all of you, living and dead, I say thank you, I touch the ground, and I pour water for you.

Most of all, I must acknowledge and thank Papa Loko Atisou and my initiatory mother, Il Fok Sa Yabofè Bon Mambo, Marie Carmel Charles, daughter of Mambo Jacqueline Anne-Marie Lubin, daughter of Kitonmin Bon Mambo Felicia Louis-Romain, who brought me out of the water and into the light.

Additional thanks are due to my editor Elysia Gallo at Llewellyn, who showed up from nowhere at a conference presentation I was doing and told me she believed we could publish a book respectful to Haitians, yet still answering the questions of a wider audience. Editor Nicole Edman put up with my sudden loss of serial commas at production time. Adrienne Zimiga, my Llewellyn artist (I have my own artist? How cool is that!) must be commended for her excellent taste in NDN star quilts and a mean *veve*, in addition to her excellent illustration work. Thank you for everything.

I need to thank the "test subjects": my friends and family who read drafts, asked questions, and gave support and advice. In addition to my *sosyete* members who helped in that process, Cristina and Craig offered copyedits when my eyes were crossing, Leah and Andy provided their shoulders for me to lean (and cry) on, and J sent me poetry and kept me smiling. I couldn't have done this without you, and I love you all.

Love and thanks for my "kids" in Sosyete Fòs Fè Yo Wè: my *hounsi* Garth, Ti-Marie, Eujenia, Mon, Scott, Salvador (oops—I mean Matt!), and Geoffrey; and my godson, Russell, for keeping me on track while I tried to work two jobs and get this book done at the same time. I'm also grateful for the contributions of my other *sosyete* members and friends who aren't initiates, who are simply curious about Haitian Vodou, or who intend to initiate in the future. Their questions and interest fueled the basis of the "beginners" part of this book, and I kept them at the front of my mind as I wrote.

Mesi anpil pou tout mwen sonje, tout mwen pa sonje.

To all those I remember and any I haven't remembered, many thanks.

Chita Tann Bon Mambo (Tamara L. Siuda)
14 November, 2011

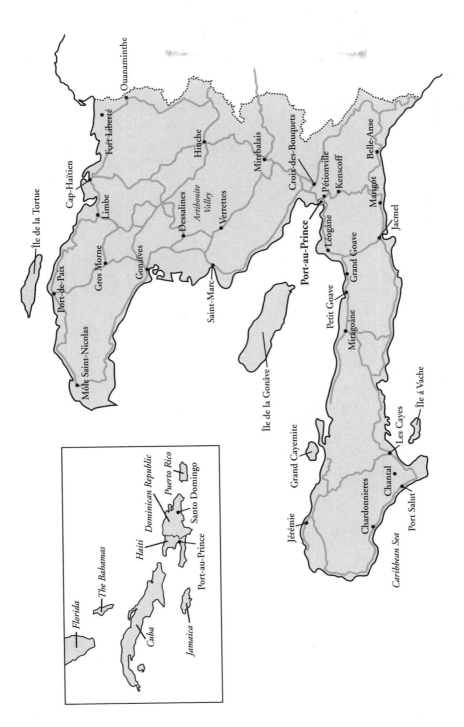

Île de la Tortue

Ouanaminthe

Fort Liberté

Cap-Haïtien

Hinche

Mirebalais

Croix-des-Bouquets

Belle-Anse

Pétionville

Kenscoff

Marigot

Limbe

Dessalines

Artibonite
Valley

Verrettes

Port-au-Prince

Jacmel

Port-de-Paix

Gros Morne

Gonaïves

Léogâne

Grand Goave

Saint-Marc

Môle Saint-Nicolas

Petit Goave

Miragoâne

Île de la Gonâve

Île à Vache

Grand Cayemite

Les Cayes

Jérémie

Chardonnieres

Chantal

Port Salut

Caribbean Sea

Florida

The Bahamas

Dominican Republic

Puerto Rico

Santo Domingo

Haiti

Port-au-Prince

Cuba

Jamaica

Introduction

I remember my godmother, Mambo Daille, as I saw her on my last trip to Haiti, almost exactly four years before the earthquake struck that took her life. When I came out of the *djevo* (the sanctuary where candidates for the Haitian Vodou initiation ceremonies called *Kanzo* are ritually secluded) on Sunday morning to attend Mass and receive my name as a priestess in the Vodou lineage, she was standing right there, shining in her brand-new clothes, tiny next to my very-tall godfather. I remember she spent a whole lot of time fussing over whether or not she thought Mama Sonia had done a good enough job of making me look good for my baptism, and she kept straightening my hat. She was impressed with the scarab beads that had been worked into the final few inches of my *kòlye* (a long beaded necklace worn by *Kanzo* initiates) in a show of respect to the ancient Egyptian gods and spirits of my Kemetic Orthodox faith. The photos that Mambo Fifi took didn't turn out very well, but Daille looked so happy and so proud, even though my Kreyòl was lousy, my French wasn't much better, and we could only communicate in broken sentences. She held on to me during the whole ceremony and both of us started crying when she told the priest what my name was: Chita Tann, a name that has been passed down more than once in our lineage and a name I still believe I have a long way to go before I live up to it.

Four years later, on January 12, 2010, Mambo Daille would be doing exactly what she did for me at my baptism—looking out for the little ones—when the earthquake came. She was inside cooking for the children of the *lakou* of Sipote Ki Di, the *peristil* in Port-au-Prince where I had been initiated in the area near the National Palace where my family lives. Daille shouted for everyone to get out, pushing them toward the doorway. Everyone got out safely except Mambo Marie-Michele, a baby boy named Hans-Cadou, and my godmother. It would be more than a week before they were all pulled from the rubble of the buildings that fell. Days of frantic phone calls with messages like "there's concrete everywhere" and "we can't find them" and "they won't let us go in" and "we just can't get to her" broke my heart.

The earthquake and its aftermath provided the impetus for me to write this book, as I grew increasingly angry and horrified in the days following January 12 at the misunderstandings and outright lies being spoken on television and even among my friends and acquaintances about Haitians and the practice of Haitian Vodou. But it was thinking about Mambo Daille and Marie-Michelle and Hans-Cadou—and three-year-old Noushka, who died a few weeks later of the injuries she sustained in the quake—that pushed me into making it happen. It's easy to make all kinds of generalizations about people whose lives you will never know or understand when you can sit in a comfortable room with permanent electricity and reliably clean water and three hundred channels on the satellite. When you know those people—when you call those people family—you want to make sure others know the truth about them and, in this case, honor their memory as best you can.

This book is not going to explain everything about Haitian Vodou. Such a task could not be done in one or one hundred books, nor could it all be written down. Vodou is part of the living, breathing, growing experience of millions of people every day, both native Haitians inside and outside of Haiti and those non-Haitians such as myself who have been given the privilege and the honor to be invited to be part of their world. Haitian Vodou, just like the Haitian people, is in no danger of dying out. It does not need to be preserved in books. It does not need to be explained to people outside of its experience because it is not a practice that seeks converts or even really cares what people who are outside it think about it. Haitian Vodou has suffered from the same losses, outright thefts, lies, and mischaracterizations that the people of Haiti have suffered since even before the world's first black democracy was founded more than two centuries ago.

Yet there is still a need to talk about Haitian Vodou and to move non-Haitians toward something other than ignorance. As the world confronts the way it has treated and continues to treat Haiti and her people, it is time for that same world to confront its misunderstandings of Haiti's culture. Haitian Vodou is a central part of that culture, even if individual Haitians do not necessarily practice. While I cannot explain everything about Haitian Vodou in these pages, I hope that I will be able to set out an understanding of what it is and is not, a basic structure of its practice, and a description of what its spirits and ceremonies are like. I provide material for further exploration in the appendices in the form of other books and cultural resources. For readers who are seriously contemplating Vodou service, I outline ways in which you can get further involved in a respectful and appropriate manner. I hope this book proves respectful to the people and culture of Haiti, to the spirits of Vodou themselves, and to the people who practice Haitian Vodou, including my family. Last but not least, I hope this book can be one small but appropriate addition to the body of knowledge that fights against ignorance as Haiti and Haitian Vodou move onward into a better future.

To fulfill my intentions, I've organized this book into three parts. Part 1 talks about what Haitian Vodou is (and is not), from its development and history (Chapter 1) into a brief explanation of its tenets and basic practices (Chapter 2). Chapter 3 touches on the subjects that everyone wants to know about in Haitian Vodou, even those (like "voodoo dolls" and zombies) that have little or nothing to do with our practices, and others (like trance possession) that seem to be a source of endless fascination. Part 2 delves into the nature and identities of the Lwa, the various spiritual beings who are served "under God" within Haitian Vodou practice. This part is divided into four chapters, each of which addresses a major division, or grouping, of spirits. In Part 3, I discuss how Haitian Vodou is practiced, both formally in ceremonies and informally in both personal practice and with magic. You'll learn how Vodou is organized and how its members are trained. The final chapter of Part 3 gives some ideas and background for those who might be interested in observing a Haitian Vodou ceremony or getting involved in Vodou in other ways.

Four appendices are also provided in addition to the information in the basic chapters. Appendix A is a full glossary of all the Kreyòl and other terms used in the book. Kreyòl (also called Haitian Creole) is one of Haiti's two official languages. Its pronunciation follows French and so does much of its vocabulary, though its spellings and word order sometimes differ, as befits a syncretic language comprising both French and various West and Central African vocabulary and grammar. A basic timeline of Haiti's history (a sort of abbreviated form of the material presented in Chapter 1) makes up Appendix B, and Appendix C provides copies of the Catholic prayers used at the beginning of every Haitian Vodou ceremony, in both English and French. Appendix D provides correspondences for various Lwa. A thorough book list is also provided for further reading, along with some Internet resources for learning more about Haiti and Haitian Vodou.

About Indigenous Spiritual Traditions and Cultural Appropriation

While I was writing this book, a fellow Vodouisant, who is a native Haitian, showed me a video by of a pair of Americans who had recently returned from Haiti. They claimed to be Haitian Vodou priests and the video was of a ritual they had performed. More shocking to me than their unrecognizable and somewhat offensive "Vodou ceremony"—which contained nothing at all of the things I have been taught to do for the spirits—was an interview included after the ceremony. In it, they were asked about why they had decided to initiate in Haitian Vodou. One of the two spent several minutes rolling his eyes and disparaging Haiti as a horrible place. When the interviewer seemed confused by this behavior and questioned it, the man added that "Vodou, though, is wonderful," and that upon his return to the United States, he had decided that his spiritual calling in life was to "bring back the spirituality of Haitian Vodou so nobody *ever* has to go to Haiti to get it again."

While I would like to think his statement was meant with good intentions, I greatly suspect it was not. Such a mindset is indicative of a particular way of thinking that many people in the First World are accustomed to. This way of thinking derives from the combined results of European, North American, and South American history—a cultural and religious extension of the social and political "winner take all" rules that often dictate human interaction. The term "cultural appropriation" is used to describe the practice of taking what one likes of another person or group's cultural beliefs and practices without being part of that culture or having any interest in becoming part of it—or even necessarily understanding it.

Simply put, cultural appropriation is a form of bigotry. Unfortunately, because of the way some people are culturally conditioned or choose to think about each other, it is not always recognized as such. Haitians are not the only people to be treated with a "we hate you but love your things" mentality. Many indigenous cultures have suffered cultural damage through this sort of "dangerous savage" myth over the centuries, where what was good about various indigenous cultures was taken while its origins were suppressed or forgotten, and what was bad about them was overemphasized so those taking the good things could justify their actions.

Over time, as people came to understand the inherent bigotry and greed of such behaviors and beliefs, they often became replaced with something that was supposedly better but was in fact just as insidious. This new myth, encouraged by an eighteenth-century philosopher named Rousseau, was of the "noble savage." Indigenous people were transformed from dangerous savages into relics of a utopian past that would never survive; since theirs was a dying breed, certain elements of their cultures and spiritualities needed to be taken and "saved" on their behalf. However, as thinking people, we should not be fooled. This was still cultural appropriation, covered in a cloak of caretaking self-righteousness.

Occasionally, and strangely enough, outsiders to Haitian Vodou have managed to invoke both the concept of the dangerous savage and the noble savage at the same time. Such paradox fills the pages of William Seabrook's 1929 *The Magic Island,* a horrible book that provides the foundation for many fictional accounts, plays, movies, and other "information" concerning Haiti and Haitian Vodou. Witness a passage from two side-by-side paragraphs:

> [T]he literary-traditional white stranger who spied from hiding in the forest, had such a one lurked nearby, would have seen all the wildest tales of Voodoo [sic] fiction justified: in the red light of torches which made the moon turn pale, leaping, screaming, writhing black bodies, blood-maddened, sex-maddened, god-maddened, drunken, whirled and danced their dark saturnalia...

> Thus also my unspying eyes beheld this scene in actuality, but I did not experience the revulsion which literary tradition prescribes. It was savage and abandoned, but it seemed to me magnificent and not devoid of a certain beauty. Something inside myself awoke and responded to it. These, of course, were individual emotional reactions, perhaps deplorable in a supposedly civilized person ...

> —*The Magic Island*,
> Paragon House, New York, 1989 reprint, page 42

Haitians may request the help of people outside their country and culture—after the earthquake of January 2010 and other current events in Haiti, this is more common—however, Haitians are not, nor have they ever been, helpless. They are not dangerous savages whose beautiful spirituality needs to be saved from depravity. Neither are they noble savages who need salvation, or to be taught to be more like the people of (insert country or culture here). Haitian Vodou is not in any danger of dying out. It is practiced by millions of people every day, inside and outside of Haiti, and even by non-Haitians such as myself. Vodou does not need me, or you, or anyone else in order to thrive. Outsiders do not need to preserve Haitian Vodou for future generations or save it from itself; it is quite capable of taking care of itself, just as the people who came together to create it are and have been since the first days of the island nation they created.

Many who read this book—perhaps the majority of my readers—will not be Haitians or even know a Haitian in their personal lives. Despite this, there is no reason you cannot be interested in Haitian Vodou, or, if the spirits should permit you, learn how to practice it. This applies no matter who you are or where you come from, no matter how light or dark your skin is, or what religious or cultural background you come from. At no time, however, must you forget that you are a guest of Haiti and her people as you learn about this tradition, until such time as you might initiate or otherwise become part of a Haitian Vodou *sosyete,* or "family." As a guest of this cultural system, you *must* be conscious of the long and often ugly treatment Haiti has received from outsiders; you must also be respectful of Haitians' natural reticence to trust strangers in light of that treatment.

These are some hard but simple facts that anyone who is not Haitian but is interested in Haitian Vodou must understand. Never forget that Haiti has no obligation to accept you, no matter how sincere you are or how respectfully you promise to act. Haitian Vodou, the people of Vodou (Vodouisants), and the Lwa owe you nothing and have no obligation to respond to your questions or your interest. If you are not a Haitian, you simply do not have an inherent right to own or borrow Haiti's spirituality, in whole or in part. Haitian Vodou is not an object you can pack in your suitcase and bring home, like the man in the video thought he could do. If you are blessed to be permitted to enter Haitian culture and/or tradition, that choice won't be up to you. Your only choice in the matter will be to accept that invitation (or not).

There will be people (myself included, for at least part of the time I spent working on this book) who think that maybe it's not the place of someone who was not born in Haiti to speak about Haitian Vodou. In fact, at one point during this writing I considered abandoning it, or at least encouraging my native Haitian elders in the tradition to write the book instead. After a lot of prayer and discussion, both to my spirits and to my elders, it was decided I should continue working on the manuscript but that they would read everything I wrote. With their guidance, I've done my best to set out a basic understanding of Haitian Vodou's cultural and religious concepts along with an explanation of their cultural context.

I can only hope I have interpreted their teachings and their advice properly, and I take full responsibility for any errors or cultural misunderstandings I may introduce through my own biases, conscious and otherwise. While I have been involved in the Haitian Vodou tradition for a little more than fifteen years, and an initiate for a decade of that, I am not arrogant enough to think I know everything there is to know. Vodou is a way of life, and my life's not over yet, so I couldn't possibly know it all.

Should you become involved in Haitian Vodou in any manner, or should you find yourself a part of a Vodou house someday, you will not be alone in your practice. In fact, you will *never* be alone in your practice, because Haitian Vodou is by its nature a family-oriented practice. From the time that it began in the early days of Haiti—from its origins in the earlier practices of the Taino Indians and the various enslaved peoples of western and central Africa—Haitian Vodou was never a solitary tradition. It was, and still is, a cultural and spiritual practice embraced by many, many people. While there are some elements that can be experienced by oneself, the majority of principles and practice of Haitian Vodou simply cannot be separated from their family and community emphasis.

If you're reading this book in hopes of learning something about the Lwa with the intention of appropriating their worship for use in a non-Vodou spiritual or magical practice, please understand that this book was not written for that purpose. While I do intend this book to be informative, so you can tell the difference between good and bad information about Haitian Vodou, I have no intention of encouraging eclectic use or service to the Lwa within other spiritual formats or religious traditions such as Wicca or Neopaganism. While Haitian Vodou is itself the result of a unique combination of beliefs and practices from different people and locations, it achieved its current form and being through struggle and centuries of practice. It is now its own tradition and deserves to be respected as such. Haiti has already lost enough over the last three hundred years; from her original people to her freedom to her resources to the lives of her children, Haiti has given and given and given. You do not have the right to take what is not given freely, and while Haitians are likely to be more than happy to share their spiritual heritage with you, you must respect that generosity. Do not take what is not yours unless and until you are given permission to do so. Sincerity and good intentions never excuse cultural theft.

Please accept this book with a full understanding of who is writing it and why, and with a bit of thought toward your own cultural background and biases as you read. Approach the subject, and the Lwa, with the respect that is due to Haiti's people and the results may surprise you.

PART ONE

What Is Haitian Vodou?

The word *Vodou* (pronounced voo-DOO or voh-DOO) comes from *Vodu* (sometimes spelled *Vodun* but pronounced the same way), a Fon word used to describe the spirits served by that West African people.

Haitian Vodou, then, is the ancestral magical practice of peoples descended from and/or influenced by the Vodu priesthood of West Africa, particularly those who were forcibly removed to work as slaves on the Caribbean island of Hispaniola (modern-day Haiti and the Dominican Republic). Haiti is named for *Ayiti* (EYE-ee-tee, "motherland" or "mountain land"), the name the indigenous Taino and Arawak peoples used for their island, which Christopher Columbus renamed Hispaniola ("Little Spain") in honor of his Spanish royal patrons.

We spell the word *Vodou* according to the grammatical rules of *Kreyòl* (or Haitian Creole), Haiti's official language and the language Vodou service is generally conducted in. The French often spell it *Voudou* or *Voudoun*, and in the United States it is often spelled *Voodoo*. In this book, I will use the *Vodou* spelling, as it is the current Kreyòl spelling and it provides a good way to distinguish Haitian Vodou from forms and derivatives of West African Vodu practiced outside Haiti, such as the very famous New Orleans Voodoo tradition.

In English, we refer to a person who practices Vodou as a *Vodouisant* (voh-DOO-wee-ZAHN), after the French word for the same term. The Kreyòl spelling of Vodouisant is *Vodouwizan,* but Haitians also universally recognize the French spelling. Bear in mind that the term is not necessarily accurate, since the use of the word *Vodou* itself differs inside and outside of the practice, as I will explain in the next section.

Is Vodou a Religion?

While many people outside Haiti refer to Vodou as a religion, if you ask a Haitian what his religion is, he is most likely to say "I'm Catholic." In fact, a running joke in Haiti says the country is 90 percent Catholic, 10 percent Protestant … and 100 percent Vodou! It is interesting—and telling—that Haitians themselves do not use the "V" word very often. The practice of Vodou is most commonly referred to within Haiti, and by Haitians living outside Haiti, not as Vodou but as *sèvi Lwa,* or "serving the Lwa." Rather than being called a Vodouisant, a Haitian who practices Vodou is either re-ferred to by their initiatory rank (see Chapter 10) or simply says *mwen sèvi Lwa* (moo-en SAY-vee luh-WA, "I serve the Lwa"). The term Lwa (lo-WAH or luh-WA), the most common term used to name the group of spirits served in Haitian Vodou, will be explained in great detail in Part 2.

Vodou is thus not really a body of *beliefs,* but a body of *practices* that illustrate particular beliefs. It is not a religion so much as a way of life, or a form of relationship and service in addition to religious practice, that one performs to one's ancestral dead (the *mo*) and family spirits (the Lwa). While the vast majority of Vodouisants profess the Roman Catholic faith and Vodou ceremonies contain Catholic elements and imagery (such as prayers to Mary and Jesus and the images of saints), it is possible to be a Vodouisant and not a Catholic, or even a Christian. What is necessary, though, is the belief in a Creator divinity and a series of lesser non-human spirits provided by that Creator to help mankind. In Vodou, we refer to the universal Creator as Bondye (bon-dYAY, only two syllables, "The Good God") and as Gran Mèt (gron MET, "the Great Master"). Bondye is hon-ored before all the ancestors and any other spirits, who are given service *aprè Bondye* (ah-PRAY bon-dYAY, "after God").

Why Do Vodou?

In Haiti, people usually practice Vodou because they have been born into Vodouisant families, and they will begin to serve the Lwa even as children. Occasionally—and more commonly as Haiti becomes increasingly urbanized and Haitians leave their hometowns and families for other countries—they may come to Vodou later in life or with other people who are not necessarily related by blood. Sometimes, a forgotten family Lwa calls them in some way to service, through a dream or a vision, or even a possession during a Vodou ceremony. Outside Haiti, non-Haitians are also being called to serve the Lwa more and more frequently as time goes by. Why this is happening, we don't quite understand, but the Lwa are happy to call people to their service and it doesn't seem to matter whether you are Haitian or not. If you are sincere in answering the call to serve the Lwa, you are welcome in Haitian Vodou, no matter who you are or where you come from.

Haitians are traditionally very pragmatic and thus serve the Lwa primarily to derive benefits from that service. Everything from a sense of spiritual well-being to wealth, health, and security have been attributed to the service of Vodou spirits. Many Haitians serve personal or family Lwa along with the more widely recognized Lwa of the traditional groupings of Rada (rah-DAH, the ancestral African and indigenous spirits), Petro (peh-TRO or peh-TWOH, the spirits of the Haitian Revolution and variations on some of the Rada Lwa), and Gede (gay-DAY, the non-ancestral or archetypal dead). Lwa come and go, change over time and service, and new Lwa are coming into existence all the time (for example, the Gede are a family of Lwa associated with dead humans who have been forgotten by their families and have thus become archetypal ancestors accessible to everyone). In-depth definitions and discussions of the Rada, Petro, and Gede Lwa follow in Part 2 of this book. For now, let's go back to the beginning—the beginning of Haiti and therefore of Haitian Vodou.

Zo li mache, li mache, li mache…
("The bones, they walk,
they walk, they walk…")
—From the *Djo* prayer sung during the
opening of most Haitian Vodou ceremonies

ONE

Zo Li Mache:
How Haiti—and Haitian
Vodou—Came to Be

One of the great loves of my life is history, and if you didn't know that before you began this chapter, you'll certainly be convinced by the time you're done. Many people, especially those who are interested in spirituality or magic, will probably take one look at this lengthy chapter, roll their eyes, and start thumbing ahead to the chapters about Vodou magic and the Lwa.

That would be a mistake. I strongly believe that if you really want to understand what Haitian Vodou is, you need to spend a little time learning about where it comes from and how it developed into what it is today. *Zansèt-yo* (zon-SET YO, "the ancestors") are central to understanding Vodou. Both the indigenous Taino and the transplanted African people who made Haiti the world's first black republic honored their ancestors in very special ways, both inside and outside of religious ceremonies. The history of Haiti, in addition to introducing you to the culture and worldview that created the practices of Haitian Vodou, also created some of our Lwa. Historical figures, including the revolutionary generals L'Ouverture and Dessalines; *maroon* (guerilla rebel) leaders like Makandal; Mayanét and Boukman, the Vodou priests who led the Bwa Kayiman ceremonies; and even the infamous Haitian President-for-Life François "Papa Doc" Duvalier are—or were at some time—equated with or actually granted status as Lwa.

Just as a Haitian Vodou ceremony begins with a ritual recitation of the history of one's lineage and concludes with a song that begins by talking about how the "bones (ancestors) are walking," this book begins with a recitation of history. Light a white candle and listen as I sing of the land of mountains where the bones still walk.

Ayiti

In December 1492, Columbus arrived on the island that contains the modern nation of Haiti. At the time, the island known as *Ayiti* (EYE-tee or EYE-ee-tee, "original land" or "mountain land") to its inhabitants was populated by the Taino (or Tayino) people. There is academic disagreement about whether or not the Taino are or are not part of the larger Arawak designation, known primarily from the nearby island of Trinidad, Guyana, and from the northern portion of South America. Some books refer to these "Indians" (Columbus's term for all the native peoples of the Western Hemisphere, after the destination he mistakenly thought he had reached) as Taino-Arawak or simply as Arawak, but all we know for certain is that they called themselves Taino and that they had some different cultural concepts than other nearby Arawak peoples. Until a few hundred years before the arrival of Europeans, Ayiti was also populated by a smaller tribe called the Ciboney (a Taino word for "people living in caves"). By the time Columbus made landfall at a Taino settlement in northern Ayiti, the Ciboney had been driven out of most of the island except for a few isolated areas in the north and west, and the survivors had long departed to Cuba.

Columbus promptly renamed the island Hispaniola in honor of his Spanish patrons and set his crews to work reaping the resources of the newfound paradise. Noticing the gold jewelry the eager, friendly natives wore and generously shared with their white visitors, he hoped to find such gold on the island, and so set up permanent settlements to seek for such wealth. They didn't know that the gold the natives wore was likely small bits found in rivers or traded from neighboring islands; the Taino had no gold mining operations.

As the Spaniards had not brought women with them on their ships, many of the voyagers married or took Taino women to have their children after they settled in Ayiti, resulting in a considerable mixed-race population. Within thirty years of the Spanish landfall, smallpox would virtually erase the Taino from Ayiti, as the island people had no natural immunity to that disease or other viruses that came with the conquerors. Additionally, those natives who were unsuccessful in rising up against the Spaniards were killed, sold into slavery, or escaped into the mountains and founded settlements as *maroons* (a word derived from the Spanish *cimarron,* "runaway"). The *maroon* settlements would figure importantly years later, during the Haitian Revolution.

When the conquerors learned there were no significant gold deposits in Ayiti—after killing many natives on the assumption that they were merely refusing to show the Spaniards where their mines were—they switched their emphasis to the *encomienda* (en-KO-myen-da, "plantation") system to farm for agricultural riches. By 1650 CE, when the Spaniards essentially ran out of native slaves to staff the cotton, tobacco (a Taino word adopted into modern languages), sugar cane, coffee, and indigo *encomiendas,* the Spanish crown authorized the importation of new slaves from Africa to make up the difference.

Voyage from *Ginen:* The Africans Arrive

Less than a decade after Columbus's first arrival, a small group of African slaves was introduced to Hispaniola from various West and Central African nations. These homelands are immortalized in mythical form in Haitian Vodou under the collective name *Ginen* (sometimes also spelled *Ginen, Ginè,* or *Guinea* but always pronounced GEE-nay with a hard *g* as in the word *go*), after the traditional name of the region of West

Africa where these slaves were placed on ships headed to the New World. The importation process accelerated in 1516, when approximately fifteen thousand slaves were transferred to Hispaniola from other slave-laden areas in the Caribbean.

Within a year of this massive island transfer—and after acknowledging Taino population losses due to sickness and revolt—King Charles I of Spain signed a formal contract to ship slaves directly from Africa to Hispaniola, and the Voyage from Ginen began in earnest. Hispaniola's labor demands instituted a new triangular trade system, whereby African kings and merchants received European luxury goods and weapons in return for slaves (who were prisoners of war, debtors, enemies of the state, rivals, criminals, or members of neighboring tribes raided for profit, sometimes with the help of European slave raiders). In the second leg of this arrangement, the slaves were shipped across the "middle passage" of the Atlantic to Hispaniola and sold in the slave markets there. Finally, the raw goods harvested by Hispaniola's slaves, including sugar (and molasses and rum derived from sugar), cotton, tobacco, cacao, and coffee, were shipped to Europe. As Hispaniola's fertile lands were covered with plantations and demand for the island's goods grew, the need for more and more people to work the plantations pushed the island's slave population to an extraordinary size over the next two centuries, growing almost faster than the harvests they worked.

Hispaniola's African slaves came from all walks of life and backgrounds, and were men, women, and children of all ages and classes. They hailed from many different areas and nations across western, central, and northern Africa and beyond. As the anthropologist Harold Courlander noted:

> There were Senegalese, Foulas, Poulards, Sosos, Bambarras, Kiambaras, Mandingos and Yolofs from north-west Africa. There were Aradas, Mahis, Haoussas [*sic*], Ibos, Anagos [*sic*] or Yorubas, Bini, Takwas, Fidas, Amines, Fantis, Agouas, Sobos, Limbas, and Adjas from the coast and interior of the great bulge of Africa. From Angola and the Congo basin came the Solongos, the Mayombes, the Moundongues [*sic*], the Bumbas, the Kangas, and others. Although there is no official

record, Haitians themselves say that there were also those tall people known as the Jangheys, or Dinkas, from the region of the Upper Nile, and Bagandas from Uganda. A few proper names that have survived, such as Ras Mede, suggest that there may have been men from Ethiopia among them. Old slavers' records show that numerous shipments were made from Madagascar and Mozambique on the East African coast.

—*The Drum and the Hoe: Life and Lore of the Haitian People,* University of California Press, Berkeley, CA, 1960, page 4

Slavery and Liberation: The Haitian Revolution (Part I)

Slavery reached incredible proportions in Hispaniola. By the time the French and Spanish divided the island between themselves in the Treaty of Ryswick of 1697 and the western third of the island was renamed Saint-Domingue, thousands of Africans had already arrived in Saint-Domingue and Santo Domingo (the Spanish name for the island's eastern two-thirds) to work the plantations. Throughout the early years of the eighteenth century, the French would improve agricultural technology in Saint-Domingue to such degree that their colony supplied 60 percent of the world's coffee and 40 percent of its sugar and was the wealthiest colony in the New World.

Life for an African in Saint-Domingue was brutal and short. Most slaves died within a few years of arrival. By 1720, there were eight thousand new slaves arriving in Saint-Domingue every year. As thousands of slaves were imported to keep up with production and replace those slaves lost to death escape, the ratio of slaves to free men kept changing. By the time of the French Revolution in 1789, there were eight to ten African slaves for every single free man in the colony of Saint-Domingue.

Effectively, twenty thousand white landowners, or *grands blancs* (GRON blonn, "big whites"), and white merchants and middle-class freedmen, or *petits blancs* (peh-TEE blonn, "little whites"), found themselves outnumbered by thirty thousand free *gens de couleur* (zhen DAY ko-LURR, "people of color," the mixed-race descendants of *blancs* of both classes and

African slaves). Additionally, both kinds of white colonists and the *gens de couleur* together were pitiful in number in comparison to Saint-Domingue's population of nearly five hundred thousand enslaved Africans.

This imbalance—and real or perceived threats between the various economic classes these different ethnic groups represented—caused a particular tension to develop in the colony. The *gens de couleur* had no desire to be equated with Africans because of their slave status (not their skin color), and thus defined themselves by class first rather than color. As there were already two well-defined classes of white colonists, *blancs* defined themselves by skin color first and class second. Thus, Saint-Domingue's *blancs* equated the *gens de couleur* with the slave population, as "blacks" in their minds. Mixed-race colonists thus existed in a difficult and uncomfortable world: they did not want to be considered African, but they weren't "white enough" (in the minds of the *blancs)* to warrant equal rights under the law. Three separate kinds of hostility and mistrust were based solely on skin tone: between *blancs* and *gens de couleur*, between *gens de couleur* and African slaves, and between *blancs* and African slaves. These prejudices became defining characteristics of the Saint-Domingue experience and would haunt the island for the rest of its history.

In Paris during 1789, the French government informed a *gens de couleur* delegation led by Julien Raimond and Vincent Ogé that all of Saint-Domingue's free citizens—including *gens de couleur*—had the same legal rights to property and elections. Both the *grands blancs* and the *petits blancs* were threatened by this decision, thinking it would only be a small step for their numerous (and profitable) African slaves to desire their freedom too. The two classes of white colonists united in refusal to recognize the *gens de couleur* as equals and rejected the order from Paris. In the autumn of 1790, a small resistance movement led by Ogé and his followers near the northern city of Cap Français was put down by white government forces. Ogé and his fellow leaders were executed in a gruesome, public "breaking on the wheel" in early 1791.

While the execution of the *gens de couleur* rebels provided a strong push for revolution among mixed-race colonists, Saint-Domingue's black slaves had been making small but significant moves toward throwing off both their white AND mixed-race masters for some time. Throughout the eighteenth century, the *maroon* colonies in Hispaniola's mountains—comprised of the descendants of Taino and mixed-race rebels who had escaped slavery during the Spanish occupation, as well as new arrivals of escaped African slaves on a continual basis over the intervening 150 years—raided plantations and took more slaves back with them to Saint-Domingue's mountainous interior.

One of the most famous *maroon* leaders was François Makandal, who established networks between various *maroon* groups and African slaves still living and working on the plantations. Makandal personally led a slave rebellion in Saint-Domingue between 1751 and 1757. In 1758, he was captured by the French and burned at the stake, but the *maroons* continued to harass plantation owners and to provide a safe haven for any slave who managed to escape. Both real and idealized concepts of *maroon* life and philosophy had profound impact on the development of Haitian Vodou, and African and Taino religious practices both played important parts in Makandal's movement. To this day, his last name is cognate to "poisoner" in several languages—Makandal's most feared method of killing plantation owners was to instruct slaves to administer various plant poisons to their food, to blow poisonous powders in their faces, or to scatter poisons where they might walk barefoot or otherwise touch them.

Bwa Kayiman Ceremony and Revolt

A few months after the end of the *gens de couleur* revolt, in August 1791, the revolution had truly come. How it really began is not easy to tell, since the events preceding the Haitian Revolution are shrouded in secrecy, legend, propaganda, and the natural confusion of many stories written after the fact and long before modern visual media. It is generally agreed that several meetings were held between slave groups in the north-central Plaine du Nord, the richest plantation land in all of Saint-Domingue, to plan an insurrection to take over the colony and gain freedom once and for all. Legend states that a Vodou ceremony dedicated to the Petro spirits was held on August 14 in Bwa Kayiman (BWAH kay-ee-MON, "Alligator Woods"; *Bois Caïman* in French) under the leadership of a *mambo* (mom-BO, a Vodou priestess) called Mayanèt and a former African slave turned *maroon* leader and *houngan* (oon-GAHN, a Vodou priest) named Boukman from the colony of Jamaica. According to that legend, Mayanèt, Boukman, and the gathered slave leaders offered one of Hispaniola's native wild pigs to the spirits and drank some of its blood in order to seal themselves in a pact to achieve their freedom. Some versions of the Bwa Kayiman legend suggest that a Petro Lwa named Ezili Danto was given the sacrificed pig; others say that Danto was actually a human being at the time—one of the slaves who attended the ceremony and helped with the sacrifice—and that she would later become a Petro Lwa alongside Mambo Mayanèt.

Regardless of the particulars of the meeting at Bwa Kayiman, violence broke out all over the Plaine du Nord within a few days of that and other slave meetings. Within ten days, the entire northern province of Saint-Domingue was under siege. While the *grands blancs* and *gens de couleur* slave owners were well armed, sheer numbers overcame them. Over the next two months, more than four thousand slave owners would be killed and hundreds of plantations burned to the ground. By 1792, the rebel slaves had complete control over one-third of Saint-Domingue and were continuing to push into other parts of the colony.

Back in France, the news of Saint-Domingue's revolt was received with terror. France had its own problems due to the ongoing changes of the French Revolution; the reasonable concern that the *grands blancs* in Saint-Domingue were starting to look to the British and the newly formed United States for support; and its own increased hostilities with Great Britain, against which it would declare war the following year. The French made a significant appeal to the colony's *gens de couleur,* many of whom were also wealthy slave owners. In hope that Saint-Domingue's mixed-race class would make peace with the two classes of whites so all three groups could join forces to put down the more serious slave revolt, France declared the *gens de couleur* of Saint-Domingue full citizens, holding all the same rights as white people. The move sent shockwaves throughout the colony as well as the rest of the white, slave-owning Western Hemisphere. At the same time, France sent a small military force to Saint-Domingue to help stop the slave rebellion.

The French gambit failed. Instead of siding with the *gens de couleur,* the colony's white government—with the full backing of both classes of white colonists—refused to recognize the *gens de couleur* a second time and repudiated France, appealing to Great Britain to protect them from the rebel slaves and agreeing to permit Great Britain to declare Saint-Domingue its own colony instead. To add insult to injury, the Spanish—who still controlled the eastern portion of the island as the colony of Santo Domingo—immediately joined the British and the united white forces against France. By 1793, the French realized they could not fight slaves *and* traitorous white colonists *and* the British *and* the Spanish all at the same time... so in an even more surprising turn of events, they decided to side with the slaves.

The Enemy of My Enemy: The Haitian Revolution (Part II)

On August 29, 1793, a French commissioner named Sonthonax, having lost half his soldiers, freed all African slaves within his jurisdiction in Saint-Domingue, and then supplied them with arms. Around the same time, General Toussaint L'Ouverture, a literate black former slave said to be a grandson of the king of Allada (the kingdom from whence Vodou's Rada nation is derived), abandoned his position as a freedman in the Spanish army, which had been sent to assist the *blancs* against Saint-Domingue's slaves. After negotiations with the French government—complete with promises that they would continue to guarantee the Africans their freedom if the British and Spanish were driven out of the colony—L'Ouverture repositioned himself as a French loyalist. As general of the united French and rebel forces, he led his troops against both the incoming Spaniards and the *blancs* and *gens de couleur* they had already been fighting.

A month later, the British arrived in Saint-Domingue in real numbers. The colony's white plantation owners welcomed them with open arms, expecting that their agreement to reinstate black slavery and strip the *gens de couleur* of all rights they had been granted under French rule would be kept. The French responded by supporting L'Ouverture and his army in a formal war against the British between 1794 and 1801. By the time this secondary war against the British began, the Haitian Revolution had already claimed the lives of at least twenty-four thousand white colonists and *gens de couleur,* and nearly four times that many African slaves.

L'Ouverture was able to push both the British and the Spanish out of Saint-Domingue. While his army (forged from a coalition of African slaves, some *gens de couleur,* and French troops) fought for the French, and while L'Ouverture himself had been promoted to major-general of all French forces in the colony, he realized that the question of slavery across the entire island would not be answered by simply breaking the plantations. He knew that the *gens de couleur* hated African slaves even more than they hated Saint-Domingue's white colonists and would never side with the slaves on a permanent basis.

In 1798, once the British had been routed from Saint-Domingue and withdrew, L'Ouverture led his forces into the neighboring Spanish colony of Santo Domingo. By the early part of 1801, he had liberated its slaves as well. L'Ouverture followed his assault by declaring all slaves on Hispaniola free people on January 3, 1801, in the first declaration of emancipation in the Western Hemisphere. After returning to Saint-Domingue, the general wrote a constitution declaring himself governor for life and setting up a pro-French (yet mostly autonomous) state, which he ruled for a short period without opposition.

But the French, now under Napoleon Bonaparte, were not ready to give up this jewel of their colonial crown. Instead of congratulating his successful major-general, Napoleon sent a huge army of eighty-two thousand soldiers under Charles Leclerc to order L'Ouverture to restore full control of Saint-Domingue to France. Predictably, the *gens de couleur*—even some of those who had become part of L'Ouverture's army and government— welcomed the French, and the general watched as his mixed-race friends and allies joined with both the remaining white colonists and the incoming French against him; it appeared the promise of money outweighed the reality of freedom. After successfully fighting off Leclerc's forces for a time, L'Ouverture agreed to a parley meeting on June 7, 1802. Instead of negotiations toward ending hostilities, the parley was a trap. L'Ouverture was captured and shipped back to France, where he would die in a prison less than a year later.

Without L'Ouverture to lead the army of freed slaves, one of his lieutenants, Jean-Jacques Dessalines, rose to take his place. The next two years would intensify the bloodbath in Saint-Domingue. Dessalines—who was not known for diplomacy and had already made his reputation as a brave, hot warrior in contrast to L'Ouverture's cooler style of military discipline—gave the French eight days to evacuate the capital of Port-au-Prince. The French military and wealthy colonists both took Dessalines's warning seriously, and most fled the island forever. Some of these refugees ended up in Cuba; others went back to France or journeyed north to settle in French-speaking areas of the United States, including Louisiana. A major defeat for the French near Cap-Français at Vertières; a British naval blockade; defections of French forces to the slaves' campaign after dishonorable actions by Leclerc's successor the Vicomte de Rochambeau; and the loss of French influence in the New World after the Louisiana Purchase all contributed to end Napoleon's attempt to put the former slaves of Saint-Domingue back to work.

After killing more than fifty thousand French soldiers and thousands of white colonists, *gens de couleur,* and British and Spanish forces in earlier stages of its long fight for freedom—and the additional deaths of an estimated one hundred thousand African slaves in the process—the world's first black republic would finally be born on January 1, 1804. The nation of Haiti (sometimes spelled Haïti, from the French spelling of the ancient Taino name of the island) was the first independent country in the Caribbean and Latin America, and the only country in the world at that time to gain independence via a successful slave revolt.

From Revolution to ... Nowhere

Jean-Jacques Dessalines, elected Governor-General for Life by his rebel leader peers, began his rule with the declaration that no slave owner (and furthermore no European) would ever control the land again. According to legend, he punctuated this resolution by taking the French tricolor, the flag of Saint-Domingue, and removing its central white stripe, leaving only the blue and the red sections for his goddaughter to sew together to create a new Haitian flag. Following up that symbolic removal, Dessalines proceeded to purge Haiti of all former slave owners who had not taken advantage of his suggestion that they leave the country. The next two months saw widespread executions. Knowing some of the *grands blancs* had managed to escape, Dessalines declared an end to the hunt just long enough for remaining white slave owners to emerge from hiding—and then had them killed as well.

Dessalines's treatment of the *grands blancs* has been recorded in various ways over time in various Haitian and world histories. Some histories portray him as a wild and violent maniac who hated white men and relished opportunities to kill them throughout and after the revolution. Others have suggested such a reading is biased toward the slave owners' perspective and ignores the reality of hundreds of years of enslaving human beings on Hispaniola as a significant moral crime, a crime that Dessalines considered punishable by death.

There is an important distinction between reading Dessalines's history as "he imposed capital punishment on slave owners" and "he killed white people," and unfortunately the latter is often how histories of Dessalines (and by extension the Haitian Revolution) have been written. In history, while his contemporary Napoleon Bonaparte is a war hero who happened to be responsible for people dying, Dessalines is often described as a "violent savage," a rebel rather than a hero, a slave who enjoys killing and murders his masters with impunity. Depictions of Dessalines also differ between Haitians and non-Haitians. In Haiti, Dessalines is a hero; Papa Dessalines is the father of his country and even became a Lwa. Outside Haiti, history focuses on how Dessalines treated French colonists and ignores the atrocities both of slavery itself (Dessalines himself had been a slave, remember) and genocides committed by Leclerc and Rochambeau against the Haitians during the revolution.

Reading Dessalines's own words shows that despite pre-conceived notions, Haiti's first ruler was both thoughtful and fair. Not only did his constitution declare full freedom of religion (L'Ouverture had enforced Catholicism), Dessalines also declared that there was to be no more racism in Haiti. His 1804 constitution specified that all citizens of Haiti, regardless of their ethnic origin or skin color, were to be considered black. And indeed, in Kreyòl, the word for "person" is *neg* (nehg), which is the same word as the word for the color black. Even the Polish and German immigrants remaining in Haiti, who were permitted to stay in the country because they were not former slave owners were considered to be black people (*neg*) under the constitution. This is a surprising event if you believe that Dessalines hated white people and wanted them all dead.

Dessalines's decision to declare all people equal and reduce Haiti's number of classes to one was well-received—except among the country's remaining *gens de couleur*, who still chafed at the idea of being equated with Africans. Despite all of Dessalines's efforts to break the skin-color castes of Saint-Domingue and finally unite its multicultural people, subtle and blatant hostility and discrimination between light-skinned and dark-skinned Haitians continues into the current day, although it has no legal backing.

From 1804, when Dessalines had himself crowned Emperor Jacques I (after Napoleon did the same back in France), dissent and dissatisfaction with the way the new country was developing grew, particularly among the *gens de couleur* concentrated mostly in the southern third of Haiti. A failed attempt to regain control over Santo Domingo, along with other despotic behaviors including the reinstatement of a form of compulsory labor not so different from the plantation slavery of the French colony, shook the army's confidence in their new emperor and tensions began to rise. In late 1806, when Haiti's predominantly lighter-skinned south rose up in revolt against its darker-skinned north, instead of supporting their leader, Dessalines's mixed-race generals had him murdered on his way to battle. Once again, a precedent was set—this time for a repetitive history of military coups and/ or assassinations between people of differing skin tones.

The North, Christophe State and Kingdom of Haiti

After Dessalines, Haiti was briefly divided in rule. Initially, L'Ouverture's friend, black general, and former slave Henri Christophe was elected president, but he was given no powers by the coup that elected him. In retaliation, he retreated to the Plaine du Nord and started his own independent government in the north. In 1811, Christophe declared himself King Henri I, the "first monarch of the New World" according to edict, and proceeded in the same manner as Dessalines had done. He renamed the important northern port city of Cap-Français "Cap Henri" in his own honor and instituted a peerage, granting land and titles to friends and allies. He also renamed the State of Haiti as the Kingdom of Haiti.

Henri I tried to restore Haiti's broken infrastructure and economy by forcing his subjects to work on corvee labor systems building roads, palaces, and the Citadelle La Ferrière, a giant fortress on the northern coast. Additionally, King Henri forced his people to work plantations, and then went to the extraordinary step of importing more Africans to work them when the economy failed to prosper quickly enough. On October 8, 1820, the 53-year-old despot king committed suicide at the palace of Sans Souci right before he was to be removed in a coup. He was buried at the fortress built by the people he had returned to a condition of near-slavery. His family survived to be influential into the future: a grandson, Pierre Nord Alexis, would be President of Haiti from 1902 to 1908, and his great-great-great granddaughter, Michèle Bennett, married the twentieth-century Haitian President Jean-Claude "Baby Doc" Duvalier.

The South, Pétion's State and Republic of Haiti

In the south, at the same time as King Henri was making plans to follow in Dessalines's footsteps, new rulership was founded by *gen de couleur* General Alexandre Pétion, the son of a Frenchman and a mixed-race mother. Pétion had already made a name for himself as an ally and sometime rival of Toussaint L'Ouverture during the revolution; when the *gens de couleur* stopped supporting the slaves, so did Pétion. For a brief time, Pétion was exiled in France, only to return to Saint-Domingue with Leclerc's army in 1802.

After the French double-crossed L'Ouverture in 1802, Pétion pledged his loyalty to the rebel leadership by siding with Dessalines and helping to retake Port-au-Prince. When Dessalines was assassinated (historians argue about whether or not Pétion was directly involved), Pétion and Christophe fought over how Haiti should be governed. While Christophe favored an autocratic government in the same model as Dessalines's failed attempt at ruling the country, Pétion felt a democratic republic would provide a better future for Haiti and her people. Their disagreement mirrored larger disagreements within the nation itself: south versus north, *gens de couleur* versus former slaves.

Unable to resolve their differences, the two men divided the country between themselves in 1810. While Christophe remade himself as King Henri in the north, Pétion was elected President of the State of Haiti in the south. Pétion tried to expand his democracy by redistributing land to individual owners, parceling tiny plots from old plantations to both peasants and allies, and starting a cycle of small-scale subsistence farming. While such generosity earned the new president many admirers, it crushed the already-broken economy, and the State of Haiti began to falter. Meanwhile, King Henri's northern kingdom prospered so much it was recognized by Britain and the United States as the "real" Haiti.

By 1816, in reaction to attempts to curtail his authority, Pétion declared himself President for Life. Two years later he disbanded his parliament in a last-ditch effort to control political power and push for conquering the oppressed (but more economically successful) northern land of King Henri. Pétion would not live to see the end of Henri's reign; he died of yellow fever in 1818. Pétion's successor, President Jean-Pierre Boyer, got off to a good start: he started the coup that caused Henri's suicide and then reunited Haiti in 1820.

Restitution to France, Final Division of Hispaniola

Boyer then invaded Santo Domingo (called *Haiti Español* or "Spanish Haiti" at this time) with fifty thousand soldiers in 1821, and consolidated his power over the entire island of Hispaniola on February 9, 1822.

President Boyer controlled both Haiti and Spanish Haiti from 1822 to 1843, trying to strike a balance between popular but risky land redistribution and the demands of his allies and the black and mixed-race leaders he needed to impress. In 1825, France offered to recognize Boyer's government and Haiti as a legitimate and independent country—but only if Haiti was willing to pay for the privilege, with a massive sum of 150 million francs (equivalent to $21.7 billion in current U.S. dollars) to be paid over five years. Perhaps because the offer was delivered by a dozen French warships with their hundreds of cannons pointed at Haiti's capital, or perhaps for some other reason, Boyer signed the agreement. He then took out a loan of 30 million francs from the French to cover the first installment, dealing a terrible blow to the Haitian economy in the process, and starting a perpetual cycle of staggering international debt, paired with dwindling agricultural resources to pay for that debt. An attempt to appease Haiti's peasants by redistributing even more valuable plantation land for subsistence farming only made things worse, and in 1843, a serious earthquake provided impetus for another revolution. Boyer left Haiti after his own government ousted him, and he died in exile in France seven years later.

Haiti's next president, mixed-race Charles Rivière-Hérard, did not even last a year. He lost control of Spanish Haiti within months, and the island would remain divided from then on: with French- and Kreyòl-speaking Haiti in the west, and the Spanish-speaking Dominican Republic in the east. Again—as under Dessalines and Christophe—Haiti's predominantly mixed-race south rose up in rebellion, but this time, the north did not come to save the president; it, too, mounted a revolt. Hérard fled to Jamaica and died in exile.

***

The rest of the nineteenth century in Haiti would be a history of repeated infighting between Haitians of various skin colors and economic backgrounds, coups, assassinations, misguided attempts at monarchy and/or dictatorships, and meddling by European and American powers. Almost without exception, the heads of state during Haiti's first century as an independent nation alternated between black descendants of African slaves and mixed-race descendants of the *gens de couleur*. With only one notable exception in President Saget, no ruler served a complete term. It is notable that President Geffrard teamed up with the Vatican to destroy Vodou temples and objects after a young girl was murdered, forcing Vodou to move underground for a time.

- Phillippe Guerrier (May 1844–Apr. 1845, died in office of natural causes)

- Jean-Louis Pierrot (Apr. 1845–Mar. 1846, removed in coup)

- Jean-Baptiste Riché (Mar. 1846–Feb. 1847, assassinated)

- Faustin Soulouque "Emperor Faustin I" (Mar. 1847–Aug. 1849 as president; Aug. 1849–Jan. 1859 as emperor, removed in coup)

- Fabre-Nicholas Geffrard (January 1859–August 1867, removed in coup)

- Sylvain Salnave (May 1867–Dec. 1869, removed in coup)

- Jean-Nicolas Nissage Saget (Dec. 1869–May 1874, only president to serve full elected term, retired)

- Michel Domingue (Jun. 1874–Apr. 1876, removed in coup)

- Pierre-Théoma Boisrond-Canal (Apr. 1876–Jul. 1879; Aug.–Oct. 1888; and May–Dec. 1902, resigned under pressure each time)

- Joseph Lamothe (Jul. 1879–Oct. 1879, removed in coup)

- Lysius Salomon (Oct. 1879–Aug. 1888, removed in coup)

- François Denys Légitime (Oct. 1888–Aug. 1889, forced to resign)

- Monpoint Jeune (Aug.–Oct. 1889, removed in coup)

- Florvil Hyppolite (Oct. 1889–Mar. 1896, died in office)

- Tirésias Antoine Auguste Simon Sam (Mar. 1896–May 1902, resigned)

Haiti in the Twentieth Century: Corruption and Occupation

Pierre Nord Alexis, the illegitimate grandson of King Henri I, took power as President of Haiti with the assistance of the United States at the end of 1902. By that time, Haiti had already suffered a century of more than a dozen different governments; war, unification with, and loss of control of its eastern neighbor; systematic agricultural failure due to ever-increasing subsistence farming; massive international debt; lack of tangible support from any other country; and continuing serious divisions between the descendants of the *gens de couleur* and the black slaves who had originally fought the *blancs,* and then each other, in the Haitian Revolution. The tumultuous opening of the twentieth century set the stage for the second century of Haitian history. Unfortunately for Haiti, Act Two was to be very similar to Act One.

By offering to support American interests in the Caribbean, President Nord Alexis finally drew the Western Hemisphere's largest political power into the Haitian world. The United States had alternated between the extremes of completely ignoring Haiti in the beginning (a nation of slave owners and plantations had severe reservations about the precedent of recognizing a nation of freedmen) and then trying, and mostly failing, to encourage African-American freedmen to emigrate to Haiti after the Civil War. Occasionally, Haiti and the United States found themselves on opposite sides of petty issues over other islands, but for the most part the two nations did not cross paths during the nineteenth century.

Now—and suddenly it seemed—Haitian presidents were more than ready to deal with the United States and its vast influence and wealth. Successive presidents opened trade and other forms of commerce with the United States, permitting Americans to purchase land and open their own plantations and factories (complete with Haitian labor!) on Haitian soil. President Francois C. Antoine Simon was elected in 1908, which is notable because his daughter was known to be a Vodou priestess. He was removed in a coup in 1911.

Some Haitian presidents lived long enough to be exiled to the United States; others were not so lucky and met their ends in violent ways. One of them, Cincinnatus Leconte (the grandson of Dessalines), was killed in an explosion that destroyed the National Palace in 1912. In July 1915, President Jean Vilbrun Guillaume Sam was dismembered by a violent mob, which paraded pieces of his corpse through Port-au-Prince's streets over a week of angry protests and riots. These riots were in response to Sam's execution of his predecessor, President Oreste Zamor. The chaos following Sam's murder led U.S. President Woodrow Wilson to invade Haiti, ostensibly because of concerns that an unstable Haiti might permit enemy German forces a foothold in the Caribbean. This first American occupation of Haiti would last for almost twenty years (1915–1934). The U.S. Navy and Marines stormed the Port-au-Prince harbor, set up a puppet government with a Haitian figurehead president named Phillippe Sudré

Dartiguenave, and then spent years fighting against rebel groups (called *cacos* after a Spanish word for a kind of frog that makes loud noises in the night) in the Haitian countryside.

By 1922, U.S. President Warren G. Harding decided to encourage the selection of a new, slightly more autonomous Haitian president, in hopes of improving the American image both in Haiti and back at home. While President Louis Borno managed to commit the Americans to help build Haiti's infrastructure and economy, this was done at a huge cost in yet more international debt and continued tension between Haitians, the occupying American force, and his own government. While Borno's government tried to convince the Haitian people it was more than a mere tool of the Americans, it also enjoyed great benefits from American money and protection.

The first president to assume full power in Haiti after the Marines left in 1930, the Spanish-Haitian lawyer Sténio Joseph Vincent, continued the general practice of repression at home paired with largesse toward the United States and its interests. Instead of stepping down at the end of his term as he had promised when elected, Vincent called a special vote and extended his term to 1941. He also changed the constitution so that all future presidents would be required to be elected by popular vote, instead of a private vote by the National Assembly.

In October 1937, Dominican Republic president Rafael Trujillo decided he would no longer tolerate Haitians living along the border or being considered natural-born citizens of the Dominican Republic. Over five days between October 2 and 8, Dominican army and police forces swept along the border, searching for Haitian migrant workers and naturalized and natural-born Haitians on the Dominican side, and slaughtering them as they went. An astonishing twenty to thirty thousand Haitians were killed during the five-day Parsley Massacre, so named because of the practice of discovering Haitians by asking them to pronounce the name of the parsley plant in Spanish (*perejil*), a method that would immediately betray a native French or Kreyòl speaker. Both Haitians and Dominicans refer to the massacre as "the Cutting," one of the bloodiest episodes ever to visit the island, rivaling the body count of much of the Haitian Revolution.

President Vincent attempted to suppress media coverage of the Parsley Massacre because he was concerned about civil unrest and had, up to that point, considered Dominican President Trujillo a friend and financial backer. Vincent's attempts failed and, as the news spread, Haitians rose up in outrage at the massacre as well as at the president's desire to suppress information about it. Vincent's further behavior, which most Haitians considered far too weak of a response to the genocide, only made things worse. Rather than sending more troops to the border, Vincent opted to place them around the National Palace, fearing a coup. Two coups were attempted and suppressed while Vincent entered private negotiations with the Dominican government for a financial settlement to the relatives of the slain Haitians—money that those relatives would never see, due to governmental corruption. All of these issues caused too many stresses on Vincent's re-election campaign; he resigned shortly before the end of his term, in hopes that the presidency could transition peacefully to someone else.

Vincent's successor, the light-skinned Élie Lescot, had served as Haiti's ambassador to both the Dominican Republic and the United States prior to his installation as President of Haiti in 1941, establishing a new pattern of presidents "elected" with the U.S. State Department's blessing. During Lescot's tenure, the power of rural police chiefs and other government agencies to suppress dissent by any means necessary grew to new and even more troubling degrees. A combination of Marxists, students, populists, and middle-class black academics went into revolt, and a military coup removed Lescot from power in 1946.

After Lescot, a succession of military men alternating with labor leaders and black-empowerment academics called *noiristes* (nwah-REESTS, from the French *noirisme,* "black-ism") attempted—and failed—to solve the problems of Haiti's economy as American exploitation, corruption, and mistrust grew. The *noiristes* reached out to growing numbers of poor black Haitians that had traded agricultural jobs in the countryside for promised blue- and white-collar jobs in the cities, jobs that had largely never materialized. Flash mobs of these urban poor, organized more quickly than ever before by using radio and newspapers, were called *woulo* (WOO-loh, "steamrollers") for the way they could galvanize Haitians into forces to push back against government repression and demonstrate the will of the people.

After President Daniel Fignolé was forcibly removed from office after a mere nineteen days in the summer of 1957, he was exiled to New York with the U.S. Central Intelligence Agency's (CIA) consent and approval. *Woulos* wandered the streets of Port-au-Prince demanding his return, and they were rewarded for speaking out with deadly violence by the interim military regime. Thousands of dissidents were killed. In September of the same year, a black medical doctor and *noiriste* named François Duvalier ran for president against a mixed-race landowner and business tycoon named Louis Déjoie. Without Fignolé on the ballot to divide the vote, Duvalier's *noiriste,* populist campaign easily carried the election. With the full support of the Haitian military—and lacking any opposition from foreign powers like the United States—the soft-spoken physician "Papa Doc" came to power.

Modern Haiti: From "Papa Doc" to January 12, 2010

It is appropriate to begin the song of modern Haitian history with the saga of Papa Doc. François Duvalier, born to middle-class parents in Port-au-Prince, received his medical degree from the University of Haiti in 1934. He benefited directly from the opportunities the American occupation gave to the educated in Haiti, and he spent a year at the University of Michigan studying public health. Over the next decade, Papa Doc was involved in U.S.-funded health programs to control contagious tropical diseases such as yaws and typhus in Haiti's agricultural interior. During this time, despite his privileged position, Papa Doc remained in touch with the black majority of Haiti through his interactions with his country patients and his involvement in the *noiriste* movement. He was also one of the founders of the *Griots* (gree-YO or gwee-YO), a group of Haitian *noiriste* intellectuals named for both the traveling bard/storytellers of West Africa and a journal of the same name published by the *noiriste* movement between 1938 and 1940.

As a *noiriste* and academic, Papa Doc studied Vodou and wrote many papers and articles about its practice; he was also rumored—probably accurately—to be an initiated *houngan* himself. As minister of health under President Estimé in the late 1940s, Papa Doc gained a good understanding of the power of Haiti's black majority against the mixed-race minority, and how that power could be used for political ends. Because of his associations with *noiriste* President Estimé, Papa Doc went into hiding until 1956, emerging only after amensty was declared and he saw a chance to run as the only pro-black candidate for president. It was Dr. Duvalier's poor black patients who gave him his innocent-sounding nickname of Papa Doc. Ironically enough, this same group of people would come to suffer the most under him as president.

Papa Doc moved quickly to consolidate power in his presidency, knowing all too well the Haitian proverb *Dlo ou pa pè, se li ki pote ou ale* (It's the water you aren't afraid of that will carry you off). He changed the constitution to promote and surround himself with loyal soldiers and government officials hand-picked from the black majority. True to Haitian history, this was not enough; within a year the military tried to stage a coup but failed. Papa Doc's reaction was to redesign his Presidential Guard—not as the army special forces it had once been, but as a special paramilitary group whose purpose was to keep Papa Doc alive and in power. Also in 1958, there was a bizarre attempt to assassinate Papa Doc and take over the palace by eight random men: three American ex-policemen, two American-born mercenaries, and three exiled Haitians. The botched invasion ended with all eight being gunned down in a National Palace outbuilding, and a diplomatic fiasco for Haitian-American relations ensued.

A year later, with the intention to expand the Presidential Guard concept into rural Haiti, Papa Doc founded a personal police force: the National Security Volunteer Militia. Its members, mimicking Vodou symbols for the Lwa Kouzin Zaka, who is a friend to all country folk, abandoned their military uniforms and instead wore the straw hats and denim shirt and pants of traditional peasant dress. Papa Doc's new and greatly feared secret police force had a popular nickname, Tonton Macoute (pronounced TONE-tone mah-KOOT, "Uncle Sack"). This referred to the name of a Haitian folk spirit, a sort of bogeyman similar to the "sack-men" of many other cultures, said to trap naughty children in his *macoute* (or *makout*, a straw bag or sack) and make them disappear.

Many of the Tonton Macoutes were *houngans*, thus continuing to conflate Vodou and its imagery with the power of the state in a way that had not really been emphasized since the Haitian Revolution. The Tonton Macoutes also sometimes dressed in the manner of Gede Lwa, surrounding themselves with imagery of death and violence to add to their fearsome reputation. Luckner Cambronne, the second director of the Tonton Macoutes, was known as the Vampire of the Caribbean for his profitable practice of supplying corpses, body parts, and blood products harvested from enemies of the state to medical schools and hospitals in the United States.

After a heart attack in May 1959, Papa Doc seemed to change. Some of the people who knew him believed that complications from the heart attack, years of diabetes and heart disease, and possible neurological damage from a nine-hour coma after the heart attack were the reason for Papa Doc's increasing paranoia and unusual behavior. By 1961, after five years in office, Papa Doc disbanded the Haitian legislature and replaced it with a single-party body of his own choosing. Then he called a completely bogus election, in which he claimed to have been re-elected by a vote of 1,320,748 to 0, despite the fact that the 1957 Haitian constitution (which he had written himself) prohibited him from standing for a second term. In June 1964, Papa Doc rigged an election a second time; this one was a "constitutional referendum" permitting him to name himself President for Life, in the Pétion tradition, with absolute powers, including the power to name his own heir. All the 1964 ballots were printed with "yes" already chosen, and Papa Doc claimed that 99.9 percent of the Haitian people cast (obviously favorable) votes.

With Haiti's military and the populace under control, and the mixed-race minority out of power, Papa Doc had one more player inside Haiti to contend with: the powerful Roman Catholic Church. During the 1960s, Papa Doc expelled almost all non-Haitian bishops from Haiti, and after refusing to permit their return, the Church excommunicated him. By 1966, he had managed to convince the Holy See to readmit him to the Church as well as permitted him to appoint all of Haiti's bishops. Papa Doc then proceeded to replace all the mixed-race Catholic authorities in Haiti with black loyalists of his own choosing.

Far stranger things than rigged elections and secret police dressed like Lwa occurred during Papa Doc's dictatorship. During the recovery from his heart attack, Papa Doc had entrusted Clement Barbot, the head of the Tonton Macoutes, with enough power to lead Haiti. Upon his return to office, Papa Doc concluded that Barbot had intended to overthrow him, and he had Barbot thrown in prison. Barbot would remain there for four years, until 1963. After his release from prison, an embittered Barbot attempted to kidnap Papa Doc's children in revenge. The attempt failed, and Barbot was forced to flee. During the manhunt, a *houngan* told Papa Doc that the reason Barbot had escaped was because he had been changed into a black dog by *wanga* (WAHN-ga, a form of Vodou magic). The president swiftly issued an order that all black dogs in Haiti be rounded up and shot.

Papa Doc started appearing in public dressed as the Lwa Baron Samedi, complete with dark sunglasses and suit and using the strong nasal accent Gede Lwa are known to speak in. The Tonton Macoutes donned sunglasses in emulation of their leader and spread the word that Papa Doc was himself a very powerful *houngan*—perhaps the most powerful *houngan* of all. The regime distributed a version of the Lord's Prayer honoring Papa Doc in the place of God; spread an image of Jesus standing next to Papa Doc with a hand on his shoulder and the statement that Duvalier had been divinely chosen to lead Haiti; and used the slogan *Papa Doc: one with the Lwa, Jesus Christ, and God Himself.* It was rumored that Papa Doc kept preserved heads in jars his office, heads belonging to former enemies who had been compelled by *wanga* to tell the secrets of their treachery.

In 1971, Papa Doc died, and the presidency of Haiti fell to his nineteen-year-old son, Jean-Claude. Baby Doc, as the younger Duvalier was publicly nicknamed, was not the politically savvy man his father had been, and he initially suggested the presidency should go to his older sister Marie-Denise. However, Baby Doc accepted the position and became the world's youngest president, contenting himself with ceremonial functions. For the most part the younger Duvalier lived as a playboy, leaving Haiti's governance in the hands of his mother, "Mama Doc" Simone Ovide Duvalier, and a committee of former Papa Doc ministers and cronies led by Luckner Cambronne. When Mama Doc forced Cambronne into exile, she and the remaining Tonton Macoutes, referred to as "the dinosaurs," continued to run Haiti largely as it had been under Papa Doc: no real governing body, total control invested in the president and the secret police, and severe penalties for any attempts at dissent.

Baby Doc made some small, mostly cosmetic efforts toward reform, and during the first few years of his regime, the United States and other countries turned a blind eye to Haiti's human rights record and poverty in return for economic benefits. Foreign countries enjoyed unprecedented business access to Haitian real estate and its workforce, as well as an increase in Haiti's role in the illicit drug trade. In addition, Baby Doc's government provided little or no regulation over hundreds of non-governmental organizations (NGOs)—mostly consisting of Protestant missions from the United States—that entered Haiti ostensibly to help with pre-existing and ongoing problems, such as erosion due to subsistence farming, substandard living conditions, and intense poverty. In 1971, U.S. President Richard Nixon restored an aid program that had been suspended under Papa Doc. Instead of investing it in the country, Baby Doc found ways to siphon off that money and other government funds for his lavish lifestyle, despite Haiti's climbing debt and worsening conditions.

In 1980, Baby Doc married Michèle Bennett, the light-skinned great-great-great granddaughter of King Henri I, in an extravagant ceremony that cost the Haitian government approximately three million U.S. dollars. Bennett's precarious class status as a mixed-race woman and a divorcée whose ex-father-in-law had attempted to overthrow Papa Doc—along with the obscene amount of public money wasted on the wedding—gave Haiti's black middle and lower classes the impression that the relatively light-skinned Baby Doc was abandoning the pro-black policies and philosophy his father had upheld.

After the wedding, Baby Doc, his wife, and her corrupt family earned even more public disapproval. The Bennetts were rumored to be involved in the drug trade and the export of Haitian cadavers to American and other foreign medical schools, and they were known to be profiting from valuable government contracts and real estate granted to Bennett-owned businesses. Baby Doc responded by cracking down on all criticism. When Michèle even managed to convince her husband to demote his own mother from running the government behind the scenes, Baby Doc also lost the support of the dinosaurs. Suddenly, his government fractured between the old guard that had been loyal to his parents and the younger governmental figures he had appointed himself, who for the most part were loyal not to Baby Doc, but to his wife and her influential, wealthy father.

Yet during all this discontent, support from the United States remained strong. Baby Doc's ability to stifle any revolution rendered Haiti relatively free of political problems, and American businesses and NGOs in Haiti continued to thrive. In 1978, after an outbreak of African swine fever, the U.S. government convinced Baby Doc that all of Haiti's pigs—the same native pigs whose sacrifice had started the Haitian Revolution in the legend of Bwa Kayiman—needed to be destroyed. The Haitian people, and particularly the thousands of peasants who made their livelihood raising the pigs, objected, but the government kept its word to the United States. Every Haitian pig was killed. Conveniently, the United States stepped in to replace the extinct Haitian pig population with swine from North America, which have no natural immunity to the tropical diseases common to Haitian livestock and require large amounts of expensive antibiotics, special foods, and care—also conveniently supplied, at a price, by U.S. businesses. The result was disaster for the Haitian agricultural sector, which has yet to recover, and the abandonment of pork farming as a viable economic resource.

In 1980, rumors that AIDS was rampant in Haiti began spreading, and the tourist trade (the economic lifeblood of many Haitians) began to fail. Subsidies of other staples such as sugar and rice, increasingly being replaced with cheaper supplies being dumped on the Haitian market by trading partners, including the United States and China, continued to erode Haiti's agricultural economy from without just as its economy was eroded from within. Deforestation to collect cooking charcoal caused a chain reaction of erosion that destroyed Haitian land acre by acre, rendering it less and less fertile. With the loss of agricultural income came more poverty, and with more poverty came malnutrition and death. The ability of Baby Doc's absentee government to stifle his growing number of critics was stretched thin.

Pope John Paul II, who had been working with U.S. President Ronald Reagan to facilitate changes in various world governments, visited Haiti in 1983. The Holy Father made several public criticisms about what he saw there, both in terms of corruption and of the systematic exploitation of the poor. After the Pope's trip to the island, the Catholic Church in Haiti picked up his call for greater social justice and for a government that listened to, and took care of, its people. By 1985, Haiti's larger cities were hosting street demonstrations too large for the Tonton Macoutes to prevent, and Baby Doc was forced to make concessions, including cuts in food pricing and changes in his cabinet. At the same time, he moved to close down opposition media (mostly radio stations) and sent both police and army personnel out to stop any rebellion.

By 1986, President Ronald Reagan's government reversed America's position on the dictatorship. Concluding that Baby Doc was no longer useful since he couldn't guarantee security in Haiti, the United States pressured him to leave. Business leaders, the government of Jamaica, and even some of the dinosaurs met with Baby Doc and told him they were in agreement with Reagan's assessment: it was time for him to go. Even though they wanted him out, the U.S. government refused to grant Baby Doc asylum, instead offering to help him leave the country. After an unsuccessful attempt to get him to leave on January 30, Baby Doc, his wife, his mother, and sixteen other family members and friends boarded a U.S. Air Force plane for France on February 7, 1986—after five other countries refused to accept them. The French permitted Baby Doc and his wife to stay but also refused to grant asylum, and life for the Duvaliers continued much as it had in Haiti until Michèle filed for divorce in 1990, taking most of their combined wealth with her in the divorce settlement. "Mama Doc" Simone Duvalier, who had been set aside years before, reconciled with her son, and the two of them lived near Paris in obscurity and relatively modest means until her death in 1997. Baby Doc would remain under the radar for more than a decade.

Following Baby Doc, Gen. Henri Namphy and Leslie Manigat traded brief presidencies marred by corruption and rioting; both men were deposed (or deposed each other) in coups. Lieutenant-General Prosper Avril, another member of the Duvalier regimes, continued the practice of "Duvalierism without Duvalier." His successor, Hérard Abraham, resigned abruptly after only three days, leaving the presidency in the lap of its first female officeholder, the chief justice of Haiti's Supreme Court, Ertha Pascal-Trouillot.

As a provisional president, Pascal-Trouillot oversaw Haiti's first truly free election in December 1990, which declared the presidency for the outspoken and popular Catholic priest Jean-Bertrand Aristide. When a group of Tonton Macoutes under Roger Lafontant attempted to stop Aristide from taking power and kidnapped President Pascal-Trouillot during the process, Aristide's supporters took to the streets in *woulos,* as Fignolé's had done decades before. The Haitian army, supported by the United States, stepped in to stop the coup and gain Pascal-Trouillot's freedom. Oddly enough, Aristide then proceeded to have Pascal-Trouillot arrested, charging that she had been complicit in the Lafontant coup, but her freedom was secured when the United States stepped in yet again and demanded she be permitted to leave the country.

As Haiti's first democratically elected president, Aristide was almost immediately overthrown in a coup led by former-general Raoul Cédras in late September 1991. Aristide fled into exile. The coup was said to be the result of displeasure at Aristide's having disbanded Haiti's influential army in favor of a national police force, as well as his stated intention to put an end to drug trafficking, a major source of the army's money and influence. For three years, the army regime under Cédras killed and terrorized many thousands of Aristide's supporters, much in the same way the Tonton Macoutes had done to government opposition figures under the Duvalier regimes. It was known that the U.S. CIA had personally trained Cédras and was privately in favor of the coup regime, despite U.S. President George H. W. Bush's administration publicly calling for its end. Once again, Haiti's eternal battle between mixed-race and black classes was demonstrated, as

Aristide's government was largely black and pro-peasant, and Haiti's light-skinned elite businessmen staffed the Cédras regime.

Following a second U.S. military invasion of Haiti by newly elected President Bill Clinton in 1994—this time accompanied by multinational peacekeepers authorized by the United Nations Security Council—Aristide returned from exile and was restored to his presidency. The following year, Father Aristide would leave the priesthood; the Vatican had recognized the Cédras government and refused to assist in Aristide's return, despite him being a son of the Church.

Despite U.S. pressure for open markets and a return of nationalized industries to the free market, Aristide only accepted a few of the demands of his American allies. He permitted the Haitian market to be flooded with subsidized American rice and other commodities, decimating the Haitian agribusiness economy, and he fought with his political party over how Haiti should be run. In 1996, when his term ended, Aristide attempted to stay in power despite the constitutional requirement that no president could serve consecutive terms; he claimed his three years in exile should not count. The government refused to recognize the lost years and called for elections. René Préval was elected by a large margin in a relatively low-turnout election. Préval was an agriculturalist who had served as Aristide's prime minister and a personal friend who accompanied Aristide in his first exile.

Préval and Aristide would trade places as prime minister and president over the next decade. Préval's first term (1996–2001) saw improvements in Haiti's condition, in addition to his agreement to U.S. demands concerning re-privatization of state-run companies, investigations into police and army brutality, and agrarian reforms. Due to infighting with a largely hostile parliament made mostly of Aristide's former political party and a new party he formed so that he would not be replaced as a presidential candidate, Préval dissolved the parliament in 1999 and ruled by decree from 1999 to 2000.

Despite the arguments between Aristide's former and current parties, Aristide was elected president a second time in a controversial low-turnout election in 2000 that was largely boycotted by opposition parties. Aristide's second presidency survived three turbulent years (2000–2003). There was continued fighting in the parliament between various parties, and Aristide's habit of irritating Haiti's powerful neighbors and allies increased to the degree that aid and trade programs were suspended by a number of governments. In 2003, facing economic disaster, Aristide demanded that France pay Haiti $21.7 billion USD in restitution for the money it had demanded from the Haitian government under President Boyer back in 1825. Aristide accused the United States of arming his opponents and the Canadians of plotting to overthrow him via their Ottawa Initiative.

In September 2003, Amiyot Metayer, an influential gang leader in Gonaïves was found murdered. Amiyot's brother, Butayer, who was also part of the gang, declared that Aristide was responsible. He renamed the gang the National Revolutionary Front for the Liberation of Haiti, sacked the city's police station, and took its weapons and vehicles as they prepared to march on Port-au-Prince. By February 2004, this rebel force had captured Cap-Haïtien, Haiti's second-largest city, and by the end of the month they had control of Port-au-Prince. Thousands of Haitians fled the country in tiny boats as they had done during instable periods since Baby Doc, desperate to reach the United States or anywhere free and safe. Foreign governments that had refused to step in to help Aristide put down the rebellion were suddenly present to convince him to leave, once again; on February 28, 2004, Aristide left Haiti for a second exile, on a flight arranged by the United States. After staying briefly in the Central African Republic, Aristide and his family flew back across the Atlantic to Jamaica for a short time, while that country negotiated permanent asylum for them in South Africa.

In the chaos, the remaining Haitian government appealed for international help and received it in the form of United Nations forces organized as the peacekeepers known as the United Nations Stabilization Mission in Haiti (known in Haiti under its French acronym, MINUSTAH). At the order of U.S. President George W. Bush, the U.S. Marines showed up the very next day, starting a third occupation of Haiti. The Marines were soon followed by troops from Canada, French, and Chile, who secured the capital while waiting for MINUSTAH to arrive.

Controversial questions remained, both in Haiti and among Haitians in exile: whether or not Aristide was involved in embezzlement schemes involving public telecommunications companies; if he was involved in the death of Amiot Metayer; if he voluntarily resigned or was forced out; whether or not the United States and other nations pressured the UN and CARICOM (Caribbean Community Secretariat) to change Haiti's government; and what exactly was the role of MINUSTAH. All that is certain is that the entire truth about the 2004 coup—and about Aristide's place in Haitian history—has yet to be understood. Haiti continued in a relatively uncomfortable interim government bolstered by foreign occupation until 2006, when Préval was re-elected president of Haiti in yet another questionable, low-turnout election.

To say that Préval's second presidency was difficult is an understatement. From initial rioting after fraudulent balloting and a runoff election, he started in the same vein as his first presidency, selecting the same man as his prime minister and trying to smooth relations with his neighbors. While Préval enjoyed the support of the urban poor who had once supported Aristide, he started to lose that support after making promises to bring Aristide back and then failing to keep them. Préval's support of presidents in Cuba, Latin America, and South America who are unfriendly to U.S. interests (such as Venezuela's Hugo Chávez) drew criticism from American sources. Still, he reached out diplomatically to the United States, France, and the Dominican Republic seeking to restore good relations.

MINUSTAH provided an additional difficulty for the Préval government. While it assists in security, and thus frees the Haitian government to put time and money into other efforts, Haitians have been treated badly by MINUSTAH soldiers and largely mistrust the peacekeeping force. There is historic ethnic tension between Brazilians (a majority of the MINUSTAH forces come from Brazil) and Haitians, and there have been significant allegations of MINUSTAH soldiers harassing and even raping and killing Haitians, then trying to blame these crimes on local gangs or seditious elements in Haitian society. I personally observed at least one such incident of MINUSTAH officers abusing Haitians during my 2006 trip to Port-au-Prince, and Haitian and foreign journalists have documented others since the 2010 earthquake.

In April 2008, facing extreme food prices and supply problems, food riots broke out in some Haitian cities. Four hurricanes hit that summer, which destroyed crops and triggered deadly floods that killed many people in the coastal regions and in and around Gonaïves. This drove the costs of basic supplies up even further. By the following summer, calls for Préval to step down were getting much louder, and my own Haitian family was starting to talk about how they worried the country would soon descend into chaos yet again.

2010 Earthquake in Haiti

That chaos would come, but not in the form of revolution. A few minutes after 5 p.m. local time on Tuesday, January 12, 2010—just before dinnertime—a magnitude 7.0 earthquake struck. This massive, shallow quake centered at Léogâne, about 20 miles west of Port-au-Prince, was followed by two weeks of aftershocks larger than many earthquake events in other places (4.5 magnitude or higher). The January 12 earthquake left Port-au-Prince and its surrounding region—the area containing Haiti's greatest population—a smoldering heap of broken concrete. Unregulated building construction, lack of infrastructure, overcrowding, and the fact that the earthquake was centered at a very shallow 8 miles below the surface all combined to make this natural disaster even more horrific. At least a million people lost their homes and an additional 316,000 people lost their lives in the initial quake. Hundreds of thousands were injured, and thousands more were trapped by the quake and its subsequent aftershocks.

Because the main MINUSTAH headquarters, Port-au-Prince hospitals, telephone and electrical service, and the governmental headquarters collapsed or were destroyed in the quake—along with the National Palace and the international airport and seaport—rescue and medical efforts over the next few days were difficult or slow to start. More people died waiting for rescue or for doctors, food, and water than perished in the initial disaster.

An unprecedented humanitarian effort raised hundreds of millions of dollars to help Haiti after the January 12 earthquake. Thanks to disagreements over how that aid should be distributed or whether or not Préval could be trusted to administer the money, given the state of his government's corruption and destruction, much of this desperately needed funding languished for more than a year (and counting) in the bank accounts of the charities and foreign governments that authorized it.

Millions of dollars authorized by the U.S. government sit locked in the desk of an Oklahoma senator who froze their authorization bill on procedural grounds completely unrelated to Haiti. Canada's government has yet to explain why the bulk of its authorizations have not been released. Major charities spent large portions of their donations on overhead and bribes to get people and supplies into the countryside. Others simply never accounted for where the money actually went. Almost two years later, people still sleep in the streets of Port-au-Prince and in tents in other parts of Haiti, waiting for help that never comes or is never enough.

After the earthquake, Haiti's condition continued to deteriorate both physically and politically. Since October 2010, MINUSTAH's Nepalese division, assigned to a post in the Artibonite Valley, has been proved culpable of causing a cholera outbreak by neglecting to locate sanitation facilities far enough away from local rivers where earthquake refugees living in tent cities get their drinking water. Rioting and protests against the MINUSTAH presence in Haiti continue, and foreign journalists have documented violent responses from MINUSTAH troops, including a recorded sexual assault of a child. (At press time, Haiti was considering asking the UN forces to leave Haiti altogether because of these incidents.) The next set of presidential elections in 2010 ended with mass protests and calls for investigation after the election commission blocked certain popular candidates from running. The electoral commission (called CEP), mostly made up of members of Préval's political party, then declared Préval's preferred candidate and fellow party member Jude Célestin to be eligible for a second round of runoff elections against front runner, Mirlande Manigat (wife of former President Leslie Manigat), despite Célestin's not having won enough votes to pass to the second round.

International election observers and the Haitian people overwhelmingly agreed that Célestin's place on the ballot should go to popular musician "Sweet Micky" Martelly instead. (Another musician, Wyclef Jean, was barred from the ballot before the first round.) Even as late as January 2011, Préval and the CEP had refused to schedule a second runoff in the midst of national and international disagreement over who the runoff candidates should be. This is despite the fact that according to the Constitution, Préval should have vacated his office before February 7.

At the close of January 2011, in a move that caught even the Haitian government by surprise, Baby Doc Duvalier flew back to Haiti from his French exile, declaring that he was back to help his country, and was met at the airport by throngs of enthusiastic Haitians. The former dictator was immediately arrested and told he would stand trial, although he was then released and has been freed to move about the country. On March 18, 2011, one day before the next round of elections was held (without Célestin on the ballot), Jean-Bertrand Aristide also returned to Haiti from South Africa. Aristide's return came despite pleas by many heads of state for him to stay away, including Préval himself (famously quoted in a Wikileaks cable as saying he did not want his former friend Aristide "anywhere in the hemisphere"). Aristide's return was somewhat surprising in Haiti as well after a long absence and little hint that he was even willing to return, and after his party had declared it was boycotting the election anyway. His supporters also came to the airport to greet him, and he has not (yet) been placed under any sort of house arrest. Cynical Haitians inside and outside Haiti threw up their hands at all this and suggested perhaps every living dictator or president should be invited back, while Préval continued to sit as president outside his constitutional term limit, and while the CEP continued to delay certifying the March 19, 2011, election results.

On April 11, 2011, the CEP finally certified that Michel Joseph "Sweet Micky" Martelly had indeed won the presidency by a wide margin in a low-turnout election, and that his installation would take place on May 14, 2011. Martelly was indeed sworn in to office on May 14, but it took him four attempts and five months to get a prime minister approved. Public opinion of both Martelly and his government is very low.

The History of Haitian Vodou

Haiti's political history is hard reading. On a visit to Haiti, it can be almost impossible to convince oneself that a land of such beauty and a people of such passion and depth have managed to survive more than three hundred years of violence and betrayal the likes of which most non-Haitians will never know. Haiti somehow manages to be beautiful and terrible at the same time; it is the hardest place I have ever loved.

The motto written on Haiti's flag and official seal, *L'union fait la force* (Unity Makes Strength), is literal. Nearly everything the Haitian people have achieved has come only through their united strength and struggle, through will and blood and sacrifice shared by all. For an outsider, it can be very easy to believe the rumors and hype told about "voodoo" as an evil practice, marked in blood and angry vengeful spirits. After all, the island has been watered in rivers of blood since Columbus first set foot on her northern shore. It can be easy to think there is nothing good left in Haiti, nothing worth seeing or knowing about or continuing, only the wreckage of betrayals, broken promises, and human cruelty littering Haiti's psychic landscape, in the same way that the rubble from the 2010 earthquake still chokes the streets of Port-au-Prince two years later.

Yet the practice of Haitian Vodou is not at all about deals with the devil, orgiastic dances, bloody sacrifices, or zombie curses, contrary to the propaganda and outright lies perpetuated about it during the first American occupation, and even centuries before that, by Haiti's first rulers eager to impress their former European overlords. Haitian Vodou is a practice united in strength; the result of a conscious, willful decision to gather all that was good about the world, all the spiritual legacies of the various people thrown together in Haiti, and make them survive. Its power was strong enough to unite hundreds of thousands of slaves—many of whom originated from enemy nations—in revolt and carry them through the dark and violent years until freedom was gained. The creation of Haitian Vodou restored and provided a common identity and history to people permitted to keep little else. Its continued existence assures that when all else is gone and everything has been forgotten, Haiti's link to spirit and to community itself will never be broken. United for strength, Vodou lives to protect the Haitian experience and give it hope.

Before the Africans came, the Taino and Ciboney of Ayiti practiced polytheistic religions recognizing the power of a Creator (called Yocahu) and other deities and spirits in all things, much as the indigenous peoples of other Western Hemisphere nations also recognize the power of the Creator in natural forces, animals, and dead and living people. Under the Creator, the spirits of the world of Ayiti were called *zemi* (zeh-MEE). Their images were carved from rocks and painted or carved into the walls of caves and the trunks of trees. Some *zemi* live in the sky and control things like rain and weather; some live in the rivers and trees and rocks and medicinal plants; some are the spirits of dead *caciques* (ka-SEE-kay, the Taino word for a chief or local king or queen) or *bohiques* (bo-HEE-kay, a word for *zemi* priests), who became *zemi* upon death. Like Mesoamerican tribes not so far to the west, the Taino of Ayiti played a sacred ball game in special stone courts and practiced ritual fasting and purging before any ritual ceremony. While Taino religion and people persist on other Caribbean islands—most notably on the island of Bohicua (called Puerto Rico today)—the Taino of Ayiti and their culture and spirits were absorbed into the multicultural Haitian culture to become part of Haitian Vodou practice.

The Taino of Ayiti drew images of the *zemi*, either in chalk or various plant powders, on their sacred rocks or even on their own bodies, to be invoked in a ceremony. They wore special clothing with feathers, paint, and skirts made by stringing many shells together. Their ceremonies were joyous, with singing and dancing in thanksgiving to the *zemi* or in celebration of various holy days or rites of passage. Before a ceremony began in earnest, a *cacique* would sing the history of his or her tribe—a practice that very likely informs the Haitian Vodou tradition of the *Priyè Ginen*, which is discussed in more detail in Chapter 7. Singing and dancing for the *zemi* was punctuated by shaking a gourd on a stick, like the modern maraca. A similar instrument called a *tcha-tcha* is still used in Vodou ceremonies for certain Lwa, including those of Taino origin, and is used by non-initiates to call the spirits and direct the singing in the same way the island's Taino did centuries ago.

Bread made from the manioc plant (also called cassava) was sacred to the Taino and is still served to the Lwa. Certain kinds of Vodou *wanga* still use the sorts of stones sacred to the *zemi*. Feathered sticks called *mayoyo* are used as invocation points and magical receptacles for spirits in some Vodou lineages, in honor of the Taino ancestors and the *zemi*. A number of Lwa have Taino origin and are served within the Rada nation and around the same portion of the ceremony, called *Djouba* (DJOO-ba), where we honor the peasant Haitian Lwa Kouzin Zaka and his escort. While the practice of tracing *veve* (VAY-VAY, the ritual diagrams indicating various Lwa) probably has been influenced from the Taino practice of drawing pictographs for their *zemi,* there are also cultural remembrances from Africa and Europe that inform the Vodou use of *veve.*

From Africa, traditionally speaking, a number of separate cultural influences came together to create Haitian Vodou. Speaking symbolically, there are said to be "twenty-one nations" of Lwa; by this numbering, nineteen parts, or nations, of the Haitian Vodou honor the spirits of African nations and cultures, and the Taino and European spirits make up nations twenty and twenty-one, respectively. One could say the vast majority of Haitian Vodou was—and remains—African, at least in origin. Of the various African legacies in Vodou, the strongest ones come from the largest ethnic groups brought to Haiti as slaves: people brought from what is now Benin in the Fon-speaking area of Dahomey (the Rada Lwa mostly come from this group); from the lands of the Yoruba-speaking Nago people of modern Benin and Nigeria (from whence Haiti gets its Nago Lwa and places like Cuba and Brazil got their *orishas*); and through modern Ghana and Togo and even into areas now considered part of Congo and North and South Sudan (homelands of the Kongo and Petro Lwa). Most of the spirits served in Haitian Vodou derive from analogous or identical spirits served by the Haitians' African ancestors, excepting the surviving Taino spirits, a handful of European spirits, and spirits of the land of Haiti itself. There are also Haitian ancestors, such as revolutionary heroes like L'Ouverture and Dessalines, and blessed family elders who are considered to have become Lwa.

From Europe, via the *blancs* and *gens de couleur* of Saint-Domingue, came various elements of European mysticism and folklore; pieces of Islam from Muslim slaves and Arab merchants; certain music and dances; and even practices like secret handshakes and passwords derived from Martinism and Freemasonry. Above all the various ethnic folk traditions and beliefs, the entire practice of Haitian Vodou was syncretized with the imagery, organization, philosophy, and practice of Roman Catholic Christianity.

As the majority white religion from the time of the Spanish and a symbol of the power of the whites to subjugate the island, Catholicism in Vodou was transformed into a power that both shielded African slaves from having to reveal their ancestral practices where it was dangerous to do so, and also represented spiritual victory over the god of the slave owners, as well as that god's devotees.

Haitian Vodou, then, in many ways, is not a single tradition at all, but represents a collection of religions and cultures and histories. In the same way, Haiti itself is a nation created from many different groups of people and difficult situations, forced together and then choosing to rise above, as in Dessalines's Haitian declaration of independence: to make their strength through unity, or die trying.

Fòk o chache konn
chemen avan ou pran rout
("You have to know the way
before you can take the road")
—Haitian Proverb

ṪWO

◇◇◇

Aprè Bondye: Basic Principles and Ethics of Haitian Vodou

In this chapter, I set out a very basic idea of the general structure of Haitian Vodou, its beliefs, and its philosophy. While this material has been written about many times by non-Haitians, it is not often discussed in books or even in conversation by Haitians themselves; even the term "Haitian Vodou" is an outsiders' term applied by anthropologists who needed some sort of label to call these practices. A Vodouisant generally does not use the *V* word. He will say *Mwen sèvi Lwa* or "I serve the Lwa," or "I serve Spirit," or "I am a *houngan,*" or something like that.

The reasons behind this apparent lack of intellectual conversation concerning Vodou amongst its own practitioners vary. Because it is largely an oral tradition—even today a fair number of Haitians are not literate— many things simply are not and have never been written down. To complicate this, in some lineages, writing down certain things is not permitted.

During the process of writing this book, I had to secure permission from my elders for every word and concept I wrote about, as I have taken vows to safeguard certain information, even in writing.

Additionally, Vodou by its nature would not be classified as a revealed religion such as Christianity or Islam or Judaism. There is no central Vodou authority, no official sacred text, and no creed that all Vodouisants necessarily embrace; nor is it taught by exposing potential devotees to sacred writings and then expecting them to comply with the tenets therein. Vodou is a cultic, or practice-oriented, tradition. Like the cultic traditions or "religions" of Buddhism or Shinto, Haitian Vodou is largely experienced through direct personal involvement as well as the personal practice of various rituals or ceremonies. Vodou is a practice that you *do,* not a creed that you *believe in.* Because of this, many Vodouisants do not feel a need to write about what they do and would be far more likely to show you or invite you to participate—or maybe, if you were respectful enough, to teach you how to do it yourself.

Despite the practice-centered and oral nature of Vodou practice, it *is* possible to discuss some things about its basic structure. Though there are significant variations in practices in various geographical areas, and even different lineages or families within the same area, a few things can be said to be universal to Vodou's practice.

Bondye and the Universe

Like many Native American, Mediterranean, and West African indigenous religious practices, Haitian Vodou can be described as monotheistic. A central, singular creator god is said to exist, but in a relatively impersonal form. This deity, called Gran Mèt (gron MET, "Great Master") or Bondye (bon-DYAY, only two syllables, "the Good God"), created the universe and continues to create the universe daily. This creator god's existence is intertwined with its creation, and its powers are part of that creation and emanate from the created beings within it. For the vast majority of Haitians, who are also Roman Catholic, it is very easy to identify Bondye with the Roman Catholic conception of God the Father, a powerful being who is nonetheless "busy" running the universe and probably not particularly concerned with the daily lives of mankind. In most Vodou houses, Bondye and the Christian God are considered one and the same. As befits the King of the Universe, Bondye is always prayed to at the start of every ceremony; all other liturgical and ritual work, whether directed to ancestors or spirits, is carried out *aprè Bondye* ("after God").

While Bondye is not particularly personal, as its name implies, it is not the "jealous god" of Biblical fame. To some, Bondye is the embodiment of cosmic order; to others, as one of my elders once described it, "Bondye is all the love in the world, real love." All fate and all destiny are in Bondye's omnipotent yet ultimately benevolent hands. While a *houngan* or *mambo* can become very powerful and have many spirits at his or her call, unless *Bondye vle* (bon-DYAY VLAY, "God wills (it)"), no amount of magic will be successful. Even the most powerful *bokor* (bo-CORE, a word used to describe an uninitiated magician) must submit to Bondye's law, and nothing can be done to alter the universe, even in small ways, without Bondye's approval.

The Lwa

At the same time, this supposedly monotheistic tradition also entertains a polytheistic belief in many sub-gods or lesser gods or spirits, who are understood to be part of the created universe in addition to Bondye. These spirits are called Lwa (luh-WAH or lo-WAH, sometimes spelled *Loa*). Religious scholars might term such a system not monotheistic in the strictest sense, but a soft polytheism or henotheism, with a hierarchy of multiple divinities; or a monolatry, a special kind of henotheism where many individualized deities can simultaneously be interpreted as parts of one godhead or abstract Creator. The Lwa of Haitian Vodou will be discussed in much more detail in Part II of this book.

Temples and Altars

Since Haitian Vodou is not a scripture-based or centrally organized practice, it lacks a central synod or authority or universal standards on how Vodou should be practiced. It does, however, have a *règleman* (ray-glay-MON, "rules")—a standard collection of guidelines about how various Lwa are served, in what order they are to be addressed, and the particulars of various ceremonies and events that should be carried out for various reasons, including initiation or other rites of passage. Like the various beliefs that came together to form Haitian Vodou, there is an initiated Vodou priesthood, complete with a *règleman* about how those priests—called *mambo* (mom-BO) if they are women and *houngan* (oon-GAHN) if they are men—are created and trained. There is also a standard regimen of training for those who wish to be initiated into various groups, called *sosyetes* (so-sah-yay-TAY, "societies"), but who are not necessarily called to the priesthood.

Haitian Vodou is not a solitary practice overall. While there are things that a person does alone to serve Bondye and the Lwa, the vast majority of Vodou service is done in community, with one's family or *sosyete,* or in larger gatherings with other families or *sosyetes.* The temple where a Vodou ceremony is held and Vodouisants gather to serve their Lwa is called a *hounfo* (oon-FO) or *houmfor(t).* This building or collection of buildings in a common compound will contain a large, clear space called a *peristil* (perry-STEEL or "peristyle," after the classical conception of the columned entryway to a temple sanctuary), where songs and dances for the Lwa are held. Most *peristil* consist of large, single-room buildings with a roof; some are outside, located in an opening in a forest or grove of trees; and still others are large roofs or tents set on columns (sometimes called a *tonelle*, toe-NELL). Some *peristil* are circular; however, most are square or rectangular. All have a central pole (or a tree in the case of an outdoor *peristil*) referred to as the *poto mitan* (po-TOE mee-TAHN, "middle pole"). The *poto mitan* is the center and heart of a Vodou ceremony, the omphalos of the Vodou universe. Ceremonies and dances revolve around the *poto mitan,* and in many houses the base of the *poto mitan* itself is planted in a concrete base that is decorated and used as an altar. The Lwa are said to climb down the *poto mitan* from the heavens and into the floor of a *peristil,* from which they then rise up through the bodies of their servants to share in the dance and appear in possessions. Many *poto mitan* are decorated either with an abstract striping pattern or the images of two intertwined snakes, representing the great Lwa Danbala-Wedo and Ayida-Wedo, who hold up the sky.

A larger *hounfo* will contain extra rooms off the *peristil,* or additional rooms or houses in the compound for various purposes. A *badji* (bah-JEE or bod-JEE) is an altar room dedicated to a group of spirits; traditionally there will be a Rada *badji* and a separate Petro *badji,* and possibly a third for the Gede Lwa. Smaller houses may only have one or two rooms for their entire *peristil.* If there are two rooms, the Gede will be placed somewhere outside the rooms; if there is only one room, all the spirits' altars will be arranged within it in a manner that still keeps the varying families of spirits separated.

Some *sosyetes* repurpose their Rada *badji* for initiation ceremonies; others keep a separate room just to be used for initiation, called a *djevo* (JAY-voh). Still other *hounfo* contain rooms for consultations (divinations or herbal treatments), rooms where a Vodouisant can sleep overnight in hopes of gaining a dream from the Lwa, or living quarters for the family that owns the *hounfo.* Smaller *hounfo* might include altar and *peristil* and *djevo* all in the same space, or they could borrow or rent spaces from a larger, related *sosyete* for big events. Like the churches or temples in revealed religions, these sacred spaces are generally permanent in nature.

Haitian Vodou altars are curious and not always beautiful things. Most working altars are indistinguishable from regular tables in a room, and covered with odds and ends. They may contain virtually anything: from candles to paper images of the saints, bowls, cups, plates, various types of bottles, food, flowers, goblets of water, oil lamps, roots, stones, weaponry, pieces of cloth, ribbon, or even the occasional human skull. What items are on an altar (and why) may not make any sense to an outsider, but a Vodouisant will be able to tell with a quick glance at an altar table which spirit(s) it is designed to serve and how.

An altar might hold a Lwa's particular favorite offerings, with a peg set in the wall behind it to hold one of her dresses for her to wear if she comes to the *peristil* in possession. For example, Legba's altar will usually include some sort of straw bag atop it or somewhere close nearby, such as hanging from a nail in the doorway or the branch of a tree near the *badji.* Watery Lwa such as Lasirèn or Simbi-Dlo generally request that cups or basins of water be kept on or near their altars at all times. Ezili Danto's altar generally features at least one baby doll for her to admire and keep and a dagger or two to threaten or protect with. Ezili Freda's wedding rings are kept on her altar.

While the majority of Vodou altars are permanent in nature, some are created explicitly for certain treatments or ceremonies, or are designed to be portable. For the *Manje Mè* (MON-jay MAY, "feeding the sea") ceremony of the Lwa Mèt Agwe, a small raft is decorated with Agwe's colors and favorite offerings, then carried in a boat out to sea, cast into the ocean at a fair distance from land, and allowed to float away on the waves. During some ceremonies, enclosed altar areas called *bila* (BEE-la) are created by draping sheets or other cloth from the *peristil* ceiling in a box-like three-sided square, with the fourth side left open so that participants can enter and exit the *bila* at will. Inside the *bila,* special items to salute the Lwa, including ritual items and images, are set up around dishes of their favorite foods and drinks. Individual Vodouisants will often keep a table or cabinet for their personal Lwa in their homes, and those who enter into a *maryaj-Lwa* (ma-REE-adj luh-WA, "spirit marriage") may set up temporary altars for their spiritual spouses on the evenings the couple shares.

Altars tend to be brightly colored, in the belief that the bright colors attract the spirits. They will generally be kept very clean (except for those few Lwa who request that their items are not washed). Bottles (*boutèy,* boo-TAY) and flags (*drapo,* dwah-PO) made from bright cloth and colored sequins, decorated with images and *veves* of the various Lwa, are used to entice the spirits to come to their altars, and these have become a form of collectible Haitian folk art among non-Vodouisants. Altars do not have to be large or elaborate and come in all sizes and shapes, depending on the Lwa included, the purpose for their construction, and the initiatory rank (or lack thereof) of their creators. I will show you how to create a temporary altar to perform a small Vodou ceremony called an *Iliminasyon* in Chapter 9.

Ethics in Vodou

One of the defining elements of most revealed religions is the existence of creeds or commandments, often moral in nature, that unite believers. Ethical documents like the Ten Commandments of Judaism or the collections of *shari'a* law in Islam serve to define appropriate behavior by believers and outline the ways in which they should or should not conduct their lives, just as secular law governs the behavior of the wider community.

Many cultic religions and practice-oriented traditions, by contrast, confuse outsiders with their seeming lack of "commandments." Since there is no standard, agreed-upon, codified rule or benchmark of behavior, they can seem lawless, disorganized, or chaotic to someone who is used to revealed religions. Haitian Vodou often appears amoral to those who are not familiar with it, partly due to its lack of an officially written or universal ethical statement and partly due to at least two centuries of propaganda associating its practice with barbarism and Satanism and other negative things.

Yet, Haitian Vodou has ethics, just as it has structure. Just as Vodou is more about what you do than what you believe in, its ethical structure is also defined by an action-based, pragmatic manner versus a codified, intellectual philosophy. Vodouisants understand, both from their personal experiences and the experience of the Haitian people over the centuries, that the universe is an orderly place, even if it is not always nice or fair. They know that those who have power are often those who take it; at the same time, they also understand that Bondye knows and sees all, and no one will get away with evil behavior forever. There is a belief in Haitian Vodou—both in an abstract sense and in the practical application of magic and ritual to one's life—that what you do is what you are, and what you give is what you will receive. It is believed that like begets like, and that the Lwa reward their servants in direct proportion to what they receive from those servants.

This is not just a simple "you scratch my back and I'll scratch yours" idea of the universe, though certainly that level of things is understood and Vodouisants would generally believe such an exchange philosophy to be true. A Vodouisant understands that the things he chooses to do or believe—as well as the things he chooses *not* to do or *not* to believe—have a direct and tangible impact on his world. The *houngan* who acts fairly and truthfully with love and respect will generally be loved and respected; a greedy and rude *mambo* will generally be ignored or treated rudely. In the most basic of terms, those people who engage in positive behavior will have a positive experience, and those who engage in negative behavior will have a negative experience.

Evil can (and does) happen in the world—no Haitian would ever be capable of believing otherwise—but Vodouisants believe that ultimately, Bondye is beyond evil and will come out on top in the end. The incidence of bad events, bad luck, or evil in one's personal life is taken not as the punishment of a jealous and vengeful god, but as a sign from the spiritual world that something is out of balance and needs to be corrected. Via divination and direct consultation with the Lwa, such problems can be identified and resolved and evil averted.

Even the legendary Bwa Kayiman ceremony and the subsequent Haitian Revolution show this philosophy and practice in microcosm. The people were suffering, so they consulted the Lwa. The Lwa told them that this suffering was not right, who it was caused by, and how to resolve it. The people then went out and fixed the problem with the help of the Lwa, giving thanks to the Lwa once they had done so.

In terms of magical practice, one could say that the Vodou philosophy is that a person is free to do as she wishes, yet responsible for all consequences. To use a common example: in Vodou, it is perfectly and ethically acceptable to do magic (or to hire someone else to do magic on your behalf) to cause a person to love you. However, if the magic is successful, can you live with the knowledge that your partner may not love you out of free will, but because you forced it to happen?

In cases where a *mambo* or *houngan* or *bokor* is hired to do magic for a client, the ethical consequences do not belong to the magician, but to the client. Just as "guns do not kill people; people kill people," Vodouisants believe that magicians for hire are not responsible for the results of their magic—the person who paid for the magic to be done is. This lack of a defined moral teaching about magic, like the "harm none" caveat in most forms of Wicca, sometimes makes outsiders think Vodouisants lack ethics or morality. In truth, the Haitian expression of ethical behavior is simply different, and it is based in a completely different worldview and experience.

THREE

Haitian Vodou Confusions and Controversies

When we are defining Haitian Vodou, we also have to talk a little bit about some other things. We need to clarify what it is not and what it does not include, due to some misunderstandings that have been perpetuated about African religious and cultural survivals across the Western Hemisphere. Most notably, it is important to explain the differences between Haitian Vodou and the practices of New Orleans Voodoo and American Hoodoo, both of which Haitian Vodou has been confused with for almost a century. We also have to talk about some of the elements of Haitian Vodou practice that have been taken out of context or completely exaggerated, most notably the concepts of making sacrifices to the Lwa (particularly animal sacrifice and allegations of human sacrifice), the "Voodoo doll," the "zombie," and trance possession.

We also have to address significant controversies, such as the place of outsiders in Haitian Vodou; the use of Roman Catholic symbolism in what is ultimately a non-Christian, African spiritual tradition; and the future of Haitian Vodou as a distinct cultural phenomenon in a multicultural, globally connected world. This chapter will hopefully make some of these confusions and controversies easier to understand within the wider context of Haitian Vodou practice as it really is.

Haitian Vodou Is Not New Orleans Voodoo

It would be impossible for me to explain the rich history and culture of New Orleans Voodoo in a few paragraphs. The subject is at least as deep as the subject of Haitian Vodou, and it deserves its own books and treatments by people far more knowledgeable about it than me. However, the two practices are called by the same word (albeit with different spellings most of the time), and more and more New Orleans Voodoo practitioners have been initiating into Haitian Vodou, thus making what they do less and less different from what we do. Because of this, it is important to give at least a basic understanding of where New Orleans Voodoo (or Louisiana Voodoo) comes from and how it differs from Vodou practiced in Haiti and by Haitians and others trained by them outside of Haiti.

Unlike the Haitian slave trade, African arrivals in Louisiana came both chronologically later and from a more homogeneous area: between 1719 and 1808, and mostly from areas that are now part of the Yoruba-language areas of the modern nation of Benin. Additionally, unlike Haiti, where African families were routinely separated in the slave markets or before, slaves who arrived in Louisiana as a family group were legally required to be sold as a group. Thus, in Louisiana, the African heritage of a particular group of slaves was more likely to be preserved, since mothers, children, siblings, and elders were kept together on the same plantations or worked for the same people in the same areas without being separated. While conditions in the Louisiana colony and subsequent United States were difficult, they were still vastly superior to those in Haiti, where a slave might expect to live a year or two before dying of overwork. Because of this, there were actual African elders in Louisiana living out their natural lives among their descendants without separation. These elders were able to keep the traditions and cultural information of their homeland alive.

New Orleans Voodoo retains its West African traditions in fairly original or slightly modified form, such as the use of actual snakes in temples and dances and its past reference to its priesthood as "queens and kings" instead of *mambos* and *houngans*. The queens and kings of Voodoo survive today only as part of the Mardi Gras tradition, which, while Voodoo-influenced, is not itself New Orleans Voodoo. Whereas Haitian Vodou melds dozens of African traditions with those of the indigenous Taino and Ciboney and the Roman Catholicism of the slave owners, New Orleans Voodoo's syncretisms come primarily from North American indigenous groups, the "spiritual churches" of the American South, and various European grimoire-based magical traditions acquired from German, French, English, Scottish, and Irish immigrants to Louisiana.

In the early twentieth century, New Orleans Voodoo responded to the horrible things coming out of books and movies being made about the American occupation of Haiti and created a sort of sensational, entertainment-only public face full of the snake brandishing, shrieking, and half-naked "African" dancing that tourists demanded to see. At the same time, authentic Voodoo practices retreated underground and became more secret, practiced quietly in Voodoo families and hidden symbolically in Mardi Gras traditions such as the marching "Indian" societies. In 1935, anthropologist and author Zora Neale Hurston would note in her research on African religious survivals in the American South that a local told her that even in New Orleans, nobody used the term "Voodoo" to describe what they did. Outsiders had imposed it on them, just as it was being imposed on the practices of Haiti at the same time. Because of this, I am reluctant to impose the name myself, though New Orleans traditions and Haitian Vodou are separate branches on the same spiritual tree.

Haitian Vodou Is Not Hoodoo nor Conjure

The same European traditions that found their way into New Orleans Voodoo also inform the practice of Hoodoo, a highly syncretic African-American tradition still practiced throughout the American South and elsewhere in the United States. While some New Orleans Voodoo practitioners and even some Haitian Vodouisants might be familiar with Hoodoo practices—

and may even practice Hoodoo alongside their Voodoo or Vodou—they are not the same things. Hoodoo, also called Conjure or sometimes Rootwork, is practiced by African-Americans and European-Americans, as well by as a growing number of people outside the United States. Hoodoo is a system of folklore and magic that is not itself religious, but almost exclusively practiced alongside various forms of Protestant Christianity, unlike Vodou and Voodoo, which are both generally syncretized to Roman Catholic Christianity where they are Christianized.

Like Vodou and Voodoo, Hoodoo derives from various sources, being an amalgamation of African-American folk magic; folk traditions from Africa, Europe, and indigenous North America; ceremonial magic; and Christian mysticism. It has no priesthood or official theology and consists more of concepts of herbal "treatments" to heal the sick and "work" such as talismanic and sympathetic magic to achieve certain ends. Unlike Voodoo or Vodou, Hoodoo has a fairly literate basis, being a combination of written and oral tradition, with "magic books" describing various recipes, treatments, or works, alongside oral teaching from a practitioner who passes his or her knowledge along as master to an apprentice in a solitary fashion. Six volumes of interviews with American Hoodoo practitioners were transcribed from audio recordings made between 1936 and 1970 by a Midwestern folklorist named Harry Middleton Hyatt, and these can still be read to learn a great deal about this uniquely American magical tradition often confused with Voodoo and/or Vodou.

Sacrifices in Vodou

Getting back to Haitian Vodou, we address perhaps the largest confusion and/or controversy that outsiders to the tradition will confront: the nature of sacrifice, particularly animal sacrifice. The Lwa of Haitian Vodou request many things as offerings or gifts as part of their ceremonies and service. Some Lwa want special candles or tangible objects like perfume, mirrors, or drums. Some Lwa might demand various drinks, from cool water to fiery *kleren* (kleh-REN, a raw, high-proof rum). Still other Lwa want various kinds of foods including fruits, vegetables, fancy pastries, breads, candies, and specially prepared dinners. Very few of our Lwa are vegetarians, and most of our Lwa eat meat, just as most Vodouisants eat meat. Remember that the practice of vegetarianism or other decisions about what to eat or not eat are generally considered luxuries in a country where food shortages and famines are far too frequent.

Because most of Haiti is rural, or possesses substandard infrastructure compared to what most people living in the industrialized world would consider standard, even now there are no grocery stores with gleaming packages of pre-cut, pre-cleaned meat products to bring home and offer to the Lwa. In many places in Haiti, reliable refrigeration is sporadic or impossible for various reasons. Even in Port-au-Prince, people often live as they did in the United States before the advent of iceboxes and butcher cuts: they hunt or fish and/or raise their own meat animals, then are personally responsible for killing, cleaning, cooking, and eating the animals they consume.

This is important to remember when confronted with what might seem to be a cruel practice of killing animals as part of a Haitian Vodou ceremony. Still photographs of thrashing animals and people or Lwa covered in blood do not convey the entire context of animal sacrifice in Haitian Vodou; they only heighten the sense of the lurid and give credence to sensational rumors started during the Marine occupation of Haiti's early twentieth century. To see some of these images might make one very well believe that Haitians carve up animals (or, Bondye forbid, humans!), gleefully splash blood all over the temples for their evil, bloodthirsty spirits, and then just toss the carcasses aside, if one doesn't know any better.

Nothing could be further from the truth.

Any animal that is given as a sacrifice in a Haitian Vodou ceremony, for any reason, has been raised for that purpose: to be a special gift and a messenger to Bondye and the spirits from the people who offer the sacrifice. It has been treated with respect and the full understanding that this animal will give up its life and its very body for a sacred act. Animal sacrifice in Haitian Vodou is a special and generally uncommon event: not every Vodou ceremony contains an animal sacrifice, and in fact, over my decade as a *mambo* thus far, I can count the number of sacrificed animals I have seen or assisted in ceremonies for on two hands. Especially in the practice of Haitian Vodou outside Haiti, where we have access to meat that doesn't necessarily require us to slaughter animals personally, the number of animal sacrifices that are incorporated in a Vodou ceremony is low; even in Haiti, it is a special occasion.

A sacrificial animal is not only raised in a respectful, humane manner; it will be treated with great dignity before, during, and after the ceremony where it will be sacrificed. It will be washed, sometimes more than once, by the participants in the ceremony and decorated with special objects, flowers, or sometimes even paint or makeup in preparation for its part in the service. The *mambo* or *houngan* who is responsible for the actual slaughter of the animal is trained in butchery; their object is to kill the animal with as little suffering or pain as possible, and every effort is made to secure a swift, respectful death for the designated animal.

Before most sacrifices, special food is set out before the animal; if it does not eat or drink of the special food, the animal will not be sacrificed, as its non-participation is taken as a sign that it is not willing to give its consent to be killed. Sometimes, the Lwa to whom an animal has been dedicated will come personally, via trance possession, to slaughter an animal and thus receive its offering. Once the animal is killed—which again, contrary to still photographs, is not dwelled upon or made into anything any more gory than the reality of butchery requires (do you really think pieces of meat in the grocery store were always so bloodless?)—a group of *hounsi* swiftly carry the animal off to be prepared as food while others clean the *peristil*. Nothing of the animal is or will be wasted or thrown away, because a life has just been given to the spirits—to waste it would be an offense not only to the spirits, but also to the spirit and body of the sacrificed animal itself. There are a very few, rare circumstances where an animal will be killed without anyone eating from its meat, but these involve an animal permitting itself to be offered as a spiritual stand-in for an individual. Such a circumstance might occur if, for example, a child was near death, and a Lwa indicated that if an animal can be found to replace that person, the child will recover. In those situations where animal sacrifice does occur in Haitian Vodou, almost universally the animal is then served as part of a communal meal to the *sosyete* that offered it, in honor of its sacrifice.

Some people find the idea of animal sacrifice abhorrent, no matter how many explanations or assurances are offered. Others are accepting of the practice but afraid that if they become involved in Haitian Vodou, they might be asked to kill an animal themselves but are unwilling or unready to consider that. I can reassure you here, perhaps, on both concepts by saying two things.

As for the practice, it is exactly like the common Christian or Neopagan practice of praying over one's meat before a meal; the only difference is that as Vodouisants, we pray over the meat before we cook it, and even before the animal is killed to provide that meat. In that way, we are directly thanking the animal personally responsible for our food. People who have a connection to what they eat are far less likely to disrespect it—ask anyone who has ever lived on a farm. It is difficult to waste meat when you know precisely where it came from and what had to happen to get it to your table. One of the saddest side-effects of modern life is that we often have a greater mental and spiritual disconnect from the things we live on and with, including the plants and animals who provide our nourishment, because we are no longer responsible for the daily work of getting our food from the fields and into our stomachs. It becomes impossible to disconnect yourself from the circle of life when you are confronted with an animal whose blood is symbolically, or even perhaps literally, on your hands.

After reading this, you may still have personal objections to the practice of animal sacrifice, in Haitian Vodou or elsewhere. I respect your objections and am happy to report that I have never known any Vodouisant to be forced to participate in animal sacrifice against his or her will, nor do I ever expect it to happen. If one had an issue with the process, it is a simple thing to not train as a butcher and thus never be asked to perform a sacrifice. Many Lwa accept *manje-sèk,* or "dry food" (food that doesn't involve meat or blood), and I am aware of vegetarian and vegan Vodouisants who are able to give *manje-sèk* to various Lwa without any repercussions. The Lwa are probably more understanding of these concepts than some humans are.

The "Voodoo Doll"

The use of dolls or other figures resembling human beings is a very ancient magical practice observed in many cultures around the world. The modern belief that Haitian Vodou uses dolls in a specific manner to cause injury or harm to human beings owes far more to an exaggeration of existing European magical practices than anything from Africa, though the first use of human figures in *execration* (cursing/harm) rituals is known from certain ritual practices of the ancient Egyptians. From Egypt, these dolls—which were abused in various ways including breaking, tying them up with string, piercing them with nails or pins, cutting them with knives, beheading them, or burying them in various places—were adopted into Græco-Roman magical practices. From there, they found their way into the early magical grimoires of medieval and Renaissance magicians. Eventually, these practices found their way even into modern witchcraft, where the dolls are often referred to as poppets.

There is a strong and well-documented practice of using dolls as part of magic in New Orleans Voodoo as well as in Hoodoo, but even in those traditions, the practice seems to derive from European roots rather than from Africa. From the Kongo nations of western and central Africa, we know about the use of a human figure carved from wood and pierced with nails called an *nkisi* (EN-KEE-see); however, *nkisi* are almost universally used as protective objects rather than to cause harm. A few Vodouisants might occasionally use crude human figures as part of various forms of individual magic, but it is not a common practice, and the entire notion of "sticking dolls with pins" comes more from horror films than from actual Haitian Vodou.

That being said, you will observe certain kinds of dolls on Haitian Vodou altars. In particular, the Lwa Ezili Danto is very fond of dolls, especially baby dolls, as she is always depicted with a child in tow. Some other Lwa enjoy dolls that either look like themselves or are dressed in their colors as part of their altar decorations. Some Vodouisants use doll parts, particularly doll heads, as part of their personal magical practices—you may occasionally see a bottle on a Gede altar that has a doll head inside. However, even these uses of dolls are not the same as the stereotypical "voodoo doll" that is designated as a magical stand-in for a particular individual to make them take harm as the doll takes harm, as when a "witch doctor" in some 1930s film jabs pins into a doll's torso to cause a hapless protagonist to sprout bleeding wounds.

The "Zombie"

In the Western African language called Kikongo, the word *nsambi* (EN-SAHM-bee) means "god" or "spirit." It can mean the Creator (like Bondye of Haitian Vodou) or any number of lesser spirits. In Haiti, this word—generally rendered *zombi* or *zonbi* and spelled *zombie* in English—persisted as a designation of spirit, and in particular, of a certain kind of spirit: the spirit of a person who has been "captured" by a magician to force it to perform his bidding.

During times of unrest in Haitian history—which is to say a majority of the time for most Haitians over the last three centuries—many rural areas relied on village elders and the *houngans* and *mambos* of their district to help them manage everyday life and society. In addition to being respected for practical and religious wisdom, these elders also performed the vital roles of policing society and enforcing the society's rules during those times when the police and the army were (at best) not present or (at worst) utterly corrupt and incapable of being trusted. A sort of parallel justice system developed in Haitian culture, alongside whatever official police force and judiciary that the government might have provided. Referred to by many names, this "secret society" or "secret police" force would make sure that order was kept by enforcing the laws in the absence of other law enforcement. If the police would not punish a murderer or stop a family feud, these secret societies would be happy to do so.

Such societies persist in Haiti today under various names including Bizango, Zobop, and Sanpwel. They are both respected and feared within Haitian culture as the ultimate authority that will punish those who have broken laws, even if the police can be bought or the government doesn't care. Part vigilante and part wizard, the members of these societies use many means to enforce public order, including the most dreaded punishment of all: zombification.

Haitians believe that in addition to the physical body and the animate force that makes a living body different from a corpse, there is also a special spirit within a person: their eternal soul. Sometimes this is called *zetwal* (zeh-TWAHL, "star"), sometimes a *bon anj* (BONE ANZH, "good angel"). Regardless of which terms are used for this spirit, the members of the secret society are believed to know how to dislodge a person's soul from his body. This is not a dislocation for a temporary purpose, as in a trance possession or when someone is under anesthesia or near death, but a semi-permanent removal that renders that person barely living, incapable of anything other than basic function. The term *zombi* has come to mean either the soul that has been stolen and enslaved (before or after actual physical death) or the living person whose soul has been stolen and enslaved in such a manner.

For a society with a history like Haiti's, the idea of being permanently enslaved, even past physical death, is terrifying. No "life sentence" or even execution by the police or the army could evoke as much horror as the idea that some unknown individual could cause you to die and then be reborn as a slave, not even capable of a desire to escape because your very soul had been stolen. Fear of zombification provides both a bogeyman to scare people into compliance with societal norms, and, on rare occasions, is used by the secret societies as an actual recourse for criminals in the society who cannot be stopped or reformed in less serious ways. As such, zombification can be understood to be a sort of last-resort form of capital punishment.

How someone is made into a *zombi* (the word is the same in the singular and the plural in Kreyòl) is a closely guarded secret. What is publicly known is that a special form of powder, made from various poisons and neurotoxic herbs, is administered to a person without his knowledge. This powder places the person into a coma so deep that even doctors will be fooled into thinking the individual has died, and then the individual will be given a funeral and buried. After a period of hours or even days, the person who administered the powder goes to the victim's grave, digs up the comatose person, and applies an antidote. The victim will regain consciousness, but damage to memory and neural systems will usually be so severe that he may not remember who he is or anything else. He will then be led off to work in the fields or perform manual labor somewhere, perhaps many miles from where he was buried, and live out the remainder of his days as a nameless *zombi* while his family believes he is still dead and buried.

The return of a *zombi* named Clairvius Narcisse to his family hundreds of miles away and decades after his "death," somewhat conscious of what had happened to him, was the basis of research conducted by a Canadian ethnobotanist named Wade Davis during the mid-1980s. His research, though considered controversial, was eventually released in the form of a book called *The Serpent and the Rainbow* (its longer, more academic form is titled *Passage of Darkness: The Ethnobiology of the Haitian Zombie).* The book became a best seller, and was eventually made into a horror film by director Wes Craven in 1988.

One wonders how (or why) an academic paper about the use of poisonous plants and animals in vigilante justice systems in a third-world country could become the subject of a horror movie. However, the "zombie," as the word is generally rendered in English, had been a star of the silver screen long before 1988. Beginning with a 1930s Broadway play called *Zombie,* which was adapted into *White Zombie* (1932), a horror film starting Bela Lugosi as an "evil voodoo master" named Murder Legendre, the zombie has been a staple of horror films and the monster movie genre for generations.

In 1929, William Seabrook's *The Magic Island* was the first book to use the term in English, describing what was (to Seabrook) a macabre practice of returning the dead to life with Vodou. As an outsider, Seabrook did not understand (or, quite possibly, was not interested in understanding) that the practice was not necessarily a Vodou practice but a Haitian cultural practice, and that zombification was neither a method of reanimating actual corpses nor was it used cavalierly. It does not help that there is an additional confusion: the live pythons honored in New Orleans Voodoo ceremonies are sometimes called *Le Gran Zombi* (after both the Kikongo word *nsambi* and a related word *simbi,* referring to water-spirits embodied in snakes) and had already been equated with "forbidden voodoo" in American cultural parlance.

Evoking the fear of the dead and the idea that the dead might be returned to life and enslaved or compelled to attack or harm the living, the zombie became just another one of the monsters of the horror genre, alongside the animated mummies of Egypt, the Frankenstein monster, or various other sorts of ghosts and ghouls. With Bela Lugosi's portrayal of an evil white Haitian using Vodou to destroy both the black slaves on his plantation and those meddling white people who interfered, *White Zombie* and other films like it were used as propaganda to reinforce both fear of Haiti as a black country and as a country with a non-Christian, African culture. Zombies and Vodou would be forever intertwined in the outside world's understanding, even long after the icon of the zombie continued to transform into the completely non-Haitian shuffling corpses of the *Night of the Living Dead* films, or modern zombies whose conditions are caused not by supernatural powers or African cults but by rogue viruses or governments.

As the secret societies of Haiti are Haitian and exist to maintain order in Haitian society, their practices and their membership are not open. While some of these sects do practice forms of Haitian Vodou or related spiritual practices from various parts of West Africa, the secret societies themselves—and zombification itself—are not Vodou societies or Vodou practices. Occasionally a Lwa (often a Gede) may mention *zombi,* particularly in reference to the idea of wandering spirits that have been "caught" and compelled to serve, such as the *zombi* mentioned by Gede Plumaj in a story I tell in Chapter 6. However, these are not the zombies of popular culture fame, and shambling corpse–style zombies do not exist in Haitian Vodou.

Trance Possession

Unlike other religious practices, where deities and spirits are always separated from the tangible world of the living and only addressed in an abstract manner, the Lwa of Haitian Vodou have a mechanism whereby they can partake of the same tangible world of their servants. Via the vehicle of trance possession, a Lwa can "ride" a Vodouisant—who, for the duration of the possession, will be referred to as a *chwal* (SHWOL, "horse") if he or she is referred to at all. During the possession, the Lwa takes over the body of its servant and uses it to eat, drink, dance, offer advice, take part in ceremonies, or otherwise interact with other Vodouisants in a physical manner. This is a temporary form of possession; once the Lwa has completed whatever it intended to do by appearing, it will leave or be asked to leave by an officiating *mambo* or *houngan* who knows how to dismiss a possession.

Most of the time, possession in Vodou occurs during Vodou ceremonies, where it is encouraged and invited by offering a Lwa its favorite songs, dances, drum beats, drinks, and offerings. Sometimes a Lwa or group of Lwa can be "called into the heads" of *chwal* to perform special acts, such as divination or herbal treatments. The Lwa very rarely appear without being asked to appear, though it can occur, such as in a case where a person is attending a Vodou ceremony but has neglected to serve a Lwa with a promised offering; that Lwa might come and demand it on the spot.

In Haitian Vodou, possession by Lwa is part of an explicitly public, community mechanism. Vodouisants do not call down the Lwa to possess their bodies when they are home alone. If they did, who would greet the Lwa when it came? Who would give it its offerings or ask it questions to benefit the gathered family? And who would dismiss it when it was time for it to go?

Additionally, while possession is an important part of Vodou ceremony, serving as a *chwal* or horse for one or more Lwa is not a personal "perk" for an individual, and it does not improve his or her status in Vodou, nor does it convey any special powers or talents. Vodouisants ignore the person whose body is being used for a particular possession, believing that that person's soul has been completely replaced by the presence of the Lwa during the possession.

If, for example, Lasirèn has come into Mambo Therese's head, she is not Mambo Therese anymore. She is Lasirèn. We will say that Lasirèn has come, that she is greeting her husbands, and that she is receiving her cake. We sprinkle water on Lasirèn, not on Mambo Therese. And when Lasirèn has gone, there will be a *mambo* or *houngan* who will make sure that Mambo Therese is all right. They will probably get her a glass of water or help her back to her chair if she is exhausted (which she most likely will be), and the ceremony will continue. The rest of the Vodouisants present will not gaze on Mambo Therese in awe or congratulate her for having been Lasirèn's horse. Neither do Vodouisants brag to each other about how many times they were able to be a horse or whether or not they are any good at it.

Serving as a horse for a Lwa is a duty that those of us who are asked to do it are honored to provide our Lwa, but it is not something that makes you special. Speaking from personal experience, if anything, it can be frustrating to serve as a horse. If you are acting as a horse for a possession, you don't get to take part in it—it is as if you fell asleep in the middle of the ceremony, only to wake up after the interesting part is over! You will not be able to talk to the Lwa or interact with it or gain its blessing while it is in your head. Some Lwa are physically hard on their horses, and you might be very tired or even sore for hours or days after a particularly vigorous possession. It is not surprising that some Vodouisants avoid certain parties for certain Lwa, leave the *peristil* during certain songs, or do things like tying a matchstick into their hair to try to avoid being possessed at times. The experience of possession, while important to our practice, is not nearly as wonderful as many imagine it would be.

Additionally, in Haitian Vodou anyone can be possessed, though initiates tend to be possessed more often and with less uncomfortable side effects than the non-initiated. Being a horse does not indicate a special rank or level of achievement; it simply means that you provided the means to an end for a spirit for a time within the community context. Possession by a Lwa is given the same amount of respect and weight as any other act you might perform for a ceremony, from helping cook the food to dancing to making a salute.

Some people wonder what being possessed by a Lwa might feel like. Generally it doesn't feel like anything at all. Before a Lwa comes into your head, you might feel dizzy or light-headed, or feel warm or cold, or maybe hear a noise or have your vision blur—that is, if you are even conscious enough to remember it at all. You might break out into a sweat or feel your teeth clench. Outside your body, other people will observe your body go rigid or slump down. You might stagger, or fall backward, or tremble as if you are having a seizure, or you might simply collapse in place. This portion of the possession is sometimes called a "crisis," where the soul of the person is gently or vigorously being pushed aside to make room for the Lwa. Those who are familiar with possession experiences, such as *mambos* and *houngans,* can often tell which Lwa is coming simply by observing what the horse's body does in the moments before the Lwa arrives.

Then, as suddenly as the strange behaviors and movements began, the person changes. Expressions, voice, body language, and mannerisms will all change, and we know the Lwa has come. The Lwa will be greeted by its servants, and will sometimes be dressed in special clothes or brightly colored kerchiefs. If the Lwa has special offerings or implements, these might be offered: Ogou might be handed a cigar to smoke, while Gede might reach for a special bottle of peppered rum. Certain Lwa like to sit in chairs, others walk around, and still others might do special things like jump into a basin of water near the *peristil* and swim, climb trees or the *poto mitan,* or even roll around or crawl around on the ground. Some Lwa speak with words in Kreyòl or other languages, some make nonverbal sounds, some scream, and some whisper. Each Lwa acts in a particular manner that is easily recognizable by the Vodouisants present and is relatively uniform throughout practice inside and outside of Haiti—a Danbala in Port-Au-Prince and a Danbala in Brooklyn both act the same way, for the most part, within certain parameters.

Once the Lwa has finished its business, it will leave. Some horses will be sat down gently before the Lwa exits the body; others might simply be tossed aside to crumple unconscious to the *peristil* floor. At ceremonies, certain Vodouisants (usually initiates) will be given the role of watching the Lwa during possessions and caring for the horses. They will make sure that eyeglasses and shoes are removed and kept safe to be returned to the horse after that Lwa has departed. They will watch and take care of the horse after the possession, if that person needs any sort of attention (a glass of water to clear the taste of alcohol the Lwa drank, a towel to dry their face if the Lwa got wet, a leg massage if the Lwa was particularly rigid, etc.). Once assured the person is all right, they will rejoin the rest of the ceremony, which continues on as soon as the Lwa leaves. Once the horse feels well enough to return to dancing and singing, he or she will return to the ceremony as well, with no ill effects.

Outsiders in Vodou

Since the Spaniards arrived in Haiti in the fifteenth century, there has been tension and sometimes bloody conflict between the servants of the Lwa and outsiders, whether they were Roman Catholic Spanish or French, the Protestant British, various Haitian governments, or Christianized forces within the Haitian population itself. Both Toussaint L'Ouverture and Jean-Jacques Dessalines eventually outlawed Vodou under their leadership, knowing first-hand how it could unite the populace to revolution. Most of the presidents following these two revolutionaries engaged in alternating between making Vodou illegal and trying to ignore its existence publicly while permitting it to go on privately.

Beginning at the Vatican's official return to Haiti in the 1860s and intensifying during the first American occupation (1915–1934), a violent anti-Vodou public campaign was carried out by the Haitian government, Church officials, and even the U.S. Marines. Drums, ritual objects, and *peristils* were confiscated and destroyed. Vodouisants themselves were arrested or killed. One of the reasons Papa Doc was so successful in gaining the respect of the majority Haitian population was that the destruction of Vodou and Vodouisants' lives and homes stopped for the most part under his regime. In recent years, missionary activities of various Protestant and other Christian organizations have resulted in new pushes to recriminalize or limit Vodou practice, despite the fact that Haitian Vodou is now legally recognized alongside Roman Catholicism as one of Haiti's official religions.

Even in the wake of the January 12, 2010, earthquake, there were people inside and outside of Haiti who sought to blame the earthquake on Vodouisants, either suggesting that the earthquake was somehow God's "punishment" on the land for its faithlessness, or that Vodou priests were profiting from the death and destruction of the quake. Several violent protests took place in Port-au-Prince, disrupting Vodouisants' attempting to bury their dead or hold memorial services; in one case, a mob of Haitian Protestants broke into a Vodou temple and beat elderly *mambos* who were trying to invoke their Lwa to help them find the dead.

If such behaviors inside Haiti were not shameful enough, televangelist Pat Robertson took to the world's airwaves and tried to suggest that the earthquake was God's vengeance for the Haitian Revolution, alleging that the slaves had sold their souls to Satan at Bwa Kayiman in return for the power to overthrow their masters. It was a low point in interfaith relations between Haitian Vodou and the rest of the world, and sadly, other than some comments about Robertson's inappropriate behavior, very few sprang to Vodou's defense. Even in my own interfaith circles, I would hear otherwise well-meaning people say really stupid things, such as that they thought it was terrible that Vodouisants were being attacked, but "maybe if they weren't sacrificing all those animals, [people] wouldn't be so afraid of them."

Add to this the treatment of historians and anthropologists who want to "study" Vodouisants and Vodou, as if detailing a pretty butterfly, a new virus, or the collected works of Shakespeare. Then add a growing number of spiritual tourists: non-Haitians with an entitlement complex who show up in a *peristil* to demand all the "secrets of Vodou," with little to no regard for their context or culture, or who want to pay a few thousand dollars for the privilege of being called a "Vodou priest" and then never come back again. Add the foreigners who read a couple of books written by those anthropologists, or who found some things on the Internet and have decided that Vodou is "neat" or that it needs to be taken out of Haiti for safekeeping. Not surprisingly, the result is an atmosphere in which many Vodouisants are inherently skeptical of or simply do not trust non-Haitians, for any reason.

With friends like these, Haitian Vodou really doesn't need enemies. Some Vodouisants are against any sort of involvement by non-Haitians, no matter what their interest, background, or level of sincerity. If you decide to try to get involved in Haitian Vodou, you will have to understand that this desire to be left alone exists; try to respect it, even if you don't understand it. You will have to persevere if you are turned down—and most likely, you will be turned down or told to go away at some point. Even once you are on the inside, as it were, some Vodouisants may still be uncomfortable with your presence until you are able to demonstrate by your behaviors and actions that, despite your non-Haitian origins, you are no longer an outsider. You will have to confront very uncomfortable concepts like white privilege, the ongoing legacy of Haitian history, and the politics of a multicultural society that has, in many ways, come to believe that the only people who can be trusted are the ones you already know (and even those not necessarily all the time). And you will have to confront these concepts regardless of your own background or skin color; for the Haitian, just as *neg* (black) is also the word for "Haitian," the word for "foreigner" is *blan* (which also means "white," and once meant "slave owner" as well). Even dark-skinned foreigners start out as *blan* in Haiti.

It can be daunting to be placed in this category, but perseverance and patience can make a change. There's a funny story I can tell about perceptions and how they can change. One afternoon in Jacmel, on my second trip to Haiti, I was shopping with one of my Haitian brothers in the Iron Market for items we would need in an upcoming ceremony. As I was paying for something, an elderly woman in the stall behind the one I had chosen to purchase from started shouting (in Kreyòl), "Hey *blan,* come look at my things!" My brother, a well-known *houngan* in town, immediately turned and said, very quietly, "That's MAMBO *blan* to you … " After a pause and much laughter from the woman I was giving my money to, the elderly woman came out from her stall, apologized, and then asked if she could show the *mambo* some of her best Vodou flags.

About Catholic Symbolism in Vodou

Some people who read this book or who have been exposed to Haitian Vodou practice or culture may find its emphasis on Roman Catholic symbolism and imagery uncomfortable. They may be confused about why Catholic prayers are said in otherwise non-Christian ceremonies, or why spirits from Africa would be symbolized with pictures of dead white men carrying crosses. Beyond simple confusion, I am also aware that some of the people reading this book may have personal issues with Christianity and may discover that these issues are consciously or subconsciously triggered by Vodou's Catholic elements.

Over the last few years, there has been considerable discussion (mostly by outsiders) about why there is so much Catholic symbolism in Vodou. If Dessalines intended to remove white people from Haiti (or so the history books tell us), then why are there still white saints and white prayers in our *peristils*? If Haitians rejected the influence of Europe, then why is the religion of Saint-Domingue's Europeans permitted to have any part at all in Haitian Vodou?

There are some who believe that the Catholic symbols and saints in Vodou are a relic of its colonial past, the "blinds" or "covers" that slaves used to hide their spiritual practices from their masters. These people will then tell you that, for example, we use an image of Saint Lazarus (an old man with a dog and a stick) to represent Legba Atibon (a Lwa also described as old man with a dog and a stick) because illiterate slaves used the images they could get their hands on. Alternatively, the explanation will be given that the slaves were amusing themselves by pulling one over on their masters, who didn't realize they were *really* praying to Papa Legba and not to a Catholic saint.

Vodou's assimilation and subsequent use of Catholic elements is considerably more interesting if you think about how religious syncretism works, and how the philosophy of Haitian Vodou adapts. While Saint-Domingue's slave population was able to overthrow its oppressors and become a free state, and while this demonstrated the power of Bondye and the Lwa to overcome evil, these people had been enslaved in the first place. The *zemi* did not protect the Taino from Columbus and his men killing most of them, directly or indirectly. In fact, the Taino welcomed the Spanish, thinking that the *zemi* had told them that these men had come from heaven to be their friends. By the same token, the spirits and gods of Africa did not protect the Africans who ended up being brought across the sea in the Middle Passage. Some of the Taino and some of the Africans who were enslaved were very powerful magicians and wise elders, and they enjoyed very good relationships with their gods and spirits. So why would such a terrible thing happen to them?

When Haitians reviewed their experience in their minds, both the Revolution itself and the events that led up to the Revolution, they felt that there had to be some reason why the white men had been able to conquer them in the first place. Because they had heard from their slave masters about the great power of their One True God, the former slaves came to the conclusion that this god and his power was so strong that it must have overcome their own spirits and gods, just as they had been overcome as people.

Whether or not this was actually true is irrelevant to what came next. Instead of denying that Christian god or complaining about how unfair it was that He had ruined their lives, the pragmatic Vodouisants declared that since the land and the people of Haiti were finally theirs to control, so was the religion of the white man. This powerful religion that could topple empires was now theirs to own and control. Instead of rejecting Catholicism, Vodou simply added it to the existing nation of Lwa, claiming all of its centuries of power and glory for Bondye. Just as the white had conquered the black, now the black was supreme, even over the white god. When the Haitian Revolution ended around 1800, the Vatican recalled its priesthood from the island. For the next sixty years, until the mid-1860s when the Church decided to return, there would be no official Catholic teaching in Haiti; only what parts of Catholicism that were already known to the Haitian people, or brought there by the European immigrants Dessalines allowed to stay in Haiti, remained. Indigenous priests combined what they already knew of Catholicism and Vodou into their own practice and kept the tradition alive, just as they had kept all the other traditions alive. Catholicism in Haiti continued without the Catholic Church, in a new and uniquely Haitian form. The intermixing of Vodou with Catholicism took place over those generations when the Church was not present to keep them separated. This is why, upon the Church's return to Haiti in the 1860s, one of its first acts was to press for officially sanctioned government anti-Vodou campaigns and to engage in the destruction of Vodou temples and their contents.

In modern Vodou, the depth and degree of Catholic imagery and symbolism in a particular *sosyete* varies. Some houses are very Catholic, with actual ordained Catholic priests serving the role of *prêt-savann* (PRETT sah-VAHN, "bush priest," from the term used for the men who acted as proxy priests during the time the Church was not present in Haiti) to baptize new initiates. Some consider Catholicism their religion and Vodou their personal magical practice. Others talk about the Catholic images in their Vodou in an archetypal way, e.g., saying that mentions of the Virgin Mary are really talking about the Lwa Ezili. Still others have started experimenting with a sort of Afro-Haitian Vodou and are trying to remove the saint images and Catholic influence from Vodou practice entirely.

For my part, I don't believe that Haitian Vodou needs to shed its Catholic elements. They are just as much part of Vodou practice as the singing of Nago songs or the making of a Kongo *wanga*. Catholicism is part of the Haitian experience, and the Catholic symbols are part of our history and the history of our ancestors.

For the potential beginner, what is important to know is that you *will* encounter both Catholicism and Catholic imagery during your journey into Haitian Vodou. If you have issues with either, you will have no choice but to confront those issues and come to some sort of peace with them. I know it is possible to do so. While I have no issues with Christianity, I am not myself a Christian, and some of my initiatory children are non-Christians. However, all of us are capable of understanding and respecting the Catholic element of Vodou practice, and we believe this is necessary to understanding Haitian Vodou.

Haitian Vodou's Future

Haiti has entered the modern world, and Haitian Vodou continues to be a living part of everyday life for Haitians, even if they do not practice Vodou personally. Haitians at home and abroad continue to attend Vodou ceremonies. The Lwa continue to listen to the prayers and songs of their servants, continue to answer, continue to come to ceremonies and down into the heads of *houngans* and *mambos* to dispense advice, heal the sick, and bless the children. The Internet has allowed Vodouisants scattered all over the globe to communicate with each other, with both encouraging and discouraging results. In more recent history, the Lwa have started calling to service people who are not from Haiti or aren't even of Haitian descent, for reasons that we do not necessarily understand.

As more outsiders get involved in Vodou, it will change and adapt, just as it did throughout history and all the changes that Haiti went through to become what it is. If the Haitian Revolution was the Big Bang of the Haitian Vodou universe and the second half of the twentieth century was the diffusion of galaxies expanding outward into space, now we see the various constellations and planets and stars trying to reach out to each other. Those who didn't drift very far shine brightest and serve as a beacon to those on the outskirts of the Vodou cosmos who are working their way back inward. We can only hope that Bondye will permit all of us to stay together on a certain level and not drift farther apart, and that as the Great Master keeps Haiti together, He also keeps all of us touched by her spirit together.

PART TWO

Lezanj: Meet the Twenty-One Nations of the Lwa

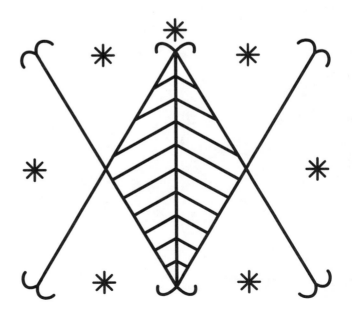

As I mentioned in the introduction to Part 1, Haitian Vodou teaches that there are many other beings in the universe that serve Bondye. Some of these divine servants are natural spirits: the life force or archetypal or symbolic force of natural elements like fire, mountains, rivers, trees, and the sea. Other spirits are the embodiments of human emotions or conditions, such as health, love, success, warfare, or wisdom. Still others are deified ancestors, gods or demigods, or the memories of African gods and spirits from ancestral practices that had been lost or changed upon arrival in Haiti, nonhuman spirits, or legendary folklore beings or figures.

Within the structure of Haitian Vodou, these spirits are called by many names. Some call them *Vodu,* a word from the Fon language meaning "invisible power" and the root of the word most commonly used by outsiders to describe the entire practice of Haitian Vodou. Others call them *miste* (mees-TAY, "mysteries"), *invisib* (in-viz-EEB, "invisibles"), *esprit* (es-PREE, "spirits"), or—in a nod to the Catholic contribution to Vodou—*lezanj* (lay-ZANZH, "angels") or *sen-yo* (SAIN-yo, "saints"). Another, more commonly encountered word used to describe these powerful spiritual beings is *Lwa* (pronounced luh-WAH or lo-WAH, and sometimes spelled *Loa*), a word I will capitalize throughout this book so that it is not misread as *iwa,* a word used for similar classes of spiritual beings by different Oceanic cultures in the Pacific.

There are thousands and perhaps hundreds of thousands of Lwa. Some are Taino *zemi*; some come from Africa, Europe, other parts of the Western Hemisphere, or even Asia. Some Lwa were discovered on the island; others came with slaves, visitors, or immigrants. Some were once human beings and/or Catholic saints who joined their ranks. All the Lwa are considered to be "the angels of God," working for Bondye to keep the universe in good order and interceding on the behalf of those who serve them, just like a Roman Catholic prays for the intercession of Jesus, Mary, the Holy Spirit, and the communion of Saints.

The Lwa are served in ceremony only after Bondye has been acknowledged. Because of the sheer number of Lwa and their individual requirements for service, including songs, dances, colors, and preferred offerings, they are organized into various families or subgroups. These subgroups are sometimes called an *esko* (ess-KO, "escort"), consisting of an individual Lwa and its immediate family, or a *nanchon* (nan-SHOWN, "nation"), a collection of *esko* known from a particular area or associated with the same concepts or service. *Nanchons* can be further grouped into divisions. Four major divisions—Rada, Petro (sometimes spelled Petwo), Kongo, and Gede—are generally acknowledged in all Vodou houses, even if the individual *nanchon, esko,* and Lwa within those divisions differ from place to place.

Each human being has personal Lwa, or a personal *esko,* in addition to Lwa of her ancestry, geographical location, family, initiation lineage if she is an initiate, or random Lwa that she might come to encounter in various ways. Learning who your personal Lwa are and how to serve them is an important and ongoing process for the beginning Vodouisant. In the vast majority of cases, the Lwa make all the decisions about those relationships. It is the Lwa who choose their servants, not the other way around.

Serving the Lwa

As the main phrase used to describe Haitian Vodou by Vodouisants, *Sèvi Lwa* (say-VEE luh-WAH), would imply, "serving the Lwa" is Vodou's central practice. The Lwa are given special offerings of foods and drinks and other objects they enjoy, and they are celebrated in joyous rituals of singing and dancing, often from dusk until dawn. *Sèvite* (say-vee-TAY, "servants," sometimes spelled *Sèviteur*, another word for Vodou practitioners that is the same in both the singular and the plural) dedicate altars for making offerings to and communicating with their Lwa. The Lwa are consulted for all sorts of reasons including healing, divination, or advice; they may answer their servants in the form of divinatory messages, dreams, or physical manifestation via temporary possession of a human body. (Possession is a topic in Haitian Vodou that is given far more attention by outsiders than insiders, and because of this confusion/controversy, it was discussed in more detail in Chapter 3.)

While we *serve* the Lwa in Haitian Vodou, it is important to understand that we do not *worship* them in the same manner as we do Bondye. The Lwa are the angels of Bondye, not gods themselves. While they appreciate attention and offerings, even their influence and help is limited by Bondye's will as well as their own lesser potencies as spiritual beings.

Detailed information on the various major/well-known Lwa makes up the chapters of this part of the book, and more information on the structure and nature of their service will follow in Part 3.

Mèt Tèt ("Master of the Head")

As each human has a personal *esko*, it is also understood that one Lwa in particular is intimately connected with each individual as a sort of guardian angel. This Lwa is considered to have been part of a person's life since birth and, once its identity is known, it can work with and for a person in ways that other Lwa will simply be unable to equal. This special guardian Lwa is called a *mèt tèt*, "owner/master of the head," after the idea that Lwa gather around the head of a living human, like the halo of a Catholic saint, and that one in particular stays closest to each person to make sure she remains happy, healthy, and safe. Some *mambos* and *houngans* have the ability to "see" people's Lwa and can tell the identity of their *esko* and *mèt tèt* Lwa instinctively; other people also think they know (or have a very good suspicion about) the identity of their own *mèt tèt*, even before they have been introduced to it.

Within Haitian Vodou, it is generally agreed that there are only a few foolproof ways to know for absolute certain which Lwa is your *mèt tèt,* including various forms of initiation or divination. It is also generally agreed that the identity of one's *mèt tèt* should be kept secret—if not totally secret, at least limited to the knowledge of certain trustworthy family members. Unlike other similar African Diasporic traditions such as Santería and Lukumi—where a person's "head spirit" is not only publicly discussed, but public initiation names indicate the identity of the person's head spirit to everyone—Vodouisants do not share this information openly or freely. Some Vodouisants will even encourage others to believe they have a totally different *mèt tèt* than they really do, on the grounds that if you do not know who their *mèt tèt really* is, you cannot possibly convince it to work against them.

Maryaj-Lwa ("Spirit Marriage")

The Lwa have various relationships with their servants, whether they are *esko* Lwa or a Vodouisant's *mèt tèt.* A unique interaction that sometimes occurs between humans and Lwa, and which is the subject of much curiosity, is the *Maryaj-Lwa* (mare-ee-AZH luh-WAH, "spirit marriage"). Lwa can enter into various agreements with their servants, for anything from promised ceremonies to special offerings to other arrangements. Occasionally, a Lwa may actually ask for a person's hand in marriage. A ceremony, also called *Maryaj-Lwa,* is then carried out, if the human agrees. Less often, a human might approach one or more Lwa seeking marriage and be accepted.

Maryaj-Lwa is exactly like what it sounds like. Like a wedding ceremony between two human beings, a *Maryaj-Lwa* ceremony is a wedding ceremony, complete with a priest, wedding rings, a marriage contract, and a reception with cake and champagne for the guests held after the nuptials. What is different is that one of the participants is not a human being, but a Lwa who has been called down for the ceremony into the head of a participant, via the mechanism of trance possession already discussed in Chapter 3. The Lwa then enters into a contractual, spiritually binding marriage with the human being, promising various benefits in return for offerings and the dedication of one or more nights a month to the spirit spouse. A human who marries a Lwa must abstain from sexual contact or even sleeping in the same bed with another human being on the promised night(s), instead sleeping alone in a special room of their *peristil* or home that has been set aside for this purpose, having prepared offerings and other things for their spiritual spouse. Starting on their wedding night, the human spouse will consummate the *maryaj* with the Lwa and will then continue to visit (and enjoy spousal benefits with) the Lwa spouse in dreams. At no time is the consummation of a *maryaj-Lwa* performed between the human and the horse that was possessed by that Lwa! This consummation occurs on a spiritual basis, during the human spouse's dream state. (There is no ritual sex in Haitian Vodou. Just as one would not have sex at a Catholic wedding Mass, one does not have sex in a *Maryaj-Lwa* ceremony, at least not until after the human bride or groom has gone to sleep on the wedding night, and then only in dreams!)

While it is never required for a Vodouisant to marry a Lwa, some Vodouisants contemplate *Maryaj-Lwa* or actually go through with marrying one or more Lwa for various reasons. Just like a human marriage, a *Maryaj-Lwa* is a very serious, expensive, time-consuming, and permanent commitment, both for the Vodouisant and the Lwa. Unlike a human marriage, there is no such thing as a "divorce-Lwa," and being willing to commit to one or more nights of celibacy per month for the rest of one's life, especially if one intends to have (or already has) a human partner, can be a difficult sacrifice.

In a few cases, a Lwa will consent to a person simply wearing a ring dedicated to that Lwa and engaging in certain practices or offerings without demanding marriage. In other cases, if a person marries one Lwa, he or she may also be required to marry other Lwa, particularly if those Lwa have a relationship, or if the Lwa have "hot" or dangerous natures and require something to balance that influence in the human life.

The most commonly married Lwa are Ezili Freda and Ezili Danto for men (almost always both, as these Lwa are intensely competitive and do not like it if one of them has more men than the other), and various members of the Ogou *esko* for women. Women who marry an Ogou usually end up also marrying a "cooler" Lwa, such as Danbala-Wedo, Mèt Agwe, Kouzin

Zaka, or a combination of the three, to balance out the fiery nature of the Ogou. Multiple *Maryaj-Lwa* may be held on the same day or at different times, though each of the Lwa that have been married receives its own commitments, special nights, wedding rings, and gifts. A few Lwa do not ever marry humans for any reason. For example, many Vodou lineages will not wed humans to the Gede spirits, lest Death decide to keep them for more than one night a month and bring them to the other side before their time.

Anonse o zanj nan dlo... ("Announce,
to the angels who are in the mirror... ")
—from a Vodou song that begins
the dancing part of a ceremony

ᵮOUR

~~~~~~
The Rada Lwa

ᵀhis chapter discusses the Rada Lwa, both as a whole group and as individual Rada spirits. In order to understand something of the Rada's character and nature, a history of the term *Rada* and its significance to the Haitian worldview is necessary.

Before there was a Haiti, before Columbus set foot on an island he named Hispaniola, and before the first slave ship reached the shores of Ayiti the mountainous island of the Taino, the seeds of the largest trees in the Haitian Vodou forest were already growing in the form of Vodu, a magical and religious practice in an area of West Africa called Arada (now part of the modern-day nation of Benin). When the coastal Aja tribe of the Arada (or Allada) kingdom conquered their neighboring inland tribes, a kingdom called Dahomey (Daomé) was born. From Dahomey came the bulk of those peoples imported as slaves into Hispaniola—the beginnings of modern Haiti's citizenry.

Arada was remembered among Haiti's former slaves as a holy place of the people who had come *nan Ginen* or "from Ginen/Guinea," the land of the blacks, across the sea in Africa. The people the Arada government sold or lost into slavery—from the tribes of the Fon, Yoruba, and Oyo among others, including its own Aja people—came to Haiti with only their bodies and spirits intact. In the creolizing cauldron of the slavery experience, these different groups of Africans merged their religious and cultural practices so that all might survive. From these tribes, from the dream of a mythical lost African world, the Rada nation of Haitian Vodou arises as a fragment of memory preserved by those ripped from their homelands, much as Jews newly exiled into Babylon must have remembered Jerusalem.

The Rada Lwa are considered to be "older," and thus in some ways more venerable, than other groups of Lwa served in Haitian Vodou. As they represent the *rasin,* or "root," Lwa that slaves brought to Haiti, the Rada form the basis of Haitian Vodou's African heritage, and in fact many of them are still served or honored in Africa (though sometimes under different names and in a different fashion). Because of the ancestral emphasis of the Rada division, those few Lwa who come to Haitian Vodou from the Taino people—the indigenous Lwa—are generally also honored as part of the Rada service, except a few that are considered to be too "hot" and are thus classified as Petro.

As befits their nature of association with what is ancestral and untouched by the violence and difficulty of life in slavery, the Rada Lwa are more archetypal in manifestation than other Lwa in many ways. Their service is more stately, their songs more formal, and their dances and drumbeats explicitly preserved from the various tribal and ethnic groups that the Rada division includes.

In Vodou, we honor the Rada Lwa before any others, immediately after praying to Bondye. The various Rada Lwa are called one at a time, starting with the royal Lwa of the Allada and ending with the martial Lwa of the Nago-speaking Yoruba nation. Within the confines of the Rada *nanchon* or nation (a term used by Vodouisants to describe a grouping of Lwa rather than a governmental structure), we encounter most of the Lwa that outsiders are aware of: Papa Legba, Danbala, Ezili Freda, the family of spirits called Ogou, and many others. The Rada are the protectors of the Vodou tradition and the mythical land of *Ginen,* the place where the ancestors live and to which initiates are invited during rituals that take place in the *djevo*, such as *Kanzo* or *Sèvis Tèt* ("Head Ceremony," see Chapter 10).

We associate the Rada Lwa with the color white and with a sense of purity and formality. Because of this, anthropologists and non-Haitians often described the Rada as the "good ancestral Lwa," while the spirits of the Petro nation of Lwa were considered "evil," or invented by slaves in Haiti, though this is extremely oversimplified. While there are Petro spirits indigenous to Haiti (or who started to appear after slaves arrived in the island), most of Vodou's Petro spirits come from the Kongo, Ibo, and Senegal nations of western and central Africa, among others; they are just as "ancestral" as any of the Rada spirits. Additionally, some Petro spirits exist as aspects or forms of the Rada Lwa, and Rada spirits are also capable of being forceful and violent.

What the Rada Lwa represent that the Petro Lwa do not is a sense of continuity from Africa, the repository of the ancestors and the African and indigenous roots of the Haitian people. The Rada represent the memory of what the various enslaved peoples were able to keep with them in their new world, while the Petro represent spirits who helped in the struggle for those slaves to adjust in a new homeland and a multicultural society. One could say that the Rada spirits look back to Africa and Ayiti and the past, while the Petro spirits look ahead to Haiti and the future.

The Order of Rada Service

Rada Lwa are particularly associated with order and tradition, and as such, there is a specific manner to how we call them in Vodou according to the *règleman* (rules). The order represents their hierarchy or relative importance to each other as well as to Vodou; as far as we know, this order has not changed since the days when the original *houngans* and *mambos* sat down and decided which Lwa should be honored in what order.

While this order is not necessarily secret, it is not often discussed outside a *sosyete*. Some houses have minor variations in the order, depending on which Lwa are served by a particular lineage, if there are any special ones, or if the Lwa request any changes; but for the most part, any Haitian Vodou ceremony you attend, inside or outside of Haiti, will observe the same order of Rada service.

The *esko* ("escorts"), or families of Lwa, also are generally unchanging, as they are specifically related to the parts of Africa and/or Ayiti that the various Rada Lwa come from.

Generally the Rada are separated from the Petro and Gede nations liturgically. Petro and Gede are always called after Rada, though some houses call Gede and then Petro, and others call Petro and then Gede; the former is more common in southern Haiti, and the latter in the Port-au-Prince area. The Rada are separated from the Petro and Gede nations literally as well, with separate *badji* (altar rooms), separate drumbeats and dances, and sometimes even separate clothing, with costume changes for different colors occurring between the calling of each spirit grouping.

As the Rada represent pristine roots, they are considered "cool" Lwa of life and growth. However, this doesn't mean that the Rada are ineffective or soft. Rada spirits have well-established demands and ritual requirements, and can be fickle as well as cool. (Some also have Petro forms or guises and are honored, separately, in both rites.) The hot, frenzied nature of the Petro and the fact that all Gedes are dead makes it unlikely for them to mix with the Rada. Some Rada Lwa even express distaste for them (e.g., Ezili Freda will usually not come to a ceremony if a Gede is already present). The Nago, or Ogou, Lwa represent a special case or exception to this general difference in "feel" between the Rada and other nations of Lwa. Most of the Nago mix freely with Petro Lwa, probably because they also represent a hot, militaristic, aggressive nature; but in a Vodou service, because they come from Africa, they are classified as Rada and not Petro. The Nago Lwa are served after all the rest of the Rada have been saluted, however, with their own songs, dances, and drum rhythms.

The Nago/Ogou nation of Lwa is also the basis of all of the spirits, sometimes called *orishas*, served in the Yoruba-derived practices called Ifa or Lukumi, also known in the Western Hemisphere as La Regla Ocha or Santería, and of several other Afro-Diasporic traditions, such as the Candomble of Brazil.

The sample order of service given here for the Rada follows the order of Rada service observed in Sosyete Fòs Fè Yo Wè. Not every Lwa we serve is given, but all the major Rada Lwa appear here. Following this order, a short description for each Lwa is given, with the Lwa's name and any alternate names or alternate spellings of their names in parentheses. In the Nago/Ogou section, equivalents to the names those Lwa are honored under in the Ifa, Lukumi, and Santería traditions are also given.

Aprè Bondye ("after God" ...)
- Papa Legba
- Marassa
- Papa Loko
- Ayizan
- Danbala-Wedo
- Ayida-Wedo
- Sobo and Badé
- Agassou
- Mèt Agwe Tawoyo
- Lasirèn
- Ezili Freda Daomé
- Bosou
- Azaka
- Osanj
- Ogou Batala
- Ogou Senjak
- Ogou Badagri
- Ogou Feray
- Ogou Achade
- Ogou Shango
- Ogou Balindjo

Papa Legba (Atibon Legba, Vye Legba)

First after *Bondye*, we call upon Papa Legba (leg-BAH), a trickster Lwa descended from an illustrious (and scandalous!) pedigree: spirits such as Elegba, Ellegua, and Eshu are associated overall with the symbol of the crossroads, the meeting place between men and gods and the seen and un-seen worlds. Papa Legba usually manifests in the Rada service of Haitian Vodou as an old man leaning on a crutch and accompanied by one or more dogs. For this reason, the saint image of Saint Lazarus (who walks down a road with a cane or walking stick and two dogs) is often associated with Legba in Rada service. Sometimes we also use Saint Peter, as the "keeper of the keys" who knows where everything is and isn't, and where everything should and shouldn't be. Papa Legba, as befits his transcendent nature, can also manifest as a Petro Lwa, and he is the first Lwa we call in the Petro ser-vice as well. As a Rada Lwa, we ask Papa Legba first and foremost to *ouvri bayè*, "open the gate," so we might experience him and all the other Lwa. Other names for Papa are Atibon (ah-tee-BONE, "good wood") and Vye (vee-YAY, "very old").

Marassa (Marassa Dosou-Dosa)

After one comes two. The Marassa (mar-AH-sa), symbolized by the twin saints Cosmas and Damian, are the manifestation of the binary power of the universe, the divine twins. Twins were considered to have special (and potentially dangerous) powers across ancient Africa, and they remain so today. Twins are considered a special phenomenon in Haiti as well. The Marassa, being both twins and children, come as innocents, and they bring joy and happiness and the power of rebirth and regrowth to a Vodou ser-vice. Their alternative name, Marassa Dosou-Dosa (mar-AH-sa doh-SOO doh-SA) in song, represents a trinity: the marassa themselves and the sin-gle child, male (*dosou*) or female (*dosa*), who follows or precedes them in birth. In Rada ritual, the third child is not always recognized; as Marassa Petro, all three will be noted as a unit. No expense is spared in keeping the Marassa happy; like fussy human children, they respond to sweets and at-tention, and they cry when they do not get their wishes. A special ceremony called *Manje Marassa* ("feeding the twins") is held at certain intervals. If the human children invited to take part in this ceremony do not enjoy the food and gifts lavished on them, it is believed that the Marassa, too, will not be satisfied, and creativity, prosperity, and fertility will not follow.

Papa Loko (Loko Atisou)

Some say Papa Loko (loh-KO) is the spirit of the very first Vodou priest. Others say he is the spirit of a *sosyete*'s ancestral land, upon which *houngans* and *mambos* are dedicated. He is also said to be (or live in) the *poto mitan,* the middle pole in a *peristil* around which all the dances go and around which all ceremonies are conducted. As a personification of the *poto mitan,* Papa Loko holds up the roof of Vodou, and he is especially honored by *houngans* and *mambos* that own or use his *asson,* or ritual rattle. We honor Papa Loko with the image of Saint Joseph, the patient worker who raised the Christ child as his own and is the traditional protector of the church.

Ayizan (Aizan, Ayizan Velekete)

Ayizan (eye-ZON or eye-ee-ZON) is the wife of Papa Loko and is sometimes called the first *mambo.* She is generally only approached during *Kanzo* ceremonies as the owner and keeper of the *djevo* or ritual seclusion space/temple, and palm fronds are especially sacred to her. Sometimes Ayizan is depicted as a shrewd old woman who owns the market and the concepts of economy and commerce. Much of the time, Ayizan is not given a saint's image, as she is embodied in the sacred palm fronds used in initiation ceremonies; in those situations where she is given an image, it is sometimes the image of the silent but strong Saint Clare of Messina.

Danbala-Wedo (Damballah)

The great white snake spirit of the city of Wedo (sometimes spelled Whydah in modern-day Benin), Danbala (don-BA-la) is said to be the world itself, a serpent made round like the ouroboros of Gnosticism. Danbala is represented by a pure white or bright green snake (a python or constrictor, not a viper). He is slow-moving but generous, kind and loving, and is often sought out by Vodouisants for help in their lives and even for marriage. His possessions are quiet and gentle but powerful and moving; during them, the horse is laid upon and then covered with clean white sheets, lest something unclean touch or even look at Danbala. The honor paid to snakes as his manifestations was misunderstood (and continues to be misunderstood) by outsiders as a sort of Satanic worship; quite to the contrary, Danbala represents the goodness of the creator. Most southern Haitian houses represent Danbala with Saint Patrick. Northern ones, noting that Saint Patrick was not fond of snakes even if his image is covered with them, use an image of Moses, the aged prophet who raised a snake of healing in the wilderness, instead. Some *sosyetes* use both images interchangeably, depending on the purpose.

Ayida-Wedo

Ayida (eye-EE-da), often formally called Ayida-Wedo (eye-EE-da way-DO), is Danbala's wife and counterpart. Where Danbala is the serpent of the earth, the curving arc of Earth's horizon, Ayida is the rainbow, a snake in the sky. She gives the rain to Earth and restores its beauty. Together, as two twisting snakes, Danbala and Ayida are depicted on Vodou drums, furniture, and even the *poto mitan* of a *peristil,* and entwined snakes appear in many other Vodou symbols. When Ayida-Wedo is given a saint's image, it is the image of the Miraculous Mother, the young Virgin Mary with a placid, peaceful smile and rainbow-colored rays of light streaming from her hands, with a green snake encircling her feet.

Sobo and Badé

In the Arada tradition, a *tohossu* (toe-HO-soo) is the spirit of a royal ancestor who is unusual in some way. Either a *tohossu* dies at birth, is stillborn, or dies while still in childhood due to a genetic defect; or is the child of an Allada or Dahomeyan king by an animal or other nonhuman spirit. Sobo (so-BO), Badé (bah-DAY), and Bosou (mentioned later in this chapter) represent the first type of *tohossu* in Haitian Vodou; and Agassou (discussed next) represents the second. Together Sobo and Badé, two brothers, are the spirits of thunder, lightning, and windstorms. They are also brothers to Bosou. Both Sobo and Badé are military-minded, depicted as generals, and honored as part of the Rada nation. As neither are generally served as personal Lwa, they do not usually get the depiction of a saint.

Agassou

Agassou (ah-gah-SOO) is a special kind of *tohossu:* the son of a Dahomeyan king by a forest spirit or the spirit of a panther or leopard. As half-man, half-cat, Agassou is a special ancestral spirit of the Fon-speaking peoples. He is honored in Haitian Vodou by those lineages with a connection to the Dahomeyan royal family, or by families that have sent members to Benin to be initiated in the panther societies that continue to exist there; he does not appear in all Vodou lineages. Where he does appear in a lineage, such as my own, Agassou comes in possession as a powerful warrior.

Mèt Agwe Tawoyo

Mèt ("Master" or "Lord") Agwe Tawoyo (met ah-GWAY ta-WOY-yo) is the owner of all the sea and its bounty. As the king of the sea and a mythical island under the sea, he is said to watch over the recently dead during the year that they spend *anba dlo* (an-bah DUH-lo, with *dlo* pronounced as a single syllable, "under the water") before their spirits are retrieved in a special memorial ceremony. Mèt Agwe is the head of a large *esko* of spirits in Haitian Vodou, among them the beautiful ladies Lasirèn, Labalenn, Mambo Filomiz, Klemezin Klemay, and Mambo Lovana; and several powerful Ogous, including Ogou Balindjo and Ogou Yamsen. Many Lwa clamor for a place on *Imamou*, Agwe's ship, depicted in the *veves* drawn for him. Mèt Agwe is a powerful and generous Lwa who greatly rewards those who serve him, is the natural patron of Haiti's numerous fishermen and sailors, and is a traditional protector of Haiti. His saint is Saint Ulrich, a bearded man of station (a bishop) holding a single fish, or the Archangel Raphael (who also holds a fish or stands next to a fish), and he is served with many things pertaining to sailing, fishing, and the sea.

Lasirèn (La Sirèn, La Sirene)

Lasirèn, (la see-REN, "the mermaid") is the wife and partner of Mèt Agwe Tawoyo. As a member of the Ezili *esko*, she is generous and beautiful, but she can be fickle and dangerous when angered. Whereas Mèt Agwe is the sea itself, Lasirèn is mistress of the sea's abundance and riches. In her alternate form of Labalenn, "the whale," Lasirèn can manifest as a powerful force of unconscious strength. Servants of Lasirèn honor her either with the image of the Diosa Del Mar ("Lady of the Sea"), a white-robed woman with a star on her head; or the image of Our Lady of Caridad del Cobre, a brightly robed Blessed Virgin shining from the clouds over a raging sea to rescue some fishermen in a boat.

Ezili Freda Daomé

Ezili Freda Daomé (eh-zee-LEE fray-DA da-OH-may), often abbreviated simply to Freda, is perhaps the first and best known of the Ezili family of spirits, all women of power and substance. Freda in particular is associated with womanhood in the sense of raw sexuality, desire, and feminine wiles. She has three official suitors (sometimes husbands)—Danbala-Wedo, Mèt Agwe Tawoyo, and Ogou Feray—and many unofficial ones, including both male Lwa and human men. She can be generous to her servants, lavishing them with material and spiritual gifts and lots of love; yet she can also be fickle, difficult, and even cruel. Freda, who is rarely called by her name in ceremony, but instead by titles such as *Metrès* ("Mistress") and *Bèl Fanm* ("Beautiful Woman"), is a very powerful Lwa, as befits her station as a woman of means. She is represented as a beautiful light-skinned woman, is alternately attracted to and jealous of other beautiful women, and will not associate with any Lwa who are peasants (such as Azaka) or members of the Gede nation. Freda is commonly served by men seeking sexual prowess or riches, and she is often assisted (or perhaps countermanded?) in this by her "sister," the Petro spirit Ezili Danto, who is a dark-skinned single mother.

Bosou

A *tohossu* like Sobo, Badé, and Agassou, Bosou (bo-SOO) has a number of manifestations, but all match his original image as a human with bull's horns. Some of the Bosou Lwa are very fierce and dangerous, and are honored as part of the Petro nation of spirits; but because of his Dahomeyan origin, Bosou is traditionally considered one of the Rada Lwa. As Bosou Twa Kon (bo-SOO twa CONE, "Three-Horned Bosou"), this Lwa is a charging bull that grants his servitors strength and magical power, as well as physical stamina and good health. As Djabolo (JO-bo-lo, "Devil") Bosou, he can destroy enemies or break challenges. If Bosou is given a saint as a representation, it is Saint Luke, the Bull of the Four Evangelists; or one of several images of Jesus Christ, depicted with three rays of light emanating from his head like horns.

Azaka (Kouzin Zaka, Azaka Mede)

Kouzin (koo-ZEN) or "cousin," is a Kreyòl term not only for actual cousins but for anyone considered part of one's extended family. Azaka (AH-za-ka) is a cousin of every Haitian, particularly those from the country. Kouzin Zaka walks the earth as a farmer, beggar, and vagabond—a Lwa who works with his hands and loves a simple, happy life. At festivals ranging from harvest feasts like *Manje Yanm* ("eating of yams") to his feast days, Kouzin and his female counterpart, *Kouzenn* (koo-ZINN), appear in possessions and dispense advice (wanted and unwanted), gossip, loan money and beg, borrow, or steal it. Azaka's presence is always a time for family and friends to enjoy. We represent him with Saint Isadore of Seville, a man in a dark blue shirt (Azaka wears the denim clothing of a Haitian peasant), carrying a sack on his back. Even Vodouisants who weren't brought up on a farm or don't consider themselves "country folk" can learn something from this passionate, joyous Lwa. Many times Azaka will come to a service alongside, or before or after, Gede Lwa due to his being a people's man and loving all Haitians, living or dead. A childlike version of this Lwa, Ti-Zaka (TEE-za-ka, "Little Zaka"), is also known in some lineages.

The Nago Nation/Ogou Family

Within the Rada pantheon of mostly Dahomeyan spirits, there is a subset of spirits from the Nago-speaking peoples of modern-day Benin and Nigeria. As mentioned earlier, these spirits make up the backbone of the Ifa/Lukumi/Santería traditions of *orisha* worship. In Vodou, all of them are considered to be in one *esko,* that of the Nago, and all the members are given the family name Ogou. This can be tricky for those coming to Vodou with previous knowledge of the *orisha* traditions; in those traditions, Ogou (which they spell Ogun) is a specific *orisha,* not a family name. For example, Osanyin, Chango, and Obatala are three very different and distinct spirits in the *orisha* traditions, and all three would never be equated with Ogun. In Haitian Vodou we refer to the same spirits as Ogou Osanj, Ogou Shango, and Ogou Batala, respectively! To help those readers with an *orisha* background, I've put the Yoruba name of each Nago spirit in brackets if there is a demonstrable, direct identification between spirits in both traditions.

Osanj (Ogou Osanj) [Ossain/Osanyin]

Ogou Osanj (oh-GOO o-SONZH) is a warrior like the rest of the Nago Lwa, but an "herbal warrior"; medicinal plants are his weapons and his war is on sickness. In my lineage, in possession he is very old and leans on a crutch or cane decorated with brightly colored ribbons.

Ogou Batala [Obatala]

Ogou Batala (oh-GOO BA-ta-la) is a venerable warrior who dispenses wisdom and is considered to be the father of all the other Nago Lwa. Despite his seemingly calm demeanor, Ogou Batala can be very powerful and convey great strength and power to his servants.

Ogou Senjak (Sen Jak Majé) [Ogun]

This is the archetypal Ogou, depicted with the image of Saint James Matamoros, or Saint James the Greater (*Sen Jak Majé* in Kreyòl) called *Santiago* in Spanish, riding to battle on a white horse. Senjak (SAIN-zhak) is a consummate warrior and very fierce protector. Some lineages understand Senjak to be the actual saint who has become a Lwa; others identify Senjak as a specific Ogou who is related to or walks with Ogou Feray.

Ogou Badagri (Badagi, Badagris)

Badagri (ba-da-GREE or ba-da-GEE with a hard *g* as in the word *go*) is a general, a warrior Ogou with a long history in Haiti as a diplomat or an instigator of wars that bring justice. One of his songs says he "throws lightning and thunder," and he is known to have a temper, yet also be fiercely loving. As one of Haiti's most beloved Ogou, Badagri's saint is Saint George the Dragonslayer. In some lineages, including my own, Ogou Badagris is a native (Taino) spirit, rather than one from Africa.

Ogou Feray [Ogun]

Ogou Feray (oh-GOO fur-EYE or oh-GOO fair-EYE, "Iron Ogou") is a very popular Lwa. He is a warrior and a blacksmith, the owner of iron and the implements of order made from it: tools and weapons. He is generally equated with the *orisha* Ogun, although unlike the *orisha,* Ogou Feray is considered an amicable soldier who fights alongside men rather than alone. In some Vodou houses, Ogou Feray is roughly equated with Senjak and/or given the same saint image; in others, Senjak is given a particular manifestation separate of Feray and is considered to be less passionate or "hot" than the owner of iron.

Ogou Achade [Ashade]

Ogou Achade (oh-GOO ah-sha-DAY) is a "boss" in the Ogou family, one of the older spirits of the Nago nation. He is said to be the father of Ogou Feray and an older, retired soldier who prefers to live in the forests alone. Like Ogou Osanj, he is an "herbal warrior" and can be good to approach about both herbal knowledge and healing.

Ogou Shango [Chango]

Ogou Chango (oh-GOO shonn-GO) is a vigorous, strong, young warrior in the Haitian Vodou tradition. He is not always honored in every house, but where he is honored, he is served with the same things the other Nago men like and is invoked for protection and strength.

Ogou Balindjo (Ogou Balendjo)

Ogou Balindjo (oh-GOO BALL-in-joe) is a Nago Lwa and a member of the Ogou group, but he is also uniquely affiliated with the *esko* of Mèt Agwe Tawoyo. Balindjo serves as the captain of *Imamou,* Mèt Agwe's ship. He is thus a Nago spirit who is also associated with the sea—with water as well as with fire. As part of his balanced nature, Ogou Balindjo is a warrior and a healer; a *mambo* in our lineage refers to him as a "combat medic." Balindjo is designated with the image of Saint James the Greater (the same image we use for Senjak of Feray) or Saint Charles Borromeo. In many lineages, he is the brother and/or twin of another Ogou, named Yamsen, who also works and lives on Agwe's ship.

Konstitisyon se papye, bayonet se fè
("The Constitution is paper,
but bayonets are steel")
—Haitian proverb

✝IVE

~~~~~~

The Petro (Petwo) Lwa

✝he division of Lwa we call Petro (sometimes spelled Petwo, after the way it is pronounced in Kreyòl) is a diverse and very large group of spirits. From the small inland tribes of Africans enslaved by their coastal neighbors to those taken by force in slave raids to the semi-divinized spirits of Haiti's revolutionary heroes to various warlike, vengeful, or "hot" aspects of some of the Lwa of the stately and "cool" Rada nation, the Petro nation comprises that part of Vodou's spirit world that does not look backward to *Ginen* or pre-Columbian Ayiti. Instead, the Petro as a group represent the history of the island from the moment of first contact, the "unity that makes strength" written on the Haitian flag.

In addition to being the spirits who listened to the cries of Saint-Domingue's enslaved masses, the Petro Lwa record the history of change. Where the Rada preserve and celebrate a peaceful memory of life before slavery, the Petro live in everyday Haiti from 1492 to today—a world often filled with violence, poverty, war, and pain. Within the Petro division are the spirits of warrior tribes like the Ibo and the Kongo. The powerful magician-spirits of the Kikongo and Bakongo people are represented in Petro as well, along with Haiti's fiercest protectors and spiritual guardians. Because the Nago nation was from *Ginen,* it is honored at the close of the Rada ceremony, but it provides a warlike, forceful introduction into the Petro rite, and many Nago Lwa have Petro aspects. Descriptive names and titles given to Petro Lwa also reflect their emphasis on strength, violence, and force: names like *Ezili Je Wouj* ("Red Eyed Ezili") and *Linglessou Basin Sang* ("Linglessou Bucket of Blood").

The evocative, forceful Petro ceremony—with its bright colors and flashing red headscarves, abundant fire, waving machetes, and loud, angry Lwa—was easily misunderstood by outsiders as the part of the ceremony for invoking "evil spirits." This is especially easy to see when Petro rites are put in comparison to the mostly lyrical, quiet, white and pastel-colored Rada ceremony. Some have suggested that Petro service is equivalent to Satanism or devil worship. Unfortunately this is not helped by the nickname, *djab* (pronounced job) or "devil," that is given to some of the hotter Petro spirits, but neither Satan nor any diabolic spirit is honored in Haitian Vodou. Strong warrior spirits do not equal evil spirits in any way.

What those who demonize the Petro do not understand is that Haiti, and Haitian Vodou, occupy both a world of peace and a world of violence, a world of calm and a world of righteous anger, at the same time. They always have. The Rada and the Petro divisions represent two parts of the Haitian experience, neither of which are accurately described as "good" or "evil." If the Rada represents that part of Haitian life worth celebrating and preserving, the Petro represents the passion, strength, and sheer guts Haitians have had to use to keep the Rada part of their world intact. Even though many of the Petro Lwa are African in origin, the rite itself is uniquely Haitian, and in many ways uniquely American—it is a ritual celebration of the reality of life in the New World and the necessity of uniting for survival.

The Order of Petro Service

We serve Petro spirits with the *tcha-tcha,* the gourd rattle that was once used both in Kongo rites and by Haiti's indigenous people, instead of the beaded-net gourd-and-bell *asson* (ah-SONE) instrument used to call the Rada spirits. Petro songs, dances, and drumbeats are hotter, faster, and less stately than Rada songs, dances, and drumbeats. The songs talk about the force of the Petro Lwa and how they can be dangerous and should be respected. Petro dances are stiffer, faster, and considerably less fluid than Rada dances (except for the boisterous, joyous patterns danced on behalf of the Kongo Lwa). Petro drumbeats are lower and more insistent, played with hands directly against the animal skins, rather than with drumsticks. During a Vodou ceremony, the Petro service generally follows the Rada service; in many houses one gets a sense that this is the portion of the ceremony where the pleasantries have been exchanged, and now it is time to get down to work. Many houses take a short break between serving Rada and Petro, and participants change their dress from white to red, or from white to multicolored.

Petro Lwa themselves come differently in possession than do their Rada counterparts. They are faster, more animated, shouting and screaming, as opposed to singing and dancing or sitting quietly and dispensing wisdom. Some play with fire, others perform feats such as eating flaming coals, spitting up blood, or stabbing themselves with knives, though their horses remain unharmed. (If you are interested in reading more about possession, please see the relevant section in Chapter 3.) Participants in the Vodou ceremony may strike the *poto mitan* or the ground with machetes or sticks, or swing them around and bash them against each other in time to the drumming. A *mambo* or *houngan* may blow a whistle—the loud, insistent sound of a slave owner telling his slaves it was time to get back to work. Cracking whips, roaring bonfires, gunfire, and small gunpowder explosions punctuate the night, calling the spirits to aid their children who are in need. To step into a Petro ceremony is to relive Bwa Kayiman, to be present when suffering people say enough is enough and ask for spiritual help to destroy the evil in their lives. It is a time of great power and promise, looking not to the past but to the present and a future unified for strength—a future that will only happen if we have the courage to stay together and make it happen.

Just like with the Rada Lwa, there is an order to how we call the Petro spirits in Vodou. The order represents their hierarchy or relative importance to each other as well as to Vodou, and—far more than the Rada order—the

Petro *règleman* seems to be divided along tribal lines, with various Petro spirits being served in sets with distinct drum rhythms, songs, and dances. This may simply be because there are many more *nanchons* under the Petro umbrella than there are in the Rada in most lineages, or it may be the result of the manner in which our lineages partitioned the order of service when they established the *règleman*.

The sample order of service given here for the Petro follows the order of Petro service observed in Sosyete Fòs Fè Yo Wè. Not every Lwa we honor is given here, but all the major Petro Lwa appear. Following this order, a short description for each Lwa is given.

Aprè Rada ("after Rada" ...)
  • Legba Petro
  • Marassa Petro
  • Mèt Kafou
  • Simbi-Dlo
  • Gran Bwa
  • Ezili Danto
  • Ti-Jean
  • Simbi-Andezo

Legba Petro

Just as the Rada ritual begins by asking Legba (leg-BA) to open the gate to the other Lwa, we invoke Legba again, to open the door to Petro. Whereas Legba in the Rada rite is an old man, Legba Petro is generally depicted as a younger man, controlling the crossroads between the spiritual world and the physical world. Instead of Saint Lazarus, the Petro version of Legba is most often depicted by Saint Peter, dressed in red and holding two keys next to a crowing rooster.

Marassa Petro

The Marassa (ma-ra-SA) in Petro are not two, but three. Their image is that of the Three Graces, sometimes called the Three Ladies of Egypt, depending on what part of Haiti the lineage is from. Petro Marassa are even more fickle and hard to impress than the Rada Marassa. In addition to the toys, candies, and sweets given to the Rada Marassa, the Petro Marassa eat meat—specifically, the meat of black pigs.

Mèt Kafou

Whereas Papa Legba controls the crossroads (*kafou*) in both Rada and Petro rites, Mèt Kafou (MET ka-FOO) is the embodiment of the crossroads itself. This Lwa opens the way to all Petro magic, knowing the secrets of the universe and being able to control them and channel them into the right places. Some lineages consider Kafou to be an unpredictable and somewhat dangerous aspect of Legba; others consider him completely separate. All agree that he should only be approached with great care, and only if he invites you to do so first. Kafou is not given a saint in many lineages.

Simbi-Dlo

Simbi (sim-BEE), like Ogou, is a title of a group or family of Lwa. The first Simbi to be called in a Petro service, Simbi-Dlo (sim-BEE duh-LO, with *dlo* pronounced as one syllable, "water Simbi") may initially seem quiet and peaceful for a Petro Lwa … but don't let appearances fool you. This Kongo spirit, believed to favor the form of a snake, is said to lurk in small pools along freshwater rivers and streams, dragging small children and the unwary either to an early grave or, if they are considered worthy, to a place where they are taught special kinds of magic. Simbi-Dlo is a powerful magician, and persons possessed by Simbi will douse themselves in water, wriggle along the ground, or sometimes leap upward without warning. I have personally observed more than one Simbi climb a tree without using the horse's hands, or suddenly jump straight up to dangle from the rafters of a *peristil* in the midst of its random, sinuous dance. Many houses use images of John the Baptist (either as a child or an adult baptizing Christ) to represent Simbi-Dlo. Others use an image of Moses lifting a snake in the wilderness; still others use an image of the Three Wise Men to indicate three common Simbi spirits (Dlo, Andezo, and Makaya) together.

Gran Bwa

Gran Bwa (gran buh-WAH, with *bwa* pronounced as one syllable, "Big Woods") is a very old, immense Kongo spirit, the spirit of all the leaves, all the trees, and all the wild forest and herbs and undergrowth of Haiti. Sometimes, he is depicted using a *veve* derived from an analogous Taino *zemi*; this *veve* resembles a blocky human figure with a heart-shaped face. Other lineages use other *veves* for Gran Bwa, but all of them recall leaves and trees and the power of herbal magic. In possession he is fast and force-ful, coming only to do herbal work and then disappearing almost before anyone notices. Sometimes he sends various healing spirits of the forest in his stead. A complex dance using crossed wooden sticks, also called *bwa,* is used as part of Gran Bwa's service in southern Haiti. Gran Bwa's saint image is Sebastian, a youth tied to a tree and impaled with wooden arrows.

Ezili Danto

Ezili Danto (eh-ZEE-lee don-TOE), often called Mami Danto by her chil-dren, is one of the most famous and universally honored Lwa in Haitian Vodou. Like the Rada Ezilis, Danto is also depicted with an image of the Blessed Virgin Mary, but in Danto's case, it is a always a Madonna figure: the Mater Salvatoris, Our Lady of Perpetual Help, or Our Lady of Czechos-towa, depending on what part of Haiti the lineage is in. Danto is always shown with a child, who in this case is not a boy like the baby Jesus, but a little girl named Anaïs (on-eye-EES). Motherhood, and the life of a mother, is a crucial part of Danto's identity. She is a single mother, a Haitian peasant who has mouths to feed, and is not going to wait for a man to handle things for her. Unlike Freda, she has no need for frills or coquetry; she drinks crème de cacao, *kleren* (raw rum), and black coffee, and she smokes a pipe and eats spicy food like *griot* (see Chapter 8).

Unlike Freda, Ezili Danto does not speak in perfect, musical French: in fact, Danto cannot speak at all. Instead she makes a sort of strangled, staccato sound, as if trying to get out a warning but is unable to. In some lineages, it is said that Danto was originally a slave who had her tongue out when she tried to warn other slaves of danger. In other lineages, they say Freda was jealous of Danto's child and the two Lwa fought. Freda ripped out Danto's tongue and scratched her face (several of the Mary images used for Danto bear three distinct scars on the Virgin's cheek). Danto favors daggers, and a set of them will usually be kept on her altar for her to hold (and swing around wildly to punctuate her attempts to speak) when she comes in possession.

Despite the initially harsh and sometimes terrifying appearance of Ezili Danto, both in iconography and in possession, she is a deeply caring, strong, fiercely dedicated Lwa that everyone who joins a Vodou house will come to know and love. Danto loves her children unconditionally and will fight for them to succeed and help them whenever they ask. She loves children in general and is a fierce guardian and protector for orphans, sick youngsters, or children who have been abused. I have never had a faster reaction to a petition of a Lwa than I did the day I asked Mami Danto to help locate a man who had murdered a woman's child and run away from the police. Quite literally, the moment I lit a candle on her altar, the phone in the next room began to ring with the news that he had been arrested.

Ti-Jean

In some lineages, Ti-Jean (tee-ZHAN, "Little John") is Mami Danto's husband; in others, he is her son; in still others there are several Ti-Jean to serve various relationships. All over Haiti, however, Ti-Jean as a specific Lwa is invoked as a powerful exorcist, healer, and magician. His possessions are extraordinary and often involve dances and other feats involving fire and burning coals. Some of the most skeptical observers to Vodou ceremonies change their minds about the reality of spirit possession after observing Ti-Jean. I have seen a Ti-Jean eat flaming logs as if they were corn on the cob, while a second Ti-Jean set the first's hair aflame. In another ceremony at another house, I watched a Ti-Jean take a bit of gasoline into his mouth, only to light it and blow flames all over a man's injured knee (the man was not burned or even singed). Then the Lwa drank the rest of the gasoline in the container, as if it were water. A first-time observer, assuming this was some sort of a staged stunt, asked Ti-Jean for the bottle, took a sip, and spent the rest of his evening outside the *peristil* vomiting. Ti-Jean is boisterous: shouting and singing, waving around logs, flares, or machetes soaked in *kleren* and set alight. But, like Danto, he is fiercely loving and takes good care of his children. Ti-Jean is usually depicted with an image of John the Baptist as a child, clutching a fluffy white lamb.

Simbi-Andezo

Andezo, or "in two waters," is the phrase describing a tidal pool—a body of water consisting of neither fresh nor salt water, but mixing both equally. It is also a metaphorical concept in Vodou, designating a thing that partakes of more than one nature or state of being, a state required for magic to be successful. Simbi-Andezo (sim-BEE on-day-ZO) is a powerful magical Lwa, even more so than his (or her, or its—some lineages believe Dlo and Andezo are interchangeably male or female) sibling Simbi-Dlo. As befits Andezo's position between the watery Simbi-Dlo and the fiery Simbi-Makaya (who is himself not often served in Vodou houses), Simbi-Andezo is usually served with the colors of both red and green, or red and teal, or red and blue, to note the mixing of those two elements in his nature. If he is given his own saint, it is usually the adult John the Baptist pouring water over Jesus Christ, or an image of Moses holding up the snake in the wilderness.

Nan Ginen m'te ye, se nan Ginen m'prale
("I was in Ginen, I will go back to Ginen")
—from a traditional Vodou song

SIX

The Gede Lwa

Everybody dies. Everybody has a relationship with the dead in some way: dead ancestors, dead relatives, the men and women buried in the cemeteries we pass every day of our lives or read about in the obituaries. Someday we will be dead people, too. Death is a natural stage of life, the final stage of our existence in this world (to our knowledge), and the Lwa also observe this natural order by having their own nation strictly for the spirits of the unknown and forgotten dead: the Gede Lwa.

When a person dies in Haiti, generally he or she will have a funeral and be buried and remembered by his or her family. If that person is a Vodouisant, he or she will be ritually honored twice after death: once at the *Dessounin* (deh-so-NEN) ceremony not long after death, and once at the *Kase-Kanari* (KAHS-ka-na-REE, "breaking of pots") ceremony that brings his or her spirit out from *anba dlo* ("under the water"). There the dead person's soul rests with Mèt Agwe for a year and a day, and then the *Kase-Kanari* elevates it to *Ginen* with the blessed ancestors who have gone before.

For whatever reason—they are not Vodouisants, they died alone or a long time ago, or their children became Protestants and refused to honor them—a soul occasionally goes under the water and is never reclaimed. Rather than being condemned to wander between this life and the next, two special Lwa gather up forgotten or lost souls and give them new purpose as the Gede (gay-DAY) Lwa, a constantly growing, innumerable horde of the dead. These Lwa are Baron Samedi and his wife Manman Brijit, the father and mother of the Gede Lwa.

Because the Gede are closer to us than any other Lwa, they have a special love and concern for life and the living. They remember what it was like to enjoy life's pleasures, and they miss them. They understand how important life and happiness are, and so they come back to visit as often as they can. We welcome the Gede and encourage them to give advice, heal the sick, divine the future, and offer their special protection and wisdom to any who will listen.

The Gede Lwa are the only Lwa in Haitian Vodou that anyone can serve regardless of their initiation status, background knowledge, or prior preparation. Unlike the other nations of Lwa, you do not have to ask Papa Legba for permission to talk to the Gede; the Gede are a natural part of life, and thus are accessible to all. They can be intensely amusing as they roam around the *peristil* cracking jokes, stealing food and money, and mimicking sexual intercourse with each other and various guests. At the same time, they can be deeply comforting, as when they are called to help a woman become pregnant or offer their advice on how to heal a sick child.

Every house has Gede and usually calls them at the end of a ceremony, if they have not already arrived on their own without invitation and been sent away several times by then. The Gede are notorious gatecrashers, delighting to show up after other possessions and attempting to hijack a ceremony by leading the congregation in highly irreverent but catchy bawdy songs. In Haitian Vodou, the Gede own the entire month of November; and the first three days of November—All Saints Day, All Souls Day, and Saint Martin De Porres' Day in Roman Catholicism, respectively—are the opening days of what we call *Fèt Gede* ("Gede Party/Festival"), one of the greatest celebrations in the Vodou year.

In many houses, the Gede are invited to the *peristil* before the beginning of an initiation cycle. This is done so that they will be satisfied and not disrupt those ceremonies, which are some of the only Vodou ceremonies the Gede Lwa are not permitted to appear at. At my own *Kanzo,* after the ritual objects were placed into seclusion on the afternoon before the first dance, the Gede came to visit, ate up all the food, and otherwise capered around before they were asked (politely of course) to make themselves scarce for the rest of the week. One of my Gede Lwa promised he would not interrupt but would make sure I was watched over—and sure enough, a moth bigger than my whole hand (insects are common Gede messengers) followed me around the entire day of the ritual baths and dances before I entered seclusion. Mambo Fifi later told me that the moth landed outside the door to the *djevo* where we were secluded and stayed there the entire time until we came out for baptism days later, when it flew in front of me as I went outside to greet the sun.

Gedes are often particularly fascinating to non-Haitians because of their universal nature—who does not know death?—and to some because of the appealing imagery of skulls and coffins and spiders and black and purple and other things we associate with the Gothic subculture and Halloween. Others are intrigued by their seeming sexual nature: Gede Lwa are known to use vulgar words and make sexual puns and comments, to dance the *banda* (a complicated dance that is an uncanny mimicry of the motions of human intercourse), and to carry around a phallus-shaped baton. Still others have heard rumors about the great Baron Samedi, who is known in other forms of African-derived magical practices in the Western Hemisphere, including the very famous New Orleans Voodoo. Modern media have used Baron's image for many years, even before he appeared as a main villain in a 1970s James Bond film.

The Gede Lwa probably enjoy this attention, since they enjoy all attention. Despite the sexual innuendo, they are harmless; they lampoon vulgarity, and while they may use dirty words, they use them in a humorous fashion, never to curse or humiliate anyone personally. They do not engage in sex. Being dead, they can no longer enjoy that particular pleasure; but they mimic it, both to get their children to laugh and to remind them, symbolically, that life and death are always one. The Gede push the boundaries of good taste and behavior, daring the world: "What are you going to do, kill me?" They provide levity for the Haitian, who for three centuries has lived a hard life and sometimes needs to be reminded that despite all its difficulties, life is still a beautiful thing worth remembering, especially after you don't have it anymore.

Fèt Gede

Fèt Gede is an incredible affair, with literally thousands of Gede wandering around Haiti's cities and countryside at any given time, while all the Vodou houses hold dances and ceremonies in their honor in their *peristils* and the cemeteries themselves. In Haiti's past, packs of singing, dancing Gede have wandered through Port-au-Prince up to the National Palace to offer advice (or insults!) to the current president, then capered off to the nearby cemetery to offer advice to their servants who come to get help for their personal lives.

During Fèt Gede, it is customary for the Catholic Rite of Commemoration of the Faithful Departed to also be celebrated by going to Mass or having it read aloud in the *peristil* by a priest. All debts to Gede are paid off for the year, and Vodouisants will visit other *sosyetes* to take part in their Gede parties as well. It is a festive and fun time of year. Even outside Haiti, many *sosyetes* hold private and public Gede celebrations and dances.

The Order of Gede Service

Just like Rada and Petro, we observe a ritual order to how we call the Gede in Vodou. While they do not have to be called in all the same ways that the Rada and Petro are, we do keep the Gede separate from those nations. In most parts of Haiti they are called last, after all the other spirits; some houses will call them on different days, completely separate from other ceremonies, or in a space between the Rada and the Petro service, with breaks between each section for changes of clothes.

We serve the Gede Lwa with the colors of purple and black, with quantities of incredibly spicy food (too spicy for the living to eat, and sometimes so spicy it even burns your skin to touch it), and with high-proof liquor. A particularly desirable drink for the Gede Lwa is *piman*, a special form of *kleren* within which twenty-one very hot Haitian peppers and other ingredients have been marinating for at least a month. Some Gede will not only drink *piman* but use it as a cologne, splashing it all over their faces and washing their underarms and other body parts in it! Considering that an ordinary human being cannot even handle *piman* without wearing gloves, handing a bottle of *piman* to someone you think might be faking a Gede possession is a good (but possibly cruel) way to check—only a truly possessed horse will emerge from that experience unscathed.

The sample order of service given here for the Gede follows the order of Gede service observed in Sosyete Fòs Fè Yo Wè. Not every Lwa is given, but all the major Gede Lwa appear. Following this order, a short description for each Lwa is given.

Aprè Petro ("after Petro" …)
- Baron-yo
- Manman Brijit
- Brav Gede
- Gede Plumaj
- Other Gede Lwa

Baron-yo (The Barons)

Baron, or Bawon (after the way it is pronounced in Kreyòl, bah-WONE), is an honorific title given both to various powerful Gedes, and specifically to Baron Samedi (bah-WONE som-DEE), himself also cognate/punned with Baron Simitye (bah-WONE sim-eet-YAY or bah-WONE sim-TYAY) in some lineages and representing two different Barons in others. All the Baron Lwa are leaders and judges of the dead, who here are not the blessed ancestors, but the unknown and forgotten dead—all the lost dead that Baron gathers together to serve as the nation of Gede. As befitting a man of his station—particularly a dead man of his station—he is dressed for the grave in a black suit and top hat. He wears dark glasses to protect himself from bright light, or with one lens broken out to demonstrate that he can see in both worlds. His food is far spicier than living people can stand, his cigarettes are strong and unfiltered, his favorite drink is *piman,* and his colors are black and purple.

Depending on the area of Haiti, Baron can be depicted with Saint Gerard Majella, the Archangel Gabriel, or Saint Expedite among others, but all his images will have skulls and/or crosses in them. While the Gede Lwa in general represent death, Baron himself represents judgment and control over death: Baron may not actually kill a man, but he can give the order for a man to live or die by withholding or granting permission to "dig his grave." While some forms of Baron can speak, some simply lay still on the ground or floor or can only speak once their jaws have been tied shut with cotton gauze, as was once done to corpses before the advent of modern embalming.

Manman Brijit

Baron's wife is named Brijit (brih-ZHEET) and called Manman (mon-MON or ma-MON) after the honorific given to very old or respectable women. There has been some anthropological speculation that she may be a form of the Irish "saint" Brighid, who is herself a Celtic deity, but this is far from proven in Haiti; while some lineages sing a song about "Manman Brijit who came from England," others do not. The imagery and functions of Manman Brijit do not really resemble those of the Irish goddess of smithcraft and poetry. Brijit lives in the largest tree of a cemetery (or the largest cross in a cemetery, which will also be where her husband, Baron, is to be found and served) and is not often seen in possession or ceremonies, being one of only a handful of female Gede. In lineages where she is given her own saint and not simply honored alongside Baron as his partner, we designate Manman Brijit with wild-haired Saint Rosalia in a cave praying to a skull, or stately crowned Saint Helena holding her giant cross.

Brav Gede (Gede Nibo, Brav Gede Nibo)

Brav Gede (BROV gay-DAY) has personal significance for me, as he was the first Lwa I ever met in possession. I was attending a service in Jacmel, and before I knew it, someone brought me to talk to this rough Lwa who had perched himself awkwardly on a chair in the Gede house on the property. He was smoking two different cigarettes at the same time—backward, with the fiery end in his mouth—and dispensing advice to various people, and I didn't quite know what to make of him. Within five minutes, he had removed all of my doubts and provided me with some important advice that would put me on the road to becoming a Vodouisant. Years later, another Gede in a totally different lineage, in a house in New York, would pick up the conversation where Brav had left off that night and give me the rest of the story. Brav Gede is Baron's "axe-man," the Lwa who carries out Baron's orders. If Baron Samedi were the head of a Mafia family, Brav would be his *consigliere,* making sure the armies of Gede were doing what they were supposed to be doing and keeping things running smoothly (in fact, at one ceremony I heard a Brav describe his job in those terms, stating that he was his boss's "enforcer"). Like most Gede, we depict Brav with Saint Gerard Majella.

Gede Plumaj

Plumaj (ploom-AZH) means "feathers," and in my lineage, this Gede has a fancy Mardi Gras masquerade-style feathered mask, which he can wear but generally chooses to leave hanging near his altar. Gede Plumaj is a typical Gede, with the rough talk and *banda* dance, but he is also a patient and competent teacher and diviner. To give an idea of what it is like to talk to a Gede, a story about Plumaj can be repeated here, since it (amazingly!) doesn't contain adult language.

At one party, out of nowhere, Plumaj walked up to me and said: "Mam'selle Mambo, I have many fine zombies for sale, would you like one?" Laughing, I asked what he meant. He frowned and then proceeded to tell me in a completely serious tone that he had been collecting lost souls (called *zombi astral,* "astral zombies") from a neglected cemetery a few blocks away from the *peristil,* and that he was training them to guard people and do other forms of magic, for a price of course. Someone else overheard this conversation and asked how many Plumaj had collected and how much he wanted for them. This same conversation was had at numerous parties over a stretch of several years. The last time I heard this conversation repeated—the *peristil* in question has since moved—Plumaj was up to "seven thousand, seven hundred and twenty-one" zombies, and wanted slightly less than $25,000 USD for each. I don't think he's sold any yet, but if he does, I think he's set for offerings for a few lifetimes...

Other Gede Lwa

There are legions of Gede, many of whom have names so vulgar they are not fit for print. Other Gede are known in certain families and not in others. Some Gede, like Gedelia (gay-DAYLEE-uh) are female; some like Ti-Mazaka (tee ma-ZA-ka) are little children. Gede Zaranyen (gay-DAY za-RON-yay, "Spider Gede") glides about like his namesake and sometimes sends swarms of actual spiders as his messengers. The night I met a man who would later become a brother *houngan* in my lineage, we were both visited by a tarantula that followed us around until we sat down to talk, and then it stayed perfectly still on the porch sill between us and watched us for hours. When either of us needs to talk to each other, Gede Zaranyen often arranges to send one of his eight-legged messengers as a reminder. Gede Hounsou (gay-DAY OON-soo) is a medical doctor and dispenses cures in English rather than Kreyòl or French, in a pitch-perfect genteel British accent. Gede Nouvavou (gay-DAY NOO-va-VOO) arranges himself in a hat and blankets like a South American native or the stereotypical Mexican bandit. Gede Vagabond, as his name implies, is a mouthy beggar.

Each Vodou lineage will have its own favorite or frequently visiting Gede; every Vodouisant has personal Gede, as well as Gede that belong to his house or his family. Gede can be dead people of any nationality and background. I have met rich Gede, poor Gede, and Gede who speak different languages. My own house has a witty Gede with an Irish brogue who claims, interestingly enough, that Baron "loaned him out" to serve as a galley cook for Mèt Agwe's ship!

Men anpil chaj pa lou
("Many hands make the work light")
—Haitian Proverb

ʂEVEN

Other Lwa

There is not enough room in this book to discuss every Lwa in Haitian Vodou. I don't even fool myself thinking that I actually know of and can serve them all, and neither does anyone in my family. Some Vodouisants say there are 401 different Lwa; others say there are many thousands more, or 401 *rasin* or "root" Lwa—401 major Lwa and thousands of local variations on the major and minor or individual family Lwa. In the Gede nation alone, no one can know all the Lwa, because new ones are created constantly. In addition to the dizzying number of local and family-only Lwa, there are variations of the greater or more popular Lwa, and lesser-known Lwa whose service is known in some areas but has been forgotten or merged into the service of better-known Lwa in others. There are Lwa who can only be served by women, some who are only served by men, and some who will only speak to the elderly or heterosexuals or children or white people or soldiers. And every person in the world has at least one kind of Lwa—because every one of us has a *mèt tèt*.

It can get overwhelming for someone new to Vodou to try to keep track of all these different Lwa and their colors and foods and dances and so on.

Then, when you go talk to someone in another house, they might tell you some *other* things about the same Lwa, or tell you about a whole bunch of Lwa you haven't heard of yet. You may wonder how anyone ever manages to become a *houngan* or *mambo,* given the sheer amount of information about the spirits that you seem to be required to keep track of.

The secret to not being overwhelmed is to remember that our Lwa are served communally. You will never be expected to serve every single Lwa in existence, even if you should become a *houngan* or *mambo.* You will be introduced to your personal Lwa and the Lwa of your family and/or lineage, and those will be the Lwa you are responsible for. From time to time, you may learn of other Lwa, or other Lwa may come to you and request attention. Vodou is a process of learning and growing. We do not do it in a vacuum; we have the support of the ancestors and our living teachers and elders, as well as the spirits themselves. Many hands make the load light, and together we manage to do what we need to do.

The *Really* "Other" Lwa

If you've read other books about Vodou, by now you've read about the "dangerous" Lwa, the ones talked about in hushed tones or hinted at by people who want to sound more powerful than they really are. Some of these Lwa are part of the Petro nation, some others seem to be outside of the traditional Vodou structure. You may have read about *djab* (job), *pwen cho* (pwenn-SHOW), or *pwen achte* (pwenn-osh-TAY): "devils," "hot points," and "bought points," respectively. These are Lwa or other lesser spirits that have been enslaved and are sold to others, to serve their new masters for eternity. Maybe you've heard about the *Anvwa Mo* (on-VWA MO, "sending the dead") ceremony, where a magician sends the spirit of an angry dead person to harm a living one. You've probably heard about the *Sanpwel* (sonn-PWELL), a secret society whispered about in books and movies like *The Serpent and the Rainbow,* that kidnaps people in the night or turns them into *zombi,* the living dead. You recognize names like Baron Kriminel and Linglessou and Mayanèt, but you don't know much of anything about them, or snippets of things that don't make sense.

There's a reason for this, and it's not because Vodouisants are just not telling you. Many experienced Vodouisants choose not to work with dangerous spirits, even if they know how, simply because dangerous things are, well, dangerous. These spirits are not dangerous in the way your mother used to tell you that if you went swimming too soon after eating, you might get a stomach cramp. They are genuinely dangerous, capricious, demanding, and hard to handle.

If you are lucky, dangerous Lwa will just ignore you if you try to communicate with them. If you're not so lucky, something worse could happen. Some of the dangerous Lwa will automatically harm those they consider strangers; it's their nature. Just because you really want to pet a snarling dog does not mean it's going to be a good idea to stick your hand through the gate and hope for the best.

I debated including information about dangerous Lwa at all in this book, as some people interpret an author saying "don't do it" as a dare to go right ahead. But I felt that I would not be responsible if I did not at least make (and explain) my warning. There are very good reasons that we consider these Lwa to be dangerous, and why we do not leave information about how to serve them just laying around for anyone to pick up.

These reasons have nothing to do with trying to deprive anyone of information. Native Haitians, even those who were born into Vodou and who have served the Lwa for generations, approach these spirits only in certain circumstances; even then, they only do so with certain training, protections, and precautions. This fact alone should give anyone who thinks to approach a dangerous Lwa pause.

Just like a responsible mother would not encourage her one-year-old son to hold a candle, no matter how pretty he thought the fire was or how still he promised to sit, there are certain things and certain spirits that really are discussed or approached strictly on a need-to-know or a when-you're-ready basis. If you need to know any of the dangerous Lwa, they will be introduced to you. At that time, you will be supplied with everything you will need to have a safe and sane relationship with them.

PART THREE

Seremoni: Haitian
Vodou Ceremonies
and Rites of Passage

Haitian Vodou is more than a collection of spirits from Africa and pre-Columbian Ayiti with a smattering of European folklore and Roman Catholicism thrown in. It is a living spiritual practice: the way of life of tens of millions of native Haitians, millions more Haitians who live outside of Haiti for various reasons, and a growing number of non-Haitians who have been called by the Lwa to join in. It is a uniquely Haitian practice, as we have discussed, being a creole (mixed) system that has brought together and assimilated many otherwise-divergent spiritual beliefs and practices and beings into a new coherent whole serving the need of an equally creole culture. In many ways Haitian Vodou is *the* "American religion," as it unites all the different cultural and religious forces that came together—willingly or unwillingly—to create the New World. As a cultic practice rather than a revealed religion, Vodou's emphasis is on ritual and action over doctrine, creed, and theology.

The central practice of Haitian Vodou is the ceremonial service of the Lwa. This can be done individually or communally, in formal rituals with special songs and dances to mark holidays and rites of passage, or in simple gestures and prayer. Vodou includes the use of magic, which is a set of ritual practices designed to effect change, and of divination, which includes various methods to discern the answers to questions that cannot be answered by conventional methods.

Magic

Magic is a loaded word in English and is often misunderstood. In the context of Haitian Vodou, I will use the Kreyòl terms for magic so I can better explain what I am discussing.

The general word used both for magic in Haitian Vodou and the act of performing magic is *travay* (truh-VIE, "work"). The same word is used to describe any other sort of work or labor in Haitian Kreyòl (or in French, where it is spelled *travaille;* the word appears in English as *travail*). This should tell you something about the Haitian magical philosophy. Nothing about Vodou magic is considered more special or supernatural, in any way, than any other sort of work/activity. Doing magic is not considered to be any more important, strange, or unusual than digging a hole to plant a plantain tree, feeding the livestock, or carrying a loaded basket to market.

Just like physical work, though, some forms of magic do require special training, talent, or expertise to perform. This training doesn't really make a person special, though, either. For example, a sophisticated *travay* is "special" only in the same way heart surgery is "special"; both require people to know what they are doing to result in success, but neither Vodou *travay* nor heart surgery is considered to be a supernatural practice.

The practice and styles of Haitian Vodou magic are the subject of Chapter 8.

Initiation

While any Vodouisant can, and does, perform *travay,* certain types of *travay* require training to learn and use properly. Additionally, certain spiritual abilities can be passed down by spirits and ancestors to be used to enhance their existing magical and spiritual talents, via special rituals. The ceremonies and *travay* that install these spiritual abilities inside a particular person, and then train him or her to use them, constitute the initiation ceremonies of Haitian Vodou. I say "ceremonies," because there are several forms of initiation, depending on the lineage of one's family and the family traditions surrounding the recognition of trained Vodouisants and/or Vodou clergy. See Chapter 9 for more information about initiation and its purpose and requirements.

Divination

Haitian Vodou uses many forms of divination and clairvoyance. Dreams are perhaps the most common form Vodouisants use to predict the future or understand messages from Bondye, the ancestors, the Lwa, and other spirits. Some Vodouisants are said to have "eyes," and can simply "see" various spirits and communicate with them about a person's questions, or they can scry for divinatory results using a glass of water and a candle, or by reading the smoke that comes off a lamp or a lit cigar. Many Vodouisants use cards to divine, but instead of the Tarot or other fancy cards used by many people outside Haiti, they usually read standard playing cards dealt out in even rows over a *layette* (lie-YETT)—a large, round, and flat woven basket. In some parts of Haiti, African methods of reading sticks, bones, or the conditions of sacrificial animals have survived in some family traditions. Some Vodouisants dispense with divinatory tools or their own biases altogether and simply consult directly with the Lwa by speaking to a Lwa during a possession.

Lavi'm nan men Bondye o Lwa yo
("My life is in the hands of
Bondye and the Lwa")
—from the *Djo* prayer sung during the
opening of most Haitian Vodou ceremonies

€IGHT

Sèvi Lwa: Serving the Lwa

Now that I've shared something about what Haitian Vodou is and about the Lwa, I can start to talk about how Vodou is practiced, or how we go about serving our Lwa. There are many ways to do Vodou, from individual to collective, small-scale to large-scale, and while I cannot possibly explain them all in a book for beginners, I can provide a good outline of basic practices and organization.

The Vodou Year

The liturgical year in Haitian Vodou begins at the same point as the Gregorian New Year. Traditionally, as the year opens, Vodouisants will still be observing a ritual rest or quiet time extending from Christmas until Epiphany (January 6, thus marking the "Twelve Days of Christmas"), though many houses take special "luck baths" made of fresh water and herbs on New Year's Day and during the Twelve Days. During the time between Christmas and Epiphany, the temples and altars are cleaned and then closed and covered with white sheets. The drums are placed in the *badji* to "sleep" until Epiphany.

On Epiphany/January 6, called *Jou de Wa* (zhoo day WA, "Day of Kings") in Haiti, most *peristyles* hold a huge ceremony and feast to open the Vodou year. The Day of Kings is a special day for the Lwa Papa Loko, owner of the *poto mitan* (the center post of the *peristil*) and the *asson* (ah-SONE, the ritual rattle and bell instrument used by *mambos* and *houngans* to call the Rada Lwa). As Papa Loko is the Lwa of Vodou priesthood, it is also a day honoring the "kings"—that is, the *mambos* and *houngans*—of the various *sosyetes*. January is also a high time to hold initiations; many *sosyetes* host a set of initiation ceremonies in the time between the Day of Kings and the beginning of Lent, a Catholic moveable feast tied to the lunar festival of Passover in the Jewish tradition. Lent generally begins sometime between mid-February and mid-March.

Most *sosyetes* will hold a final ceremony on *Gwo Madi* (Mardi Gras, or "Fat Tuesday") or the Saturday before, and then close their *peristil* on the following day, Ash Wednesday. Traditionally no "hot" work (magic involving anything dangerous or coercive) is done during Lent. Some *mambos* and *houngans* do not do any magic or host any ceremonies at all during the forty days of Lent; others opt only to refrain from this during Holy Week, the period between Palm Sunday and Easter Sunday. Most Vodou *sosyetes* also do not perform initiations during Lent. A few may divine to decide if it is appropriate to do so in special cases, but for most Vodouisants, Lent is considered a time to focus on prayer and gaining forgiveness for one's sins. During the Lenten season, many Vodouisants take part in *Rara,* a sort of traveling music tradition where groups of musicians playing drums, bamboo flutes, trumpets, and other simple instruments, accompanied by singers, go from town to town across Haiti, singing traditional songs and competing in contests for cash and other prizes, or offering performances at private and public venues. While *Rara* music is generally separate from Vodou's liturgical music, it comes from the same roots, and *Rara's* costume and dancing has heavy Vodou influence.

Once Easter has passed, Vodou's liturgical cycle resumes, and various dances for the Lwa are held on their saints' feast days or other days. Spring and early summer are common times for another initiation cycle and trips to the lineage's home temple(s) or hometowns to serve the ancestral Lwa. Near the end of April, community ceremonies are held to bless and release the spirits of those who died the previous year. In April or May, most houses hold a feast with dancing and singing in honor of the Djouba *esko* of Lwa, particularly Kouzen Zaka (or Azaka Mede), the divine peasant who blesses the planting and working in the fields that is going on all over Haiti. As spring turns to summer, various pilgrimages are made to special streams, rivers, waterfalls, mountains, and other sacred places. One of these annual pilgrimages, the July festival of Saut-d'Eau in the Arbonite Valley, draws millions of people who come to bathe in the sacred waterfall and ask for the blessing of its Lwa.

Summer changes to fall, and initiations and other ceremonies in honor of a house's Lwa are held through the warm evenings. *Manje Yanm* (mon-ZHAY YOM, "eating yams") is a harvest festival in honor of all of a house's Lwa and is often held in September or October. As of November 1, *Fèt Gede* season is in full swing, and all Haiti is dancing and singing for the Baron and his children. December begins with the *Manje Mè* (mon-ZHAY MAY, "feeding the ocean") and ritual offerings and visitations to the sea in honor of Mèt Agwe Tawoyo and his *esko,* and then Christmas comes and the cycle starts all over again.

Vodou ceremonies are not limited to huge groups or special days of the year. Other than the general *règleman* ("rules") that one does not hold ceremonies on Sundays, during the Twelve Days of Christmas, or during part or all of the forty days of Lent, ceremonies can be held at any time. Ceremonies for the Lwa can consist of something as small as a single person lighting candles and praying (called *Iliminasyon*) or as large as huge dances with teams of drummers and hundreds of guests that go from mid-afternoon until sunrise, or the massive public celebrations of *Fèt Gede*, initiation cycles, or various pilgrimages that can go for days or weeks on end.

These ceremonies can be dedicated to a specific Lwa or group of Lwa (called a *Manje Lwa*), given in thanksgiving for help, or performed to keep a promise made to a Lwa in return for a favor granted, called an *aksyon de gras* (ock-SHOWN day GRAHS, "action of or for blessing/grace").

Weddings and their receptions can be held in a *peristil*, particularly when the wedding is between a person and a Lwa (*Maryaj-Lwa*, see Part 2). Even when there are no ceremonies going on, a *peristil* is still often a busy place, where members of that Vodou community will gather to learn about the Lwa, receive a divination or a healing treatment, prepare for an upcoming ceremony or event, share news, talk, sleep, cook food, watch their children play, or simply enjoy a nap in the shade.

Règleman and the Order of Service

How a Vodou ceremony is conducted is dictated by a series of unwritten but generally agreed-upon guidelines referred to collectively as *règleman* ("the rules")—the order and manner in which Vodou service is carried out, which was mentioned earlier in the book. Vodou's *règleman*, it is believed, was established long ago by Vodou elders, and each successive generation of Vodouisants and Vodou clergy are taught the *règleman* by their *sosyetes* so that they can pass these traditions on to their own next generation and thus perpetuate Haitian Vodou's practice. While natural and deliberate changes do creep into Vodou practice from house to house and location to location, the things that are done in every house in every ceremony are fairly universal to Haitian Vodou. These things distinguish Vodou both from the religions it gathered its elements from and from other African Diaspora traditions and American religions and spiritual practices. Knowing something about the *règleman* can help a beginner to discern what is really Haitian Vodou and what is not, and provide a very useful judgment tool if one wishes to join a *sosyete* and has opportunity to observe a ceremony (see Chapter 11).

The *Priyè Ginen*

Before Columbus, the Taino of Ayiti began religious ceremonies with a special ceremony also practiced by many other native American nations: the *cacique* or *bohique* (priest/priestess or leader) would recite or sing a history of the tribe, reminding all the participants of their place in space and time and how they came to be there at that particular sacred moment. Haitian Vodou has retained this practice and analogous storytelling practices in various African rituals in the form of a very special and beautiful collection of prayers and songs collectively referred to as the *Priyè Ginen* (pree-YAY gee-NEN, "Ginen Prayer"), sometimes simply called the *Priyè*. This special prayer is sung and spoken in its dozens of verses at the outset of every community Vodou ceremony. Depending on the purpose, emphasis, lineage, and requirements of a particular ceremony, a *sosyete's Priyè Ginen* may take anywhere from half an hour to several days to recite and sing. While the order of each element of the *Priyè* is always the same, some parts may be abbreviated or omitted from some ceremonies and included in others. The *Priyè,* and thus all Vodou ceremonies, commence with the Vodou clergy and congregation seated quietly before the altar(s), with bare feet and bowed heads, just as would have been done long ago on Sunday morning on the plantations.

Following from that point of origin, the first part of the *Priyè Ginen* is called the *Priyè Katolik* ("Catholic Prayer"). It begins with making the Sign of the Cross, and proceeds into a recitation of the Lord's Prayer, the Hail Mary, and the Apostle's Creed. A nod to Vodou's Catholic origins has all of these prayers spoken in the formal French they would have been said in by priests and slave masters, rather than the Kreyòl of everyday speech (see Appendix C). Another nod, this time to Vodou's African origins, has these prayers said in duplicate, in a call-and-response pattern; the leading *mambo* or *houngan* says the prayers or portions of the prayers alone, and then the congregation joins in a litany response afterward.

Once the spoken prayers have been said, the leading *mambo* or *houngan* takes up the *asson*—the beaded gourd rattle and bell instrument used to call the Rada Lwa and the emblem of Vodou priesthood—and proceeds to ring the bell and shake the *asson* while the congregation softly applauds. If the drums are already present (in some houses the drums will not be not set up until the end of the *Priyè Katolik,* since there are no drums in Catholic churches), the drummers may tap very softly on them to add to the soft, rolling sound. This brief percussion is said to stir the spirits and prepare the way for them to arrive *aprè Bondye* ("after God"), and it may be repeated from time to time during the rest of the *Priyè Katolik* at the leader's discretion. Then the singing begins, with a line of French: *L'Ange du Seigneur dit à Marie,* "The Angel of the Lord said to Mary ... ," also the first line of the

Angelus prayer said multiple times per day by the Roman Catholic faithful. Many beautiful songs follow this line, greeting in turn Bondye, the Blessed Virgin, Jesus Christ, and the body of saints. These songs are all in French, as befits their Catholic nature.

Even an observer who does not understand French will be able to tell when the *Priyè Ginen* enters its second phase, the *Priyè Afriken* ("African Prayer"). The leading *mambo* or *houngan* will put down the *asson* and pick up a *tcha-tcha*, the rattle used by both Taino and Africans to call their spirits in need. The drumming and applause gets louder. The songs and melodies change tempo (they get progressively faster and often change key) and language. Unlike the mostly French *Priyè Katolik*, the *Priyè Afriken* is sung in a combination of Kreyòl and *langaj* (lawn-GAZH, a collection of various African words, a few of which are not entirely translatable). Some of the first Kreyòl words that can be made out include the often-repeated phrase *zo-a li mache* (ZO-wa lee ma-SHAY, "[the] bones are walking"), a reference to the ancestors, and the history continues on. The call-and-response phrasing is more urgent and participatory, particularly in the section sometimes called the "*Djo* Prayer" because of its rather lengthy litany beginning with the *langaj* words *Djo e* (JO-ay).

As the *Priyè* draws to a close, the congregation will stand and put away the chairs, clearing the floor of the *peristil* for the upcoming dance. A song begins *Anonse o zanj nan dlo*, "Announce to the angels in the mirror … " referring to the Lwa, the spirits who live in the mirror world of *Ginen*. And the ceremony begins.

A Vodou Ceremony

The body of a standard Vodou ceremony—once the *Priyè* is said and the chairs have been cleared away—is a long communal dance. Traditional dances start around sunset, just as they would have back in plantation days, and often go all night, ending with the congregation simply laying down to rest on mats spread out across the *peristil* floor for a few hours before getting up and heading home. The dances are as joyous and beautiful as they are expensive and exhausting—to call the Lwa requires sacrifices but gains much, as the Lwa will listen to the singing and drumming and come down through the *poto mitan* to dance along with their children. If the situation is just right, a Lwa may choose a Vodouisant to serve as its vessel for possession, described as a Lwa riding a *chwal,* or horse, the word most commonly used to describe a person who is possessed.

While a horse is being ridden by a Lwa—that is to say, during the time that a Lwa is in possession of a person—for practical purposes, that person ceases to exist. No one at a ceremony will talk about what Houngan Pierre did when Ogou was on him. They will say "Ogou drank this rum," or "Ogou told me I'd better give him that party I promised him four years ago, or he's going to make me lose my job." A horse *is* the Lwa, for the duration of the time the Lwa is riding that person. The horse does not speak about him- or herself, except obliquely; the Lwa has come and is doing all the actions and giving all the advice, and it is not about the horse at all. Metaphysically speaking, Vodouisants believe that the soul of the horse has been completely displaced by the spirit of the Lwa, and so that person is not even present to experience the possession. The soul of the horse will return after the Lwa leaves, and the person will be as before the possession, although exhausted and disoriented for a time. Then she may join the dance once again, in hopes that maybe more Lwa will come—perhaps in someone else's head so she can talk to a Lwa, too!

Many outsiders seem to think it must be a great honor to serve as a horse for a Lwa, and in some ways it is a deeply meaningful service to offer to one's family and community. However, it is not necessarily a desired end. The Lwa are not human, and they are sometimes very strong and do physically taxing things. In Vodou, possession is usually a physically grueling and potentially painful experience that the possessed person does not even get to enjoy on a personal level. Vodouisants do not congratulate other Vodouisants on their ability to serve as *chwal,* just as people do not usually congratulate their cars for arriving at the grocery store or their coffee mugs for holding this morning's caffeine. A horse is a tool used by the Lwa, nothing more. Anyone in Vodou can serve as a horse, and so it is not considered something one would necessarily aspire to do, or something one would gain special benefit from being able to do.

Despite this, we are grateful that the Lwa come to share ceremonies with us. One at a time, after songs are sung to gather the family and open the ways between the spiritual and physical worlds, songs are "thrown" out to the various Lwa and their families, one at a time. We start with Papa Legba, who is asked to *ouvri bayè* or "open the gate," so all the other Lwa can come. The songs continue all night long, usually in sets of three, through the *règleman* listing all the house's Rada Lwa to the Nago Lwa, and then to the Petro Lwa, and eventually ending with the Gede Lwa (or Gede then Petro in a few lineages I have encountered). There are breaks to change drums, get something to drink or eat, or listen to various Lwa who come to give advice or do work on the congregation's behalf. As each set of songs is sung, servants of the particular Lwa being called may make offerings and salutes to the cardinal directions, drums, and altars to further entice that Lwa to visit. During the series of songs for Papa Loko, visiting *mambos* and *houngans* will be greeted and greet each other and the congregation, and all initiates will perform special dance steps and ritual movements to demonstrate their relative ranks and salute each other as keepers of the Vodou tradition. A careful observer will be able to tell the relative rank and importance of the attending Vodouisants and Vodou clergy by watching how the various participants salute and bow to each other during Papa Loko's portion of the service. If a dance is being held in honor of a particular Lwa, or a house has a special patron Lwa, that Lwa might be given more than three songs, or special time set aside for him or her to come and meet with the congregation.

Vodou ceremonies are deeply participatory. Everyone present is welcome to dance and sing and take part in saluting the Lwa. Visiting *mambos* and *houngans,* as a token of respect, are often invited to give salutes to their personal Lwa or house Lwa when that portion of the ceremony arrives. Anyone in the house, including people sitting along the sides observing the ceremony, can potentially be possessed by a Lwa and end up as part of the ceremony, even if they had not originally intended to do so. Most of the time, however, the leading *mambo* and *houngan* and certain *hounsi* (the house's initiated non-clergy members) will be the ones who are possessed.

Mambos and *houngans* have knowledge of how to stop a possession as well, in the event someone does not wish to act as a horse for whatever reason.

Since ceremonies are so long and involve the dance as well as a celebration of the Lwa, there is usually lots of food present. There will be food on the altars as offerings to the Lwa themselves and other food that the *hounsi* may have spent several days preparing in advance, or food prepared by some of the *hounsi* during the ceremony using the offered food and animals. For example, a house might have a small ceremony offering a pig to Danto in the afternoon, and when the larger dance and ceremony are held that evening, plates of the cooked pig will be passed out to all the participants during Danto's portion of the ceremony so she can "share" her food with everyone. In my initiatory mother's house, the Lwa Ogou Badagri has a tradition of serving food at the end of his section of the ceremony. He will sit for as long as it takes to make sure every single person present has received at least one plate of food, which he personally dishes up out of pots the *hounsi* stack in front of him, before he then goes off, cigar in hand, to answer his children's questions and help with their problems.

Foods for the Lwa: Some Haitian Recipes

Haitian cooking, like Haitian culture and Haitian Vodou, is also a mix of native, French, and African dishes, as well as some Asian and Middle Eastern recipes introduced by visitors and immigrants from those parts of the world. Some common dishes are given as traditional offerings to Lwa, and cooking them is not so difficult, though it can be time-consuming. Here are some of the more popular recipes for those who might like to try some Haitian cuisine.

Riz ak Pwa (REEZ ock PWAH, "Rice and Beans")

This is one of Haiti's traditional staple foods and is considered the "national dish." *Note: this recipe makes enough rice and beans to feed you AND your Lwa; divide the recipe if necessary.*

2 cups dry red beans (kidney beans)

10–12 cups water (and a pot big enough to boil that much water in)

3 teaspoons salt

3 teaspoons black pepper (freshly ground tastes better)

6 tablespoons lard (butter or margarine can be substituted)

4 cups uncooked long-grain white rice

Put the beans in a colander and rinse them until the water is no longer red. Pour the water into a big pot along with half the salt and pepper, and then add the beans. Bring to a boil, cover the pot except for a small opening to release steam, and allow the beans to simmer on low heat for about 90 minutes, or until they are soft but not quite falling apart. Drain the cooked beans and set them aside, but save the drained water.

Using a large frying pan or skillet, melt half the lard and add in the beans slowly. Stir them frequently so they are covered and shiny, but don't let them burn. Remove the beans from the pan and set them aside. Now, repeat the process with the rice: first melt the rest of the lard, then stir in the dry rice until it is somewhat opaque but not burned. Remove the rice from the skillet. Measure 8 cups of the water you boiled the beans in, and put it back in the original pot. Stir in the remaining salt and pepper and the rice, and bring the pot to a hard boil. Then add the beans and stir. Reduce to very low heat (so the bottom does not burn), cover, and simmer until the rice is tender and has absorbed all the liquid; this usually takes about 30 minutes. Add cayenne, more salt and pepper, or hot sauce to taste. Fluff the rice and serve.

Tchaka (CHA-ka)

Tchaka is Kouzen Zaka's favorite food, and it can also be served to some other Rada and Nago Lwa. It may be a descendant of a Taino dish and is made with different ingredients in some areas, but a basic *tchaka* is made like this:

4 cups dried unsalted corn

2 cups dry red beans (kidney beans)

½ lb. pork or beef, finely minced (omit for
    vegetarian version)

¼ cup olive oil

3 cloves garlic, chopped fine

2 small white onions, finely chopped

1 large hot pepper, chopped (a Scotch bonnet
    or habañero or jalapeño pepper will work)

Salt and pepper to taste

2 tablespoons butter

Boil the corn, beans, and half the pork in a soup pot or stockpot until
they are tender (use only enough water to cover the dry ingredients in the
pot and do not add water during the process). Drain off any extra water,
but keep it to the side.

Sauté the cooked and drained vegetable/pork mixture in the olive oil in
a second deep saucepan or pot. Add garlic and onion and the hot pepper;
stir in the rest of the meat. Add salt and pepper to taste. Simmer until all ingredients are cooked thoroughly. Add the butter and stir until it is melted.
If the final product in the second pot seems too dry, stir in small amounts
of the water from the stockpot until the end result is moist and saucy. Note
that some Haitians will mince pork for the second cooking phase but will
use a ham hock or a couple of pig's feet (well-cleaned) for boiling with the
beans and corn.

Labouyi (or La Bwi) Bannann
(la BWEE buh-NONN, "Plantain Porridge")

Labouyi bannann is a soft, creamy white pudding that can be served to any
of the Rada Lwa. Traditionally, it uses flour made from the plantain (*bannann* in Kreyòl; not to be confused with English banana) plant.

1 cup milk

1 cup evaporated milk (NOT sweetened
   condensed milk)

1 cup water

3 cinnamon sticks

Handful of star anise

1 cup plantain flour (fine corn flour/farina
   or wheat flour can be substituted; then
   this dish is called *akasan*)

1 teaspoon vanilla extract

1 teaspoon butter

Boil both types of milk and water with the star anise and cinnamon sticks in a saucepan, being careful not to let the milk scorch. Slowly stir in enough flour for the mixture to become thickened, and then add the vanilla and butter one at a time. (To avoid lumps, mix the flour in a small amount of cold water first, before putting it into the boiling pot). Turn to lowest setting and heat until the mixture starts to bubble, approximately 5 minutes, stirring frequently to avoid lumps or scorching. Remove from heat and allow the mixture to cool. It will continue to thicken upon standing, and should be the consistency of pudding. Remove the cinnamon sticks and star anise and serve.

If you are serving this to the Lwa, let it cool until it is room temperature. Do not serve it to your Lwa either heated or refrigerated, though both combinations, along with whipping cream, milk, and fresh fruit, are delicious for humans! If made with regular flour or corn flour (*farinn*), this very tasty dessert or breakfast food is more properly called *akasan*.

Soup/Bouyon Poul (SOOP/boo-YONE POOL, "Chicken Soup")

1 whole chicken (a cut-up fryer is fine [no giblets]
   if you want to skip the traditional preparation)

Optional: 1–2 limes or blood oranges (for preparing
   the whole chicken)

4–5 whole carrots, cut

3 small red potatoes, cut

1–2 plantains, peeled and cut (note instructions
    on how to peel; despite their resemblance to
    bananas, plantains are much harder to peel.
    Green [unripened] bananas can be used if you
    absolutely cannot get plantains where you
    live, though they are usually sold by Latino or
    Caribbean groceries throughout the world)

1 small red onion, cut

1 small white onion, cut

1 handful fresh watercress leaves, shredded

2 tablespoons butter (or margarine)

1 teaspoon each salt and fresh black pepper

To prepare your chicken the Haitian way, wash it in the sink with cool water, using your hands and a tiny amount of soap, just as you would wash your body. (If you do this, make sure that ALL the soap is thoroughly rinsed from the meat.) Then cut limes or blood oranges (not both) in halves or quarters and use them to scrub the meat, pressing vigorously until the juice runs all over the meat. Rinse the meat and place in a stockpot (or Dutch oven or crock pot) for cooking soup. Cover with water until the chicken is completely submerged, and then boil about 90 minutes until chicken is thoroughly cooked. Remove the chicken from the water and set it aside to cool.

Cut up all the vegetables, shred the watercress, and put them into the pot. Remove the bones and skin from the chicken, and add the meat to the pot as well. Return to a boil and make sure the butter has melted. Season with salt and pepper. Cover and simmer at medium heat for an additional 30 minutes, or until the vegetables are tender.

Soup Joumou (SOOP zhoo-MOO, "Pumpkin Soup"),
a lucky soup for New Year's Day and other special occasions

- 1 lb. boneless beef (pot roast, stew meat, or fajita
    meat will do)
- 1 lb. boneless chicken breasts or thighs, or both
    (to taste)
- 1 tablespoon white vinegar (or lemon juice)
- 2 lbs. *joumou* (Haitian pumpkin; you can substitute
    yellow squash or zucchini), cut
- 1 lb. green cabbage, cut
- 3 large carrots, cut
- 4 large red potatoes, cut
- 1 onion, cut
- Black cloves (2–4)
- 1 large turnip (or 2–3 small turnips), cut
- 1 whole hot pepper (pimiento or jalapeño),
    do not break or cut
- Part of a box (approx. ¼ lb.) spaghetti or vermicelli

Put beef and chicken together in a large stockpot (or pressure cooker or crock pot if you choose) with the vinegar and cover with enough water to boil it until tender (1 ½ to 2 hours in most cases). Skim off any fat/grease that floats to the top. Add all the vegetables in small chunks and boil another 30 minutes, or until vegetables are tender. Remove from heat and remove meat from the pot. Cut the meat into cubes and strain the vegetables, saving the water. Set the vegetables aside. Add the meat back to the water in the pot and bring back to a boil. Drop in the pepper, being very careful not to break it; it is for aroma, not taste. Add the spaghetti and cook according to package directions. Once the pasta is tender, add the vegetables back to the soup, bring to a final boil, cool, and serve warm. Do not eat the pepper!

Sòs Ti-Malis (SAUCE tee-ma-LEASE, "Little Malice Sauce"), a very spicy sauce for meat and other things

    2 cups fresh lime juice (no pulp or seeds)

    4 cups onions, chopped fine

    1 stick butter or margarine

    3 teaspoons fresh garlic, chopped fine

    5 teaspoons hot chili peppers, chopped fine

    4 teaspoons salt

Marinate the onions in the lime juice for at least an hour (less time if the room is warmer than room temperature). Melt butter in a heavy frying pan, being careful not to let it brown or burn. Strain the onions from the lime juice, but don't throw the juice away. Add the onions to the melted butter, and cook until they are soft and transparent, stirring constantly. Do not let the onions brown.

Add garlic and peppers and cover the pan, cooking on low for about 10 minutes or until the peppers are soft. Turn off the heat and add the salt and reserved lime juice, stirring thoroughly. Let stand until the sauce cools off (it is served at room temperature). Refrigerate what you do not use right away; it will keep for about five days.

Griot (gwee-YO, "Braised Pork"), one of Ezili Danto's favorite dishes

    Small amount (less than ½ cup) vegetable oil

    1 lb. boneless pork loin, cubed

    1 lime

    1 orange or blood orange

    Optional: additional lime, orange, or blood orange
        for washing the pork (see instructions)

    3–4 shallots (scallions can be substituted)

    1 large onion

    1 small hot pepper (Scotch bonnet, habañero,
        or jalapeño)

½ teaspoon black pepper

Pinch of thyme (fresh crushed leaves are preferable)

Pinch of salt

½ cup water

Optionally, you can "wash" the pork before cooking it by cutting a lime, orange, or blood orange in half and using the halves as "brushes" to scrub the meat until the juice runs; if you choose to do this, throw that fruit away when you are done and use different fruit(s) for the actual recipe. Brown the pork in a skillet using the vegetable oil: be careful not to let the vegetable oil or the pork burn. Juice the lime and the orange, being sure to strain out any seeds or pulp, and chop the onion and shallots so that you have approximately ¼ cup of each. Divide the pepper in half (be sure to use gloves and wash your hands afterward), and then chop up half the pepper very finely. Once the pork is thoroughly and evenly browned, add the black pepper, shallots, lime juice, orange juice, thyme, salt, and water. Stir the hot pepper in carefully. Bring to a boil, then cover and simmer for 30 minutes.

Uncover the pan and turn the heat back up to high, stirring frequently for another 10 minutes, as the sauce thickens to a glaze. Use the half of the hot pepper you did not put in the recipe as garnish, or leave it out if you're afraid of more heat!

Yo bay mwen pwen-a
se poům mache la nwit
("They made me a pwen
so I can walk around in the night")
—from a ceremonial song about the
magic of the Lwa Simbi Andezo

NINE

Wanga: Haitian Vodou Magic

A s I mentioned in the introduction to this section of the book, I am using the Haitian word for magic, *travay,* along with its definitions, in this chapter. Linguistically, there is nothing in this word to separate its meaning from any sort of mundane "work," but in Vodou philosophy, *travay* as magic is a specific thing.

The thing that sets Vodou *travay* apart from other sorts of *travay* is that it is *spiritual* work, effort put forth by a *mambo* or *houngan* or other Vodouisant to gain the employment of the spiritual world to assist in the physical realm. *Travay* involves tangible as well as intangible elements: a prayer and the lighting of a candle; a possession of a spirit in the head of a *mambo,* who then uses the *mambo's* hands to administer an herbal treatment or bath to a sick child; or an invocation of various Lwa while dancing or singing or drumming, or doing all three at the same time. *Travay* can be simple or very complicated, can be easy or difficult to do, and can be completed quickly or take a lifetime. There are as many different sorts of *travay* as there are problems needing solutions.

Nothing in the universe is free. Not even Bondye reaches down from the sky and hands us what we want or need for nothing, no matter how hard we pray or how virtuous we are. The reason Vodouisants call magic "work" in the first place is because we understand that if you want something in life, you have to work for it! Thus, magic is not a replacement for effort, so much as it is a way to enhance or multiply our effort—a community attempt to get as many helping hands as we can get into a situation, so that the load can be lessened and the results achieved. If life is a sailboat and fate or chance or destiny are the winds that fill that ship's sails, magic's place is in the rigging and the sailors, who know how to move the sails or turn them to catch the best wind or enhance the occasional weak breeze, and who keep the ship moving where we want it to go.

The sailboat metaphor is also a good one for explaining how magic works in Haitian Vodou. We can alter course or change a ship's speed by controlling the sails; with great effort we might even be able to move against the wind (for example, if we break out the oars, or trim the sail, or turn the wheel or rudder, or, if it's a modern sailboat, engage the motor). But inside the boat, we are still limited to certain parameters. Whether or not the boat will actually make it to shore will depend on the skill of its captain and crew, the boat's physical condition, and all the factors outside the boat that we can't control at all, like water and wind and weather.

In the same way, magic is successful or unsuccessful according to factors, including the amount of effort put into the *travay*, the expertise of the person who performs the *travay*, and whether or not any Lwa or Bondye Himself will support or oppose the *travay* once it's made. Even the most powerful *houngan* or *mambo* will tell you they can guarantee their work only so far as *se Bondye vle* ("God (is) willing"), and sometimes several *travay*, or different kinds of *travay* at different stages, may be required to help in difficult situations. Alongside *travay*, a Vodouisant will often use divination to get a better understanding of the extent and root causes of a problem, what sorts of assistance the Lwa can or will give in solving it, and how to go about *travay* in the way most likely to have a successful result.

While there are many kinds of *travay*, a few are worth mentioning since they are very common to Haitian Vodou.

Almost all Vodouisants create *wanga* (WAHN-guh), which are talismans, pieces of jewelry, *pakets* (pa-KATES) (objects tied together in a cloth or placed in a bottle or other container), or other ritual receptacles designed to permit a spirit to reside within, either temporarily or permanently. Some common *wanga,* such as *Pakets Kongo* (pa-KATES cone-GO, "Kongo packets")—*pakets* that contain herbs and natural and manmade objects combined in a bag or cloth receptacle, itself decorated with mirrors, sequins, feathers, ritual implements, and/or various other objects for artistic and magical purposes—are created for use on Vodou altars to act as *repozwa* (wee-POSE-wah, "resting places") or homes for the Lwa whose altars they belong to. Some *wanga* are designed to be worn by initiates as jewelry; others are made to be worn about the person or placed in certain locations. The term is also used for the similar "*wanga* bag" (also called a *mojo bag* or a *gris-gris*) of New Orleans Voodoo and African-American rootwork traditions, and similar items are still constructed in West Africa by indigenous peoples for similar or identical reasons.

Other more complicated *repozwa* are also created for Lwa and for other spirits, the spirits of the dead, and even natural spirits for various reasons. These are sometimes also just called *wanga* or sometimes by the term *pwen* (poo-WEN, one syllable, "point"), meaning any object that can be used as a ritual focus or dwelling place for a spirit. A *pwen* can be a constructed object like a *Paket Kongo,* or it can be an already-existing natural or manmade item, such as a thunderstone, a shell, a clay pipe, or a fancy dagger. *Pwen* can be made for Lwa and kept on their altars. They can be created for specific purposes and then given or sold to others (sometimes called *pwen achte,* "bought points"), or they can be used to imprison or enslave a spirit, much like the "genie bottle" of Islamic magic. In this case, the *pwen* are often called *pwen cho* (poo-WEN SHO, "hot points"), which some *mambos* and *houngans* refuse to make due to the ethical gray area this sort of *travay* falls into. Many Vodouisants leave the creation of *pwen cho* and other such *pwen* to the domain of the *bokor,* or non-initiate magician.

Some forms of *travay* are less tangible. A person can make a *pwomès* (pwo-MESS, "promise") or agreement with a Lwa or group of Lwa, offering certain ritual objects or actions in return for favors granted. *Mambos* and *houngans* are skilled in the use of herbal and spiritual *trêteman* (tret-MON, "treatments," just as the word is used by doctors) to cleanse a person of negative energies, bad luck, or illness. They know how to create *gad* (GAHD, "guards"), *pwen* dedicated to various Lwa that protect their bearers from any sort of harm. Some Lwa are willing to enter into spiritual marriage with a human being via the ceremony of *Maryaj-Lwa*, which is exactly like a Catholic wedding Mass, except that one of the participants is a Lwa in possession and there is no such thing as a "divorce-Lwa" or annulment of such a spiritual marriage (see Part 2).

Iliminasyon (Vodou Lamp Service)

A very simple Vodou service that anyone can do, regardless of their initiatory status or even depth of knowledge in serving the spirits, is called an *Iliminasyon* ("candle-lighting," pronounced the same as the English *illumination,* with the same meaning) ceremony. It involves the setting of a special lamp in a ritually prepared space to attract the attention of and communication from the Lwa or the blessed dead, and it is something that you can do as a beginner in Haitian Vodou, if you are interested. It is an excellent way both to get dream messages from your ancestors and/or to get to know a Lwa or two when you are just starting out.

What you'll need

- One metal pan or basin. This can be a baking pan, a stockpot, or a saucepan. If you want to do it the way Haitians do it, you'll want to acquire a *kivet* (kee-VETT), an enameled-steel basin, like those used to wash dishes in houses without running water. The basin doesn't have to be huge, but it does need to be made of metal and thus fireproof. If you don't use a *kivet,* avoid using a pan that is Teflon-lined or non-stick, nor should it be black, red, or a dark color. (Try for silver, white, or ivory.) It needs to be at least 6 inches deep.

- One plate, either (traditionally) an enameled tin plate, or a sturdy but lightweight Corningware® or other glass plate that is heat-safe. This plate needs to be white in color , undecorated, and light enough to float on water. It also needs to be slightly concave or have a lip; if it is perfectly flat, it will not be able to hold the small bit of oil it needs to hold to create the lamp. If you cannot find a suitable plate, a shallow, wide bowl (a salad bowl or a pasta bowl) will also work, but again, it must be white in color, light enough to float, and heat-safe. Do not use a paper, wood, or plastic plate under any circumstances—the plate must be fireproof, as it will be holding the lamp wicks for this ceremony.

- A handful of fresh basil leaves (dried or crushed leaves will not work). If you do not pick the basil yourself, remove it from the container you purchased it in and rinse it very gently in cool (not cold or hot) water.

- One white penny candle (or Sabbath candle): this is a paraffin candle 4–6 inches long and about ¾ inch in diameter. If you cannot find a penny candle, a white taper or a white votive candle will work. It needs to be new and completely white. You will also need matches or a lighter to light this candle and your lamp.

- Enough clean spring water to fill the basin halfway (do not use distilled water). Allow the water to come to room temperature; do not refrigerate the water before use.

- One small bottle of olive oil. Brand and grade do not matter, as long as it's pure olive oil (with no salt, spices, or herbs inside). Haitians often add other kinds of oils to their lamps, but at this stage, as you are just starting out, you don't need to worry about that.

- Cotton to make the wicks. You can get this at a pharmacy; it is sold as "raw cotton" in large sheets wrapped in paper in the first-aid section. Cotton balls are both bleached and machined, and are usually too small to serve our needs. Make sure there is nothing on or in the cotton (don't use cotton that has been coated in colored dye, antiseptic, or powder).

- Some shiny, clean coins. Some houses recommend using 41 U.S. cents, divided further as one penny, one nickel, one dime, and one quarter, but obviously Haitian coins don't add up to this number, nor do coins in other countries necessarily. Either seven coins, or coins that add up to a number divisible by 7, is also a common way of doing this.

- Two clean (and/or new) FLAT (not fitted) white sheets, full or queen size.

- Clean white clothes, including underclothes, and a white cloth, soft white hat, or bonnet to cover your head. Vodouisants usually use a shiny white satin headwrap called a *moushwa* (moo-SHWA).

- Spiritual perfume (traditionally *Lotion Pompeia,* a French perfume sold in many botanicas and spiritual stores; or another common spiritual perfume called Florida Water). If you absolutely cannot acquire either of these perfumes, use something with a very soft floral scent, such as rosewater or jasmine perfume. Avoid musks, heavy colognes, or anything that has a spicy smell; think soft flower scents and the sort of thing your great-grandmother might have worn.

Making Iliminasyon

My common sense note before you begin: *Iliminasyon* involves candles and oil lamps, as well as cloth and perfume. It also involves sleeping in a room with an oil lamp while it is burning.

Do not perform this ceremony alone or unattended if you have pets, small children, or can't guarantee your lamp will not be disturbed while you sleep. Make sure your space has adequate ventilation but is not drafty, as this will affect the lamp's burning and could cause a potential for fire. Do not use more oil or perfume than I recommend, as both items are flammable. Make sure to keep yourself, your hair and clothing, and all bedding and other cloth materials (such as the raw cotton) away from the lamp or candle flames, except for the wicks that are supposed to be burning. Make sure you have a working smoke detector and a method of fire extinguishment (an actual extinguisher, or a bowl of clean sand or cat litter) handy. Be smart and be safe. The Lwa do not want anyone to burn their house down, and neither do I.

You want to do this right before going to sleep at night. If you already have an altar to your Lwa, clear a space on the floor in front of the altar big enough for you to lay down in, and for the basin and lamp to sit in, without anything else catching on fire. If you do not have an altar to your Lwa, you can do this in a bedroom or any other quiet place where you can sleep undisturbed for the night. You can place an image of the Lwa you wish to make *Iliminasyon* to next to the basin, or set up a temporary altar for that Lwa. Whether or not you have an altar in addition to this setup itself, bear in mind that if you do this ceremony in a room that already has a bed in it, you will not be sleeping in the bed, but on the floor near the lamp.

Take a bath or shower and be very clean. Dress in the white clothes and put on the white hat or *moushwa*. Think about the reasons why you are doing this ceremony while you get ready. Leave your feet bare (if it's cold, you can wear clean white socks, but don't wear shoes).

Make your bed for the evening. Take the sheets and spread them out on the floor in front of the altar, leaving room for the basin and the lamp plate between the top of the sheet and the altar. Your head should be situated at the top of the sheet and in front of the lamp, as indicated in the following diagram. The second sheet is to cover yourself with when you lay down. It's okay to test the "bed" and make sure you will fit comfortably in it when the ceremony is completed.

Iliminasyon *setup.*

Put the coins in the bottom of the basin. Fill the basin halfway with the spring water and shred the basil leaves until you can smell the basil and feel its oils on your hands. Place the shredded leaves into the water and stir it with your right hand. If you have Florida Water, add a tiny splash of this to the basin as well. Set the basin at the head of the bed. If you are an initiate or in a Vodou house, you can add a *veve* of the Rada star underneath the basin; if you are not, don't worry about this part for now.

Put a small amount of olive oil in the plate (perhaps ⅛ inch). Sprinkle a little bit of the spiritual perfume on your hands and on your body (not your face or head).

Light the white candle and pray. Traditionally, this is the Sign of the Cross, the Our Father, the Hail Mary, and the Apostle's Creed, followed by a heartfelt prayer of your own to Bondye. Ask Bondye, the ancestors, and the Lwa to bless your basin and your bed and help you to make your *Iliminasyon*. If you are an initiate or in a Vodou house and you have been shown how to do it, *jete dlo* ("throw water") for Bondye, *zansèt-yo* (ancestors), and your Lwa in the manner of your lineage when you pray.

Set the candle down next to the basin (if need be, you can place it in a candle holder if fire safety is a question; Vodouisants usually simply tip the candle so it drops a bit of wax on the floor, then set the candle upright on top of the melted wax so it will stick in place). Take up the cotton to make the wicks, called *ti-mesh* (tee-MESH). Tear off a hunk of cotton with your fingers, maybe the size of two cotton balls, and then twist one end of it until it is compact and pointed; leave the other end fluffy and loose. If you can do this without using your index fingers, all the better. Traditionally, Vodouisants don't touch a *ti-mesh* with the index fingers so that any potentially disruptive influences will not enter through those fingers, which are considered magically active. It takes some practice to learn to use your second and third fingers to pull and twist a *ti-mesh*, but once you learn how to do it, it's not so difficult. If you've left the candle on the floor near you while you work, be sure not to kick it over onto the sheets or altar, or into your lap as you work on the wicks. If possible, allow the candle to burn down naturally as you work on the wicks, and then you can use it to light them when the time comes. The lit candle calls the Lwa and puts their attention on what you are doing.

When you are done twisting one end of a *ti-mesh,* set the fluffy (untwisted) end down into the oil in the plate, so that it is soaking up the oil and the pointy end sticks up like a tiny candle for you to light. For this particular *Iliminasyon* ceremony, you want to make seven wicks; other ceremonies call for different numbers. While you're twisting the wicks, talk to your Lwa out loud about what you are hoping to learn in your dreams. You can either talk about the same thing for all seven wicks or specify something different for each one. If you don't know who your Lwa are, talk to them in general ("my Lwa"), or ask Bondye and your ancestors to help.

Once all seven wicks have been set in the oil, a little bit apart from each other so their flames won't combine, hold the plate up in front of you, at about the level of your solar plexus, and present it to the four directions (east, then west, then south, then north). If you are an initiate or a member of a Vodou house, you can add the lineage's standard turns and salutes as well, if you know them. Set the plate down and do the same with the basin full of water and basil. Then put the basin down, place the plate inside it so it is floating on the surface of the water, and carefully light the wicks.

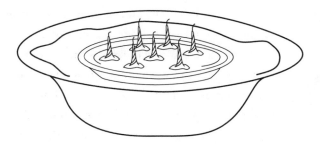

Ti-mesh *in a plate of oil that floats in the basin.*

Because of the small amount of oil you have put in the plate, the lamp should not burn for more than six or seven hours. Do not add any more oil to the lamp if it goes out; let it extinguish itself naturally as it exhausts its oil supply. It is natural for the wicks to burn at different rates, or to make snapping or popping sounds, or to burn in various colors. Take note of how your *ti-mesh* burn; this may be a way the Lwa are communicating with you. It could also be an indication that you've used too much oil, not twisted the wicks tightly enough, or that your olive oil is rancid, among other things. If you have problems with too much smoke or soot coming from your *ti-mesh,* the next time you make a lamp, add a tiny amount of sugar water (no more than 2–3 tablespoons) to the oil mixture in the plate, and stir carefully.

This lamp will give off a certain amount of smoke, but this should not be so much that it sets off a smoke detector, unless the detector is right above the lamp. If, for some reason, you should have an emergency and need to extinguish the lamp before it goes out on its own, do NOT tip it into the water, as the oil and wicks will simply float to the top and keep burning. Consider keeping a bowl of clean sand or clean cat litter (or coarse salt) in the room, and sprinkle this over the fire. The fire will go out, and the plate will become heavier and sink to the bottom of the basin, extinguishing any remaining embers. With the very small amount of oil you should be using in this lamp, fire should not be a problem. That's a hint—don't go overboard on the oil in the lamp; even ¼ inch of oil will keep the wicks burning brightly for several hours.

Lay down and go to sleep, with the basin near to (but not close enough to touch or catch fire to) your head. The Lwa and/or your ancestors will come in your sleep and give you messages in your dreams. You may wish to keep pen and paper handy near the bed to write down these messages when you wake up the next morning. If you wake up in the middle of the night, that is fine; just make sure to extinguish the lamp when you leave the bed for the day. You may also want to keep track of how the wicks burn, whether they go out, or if anything else happens during the night and talk with a *mambo* or *houngan* about it afterward.

Lafanmi samble! Krèyol nou la e …
("Assemble the family!
We are Creoles now …")
—from a ceremonial song

TEN

Sosyete: The Vodou Family, Initiation, and Practice

Unlike some spiritual paths, Haitian Vodou has no central authority. As Vodouisants, we have no single leader to tell us what to do or to codify our practices into strict dogmas or commandments. As a result, some of what we do varies from house to house and family to family, and even from Vodouisant to Vodouisant, though there are uniform rules under the *règleman* for certain types of formal ceremonies and the Vodou priesthood's hierarchy and initiation.

All Haitian Vodou houses will observe those practices classified as *règleman,* even if some other practices vary, and most houses have a "live and let live" attitude toward the practices and beliefs of other houses. This attitude is summed up best in a proverb: *Chak houngan se houngan lakay li,* "Every *houngan* is the *houngan* in his own house."

The Vodou House or *Sosyete: Asson* Lineage

Houses (or *sosyetes;* the words are interchangeable) contain three ranks of Vodouisants in the standard *asson* lineage of Port-au-Prince and other urban areas. This is a specific kind of Haitian Vodou, often mistaken to be the "only Vodou" or the "real Vodou" by outsiders, because it is the form most anthropologists and early foreigners who came to Haiti were permitted to observe. However, the *asson* lineage—so named for the *asson* rattle-and-bell instrument that is the lineage priesthood's badge of office—is not the only way Haiti's Vodouisants are organized. I will describe the *asson* lineage in detail here, because it is most likely to be the kind of Vodou that non-Haitians will encounter.

- *Hounsi*—This is the rank of the vast majority of Haiti's Vodouisants, both inside and outside the *asson* lineage. The word means "bride of the spirits," and is used for both males and females. It indicates entry-level involvement or initiation into Haitian Vodou. It can be used to refer to people who are not initiated at all, but it is more commonly used to refer to those who have gone through one of two types of initiations: the *Sèvis Tèt* initiated are called *hounsi senp* or "simple hounsi"; those who go through the *Kanzo* initiation are called *hounsi Kanzo.* In many *asson*-lineage *sosyetes* south of Port-au-Prince, *Sèvis Tèt* is not offered, and so they do not have *hounsi senp* at all.

  Every Vodou *sosyete* needs—and depends on—a body of *hounsi* to carry its ceremonies. They do this by singing, dancing, helping to prepare services, cooking the spirits' preferred foods, or performing other necessary tasks before, during, and after a ceremony. Since *houngans* and *mambos* are often busy with the spiritual and magical work to be done, a house's *hounsi* are most likely to be possessed and to be able to talk to Lwa when they arrive. Even though his or her rank is technically "lower" than the ranks of Vodou priesthood, nobody looks down on a *hounsi*.

  Some houses refer to members who have not initiated (either via *Kanzo* or *Sèvis Tèt*) as *hounsi bossal* or "wild hounsi," after the difficulty that these Vodouisants generally show being used as *chwal*, the possessory vessels for visiting Lwa. It is telling that *bossal* was also once used as a derisive term for newly arrived, and thus "unbroken," slaves. Sometimes *hounsi*, whether initiated or not, are also called *ti-fèy* (tee-FAY, "little leaves"), with the idea that a Vodou *sosyete* is like a tree; or in a pun, *ti-feux* (tee-FO, "little lights/fires"), with the idea that each *hounsi* is a candle illuminating the altar of his or her house.

- *Mambo/Houngan Si Pwen*—A *mambo* (female) or *houngan* (male) is a Vodou priest who has been trained to assist at and conduct services and initiated via the *Kanzo* ceremony. *Si Pwen* (or *sur pwen*, both pronounced suh PWENN, "on the point") is a junior priest(ess), in the middle of the initiatory hierarchy of the *asson* lineage. Some Kreyòl dialects spell the terms *mambo* and *houngan* as *manbo* and *ou(n)gan*, but in both cases, they are pronounced the same way: mom-BO and oon-GAHN.

  Over time, a *si pwen* learns to work with and on behalf of their *mèt tèt* ("master of the head"), one's personal, special Lwa. As a *si pwen*, the *mambo* or *houngan* works very closely with both the *mèt tèt* and the patron Lwa of the *sosyete's* lineage. While a *si pwen* may be presented with an *asson* (the intricately beaded ritual rattle used to call Rada Lwa) during *Kanzo* initiation, he is considered to have it on loan and not to "own" it—that is, he is not permitted to initiate others into the lineage. This does not mean a *si pwen* is not an effective priest. It just means he does not possess the additional spiritual training or authority to initiate others into the *asson* lineage of Haitian Vodou.

- *Mambo/Houngan Asogwe*—Asogwe (ah-so-GWAY) is the highest rank of the Haitian Vodou priesthood in the *asson* lineage, and this is considered the ultimate clergy rank in Haitian Vodou by most Haitians, regardless of lineage. Tradition states that the *asogwe* priesthood derives its authority directly from the ancient royal houses of Dahomey. A *mambo* or *houngan asogwe* is expected to know and serve all the Lwa of *Ginen* in addition to his or her *mèt tèt* and lineage, and to serve the people of the *sosyete* as well as its ancestors and spirits. As an owner of Papa

Loko's *asson*, an *asogwe* is permitted and encouraged to initiate others and to found his or her own house or *sosyete* as a mother or father to initiatory children.

The Vodou House or *Sosyete:* Non-*Asson* Lineage

The vast majority of non-*asson* lineage Vodouisants—who sometimes call themselves *fran Ginen* ("true Africans") or *Deka Vodou*—practice in small family or village *sosyetes*, and they are generally not at all interested in teaching Vodou to outsiders, even other Haitians. Each non-*asson* house will have its own idiosyncrasies and variations on practice, based on the location(s) within Haiti and the location(s) from which its African ancestors came. The largest concentrations of non-*asson* lineage houses are in Haiti's north and extreme southwest, in the Artibonite Valley, and around the smaller cities of Cap-Haïtien, Saint Marc, Gonaïves, Souvenance, Léogâne, Jérémie, and Les Cayes.

Occasionally, you may encounter a house that has more than one kind of Vodou practice. My own family has one such lineage, containing *asson* tradition elements from our family in Port-au-Prince and its suburbs, as well as non-*asson* traditions from the family's ancestral homes outside the capital, in Kenscoff and La Pleine. This mixing of *asson* and non-*asson* traditions is becoming more common in modern Vodou, as people inside and outside Haiti move around and interact.

Initiation

In the majority of Haitian Vodou practice, being an initiate is not necessary for success. Anyone can serve Bondye, the ancestors, and the Lwa without being formally initiated. Anyone can have divinatory talents or speak to Lwa at a ceremony, and, with a sincere attitude and proper guidance, anyone can develop a personal relationship with the Lwa and gain messages and blessings from them.

A few people (perhaps less than one-tenth of all Vodouisants) are either encouraged by their families or the spirits or make an agreement with the spirits to take a further commitment to learn special techniques or *travay*. Sometimes a person undergoes initiation because a Lwa demands it of them; sometimes it is done to restore health, keep a promise, or prevent a potential calamity in that person's life.

This is a very different situation than, for example, the Wiccan conception of a right to or need for a universal priesthood. Unlike initiation in many Neopagan traditions, where a person has a "calling" or vocation to become a priest and is ordained by a group of elders or dedicates themselves as a priest, sometimes your opinion about whether or not you should be initiated in Haitian Vodou (or what rank to initiate in) is not even part of the equation.

Initiation in Vodou is something that is done TO you and FOR you, on your behalf, so that you can serve the Lwa in the fashion they require. It involves significant hardship and sacrifice, from the many thousands of dollars it costs to hire the people and purchase the objects required to carry out nearly two weeks of continuous ceremonies in their most involved form, to the permanent physical and spiritual commitments and taboos that will be your responsibility as an initiate for the rest of your life. Just like there is no divorce from a *Maryaj-Lwa,* one cannot be un-initiated from Haitian Vodou.

As a non-initiate Vodouisant, you are in total control of the depth and breadth of your responsibilities to the Lwa. If you consent to take the extra steps to become a Vodou initiate, you will have no choice but to serve the Lwa from then on, as befits the rank of initiation you receive. To make an initiation agreement with the Lwa is permanent, and since it is not mandatory to be an initiate in order to serve the Lwa, most Vodouisants simply never take this step.

There are two major initiation ceremonies in Haitian Vodou that can be discussed in any depth: the *Sèvis Tèt* and the *Kanzo* initiations. *Sèvis Tèt* is normally reserved for non-*asson* lineages and *Kanzo* for the *asson* lineages, though some houses (like my own) perform both initiations.

Sèvis Tèt Initiation

A *Sèvis Tèt* ("head service") is the primary form of initiation in the non-*asson* lineage of Haitian Vodou. In all of the houses that perform it, *Sèvis Tèt* creates *hounsi.* In some houses, it can also include extra ceremonies that permit the creation of *mambos* and *houngans*. In my own house, which combines both *asson* and non-*asson* lineage backgrounds, we use *Sèvis Tèt* strictly to create *hounsi*. For us, the *Sèvis Tèt* provides an opportunity for people who wish to be initiated further than simply dedicating himself or herself or joining a house, but who do not want or need to be initiated into the priesthood.

Any *hounsi* made by *Sèvis Tèt* are referred to as *hounsi senp* or "simple *hounsi*," to distinguish them from *hounsi* created by *Kanzo* ceremonies (*hounsi Kanzo*). In our lineage, *Sèvis Tèt* can be performed outside of Haiti and takes less time (four to six days) and resources to achieve than *Kanzo*, making it a viable alternative to those who cannot commit to the greater *Kanzo*, or who wish to be initiated into Vodou with less responsibility or commitment than *Kanzo* requires.

Sèvis Tèt requires ritual seclusion of the candidates in the *djevo*, a ritual space in the *badji* set aside for the initiation of Vodouisants in both *Sèvis Tèt* and *Kanzo* ceremonies. This space is ritually prepared by the *houngans* and *mambos*, and once it is ready, no one may enter except the candidates themselves and others who have also "passed the *djevo*." Outside the *djevo*, the *sosyete* will prepare (usually on a Tuesday or Wednesday afternoon and that evening) a huge dance in honor of the spirits and the candidates. At the end of the dance, the candidates are taken inside the *djevo*, and their ritual seclusion begins.

Everything that occurs inside the *djevo* during initiation is secret, whether it is a *Sèvis Tèt* initiation or a *Kanzo* initiation, and these things cannot be discussed in any detail. I can say that the candidates spend their time praying and resting and going through ceremonies and teachings that strengthen them and connect them more strongly to the lineage and to their Lwa. On Saturday morning, the candidates are dressed in their best new white clothing and brought out of the *djevo* to be baptized as *hounsi* of the house in a special ceremony, followed by another dance. The new *hounsi* are expected to observe a short period of purification taboos, and then afterward are considered to be full *hounsi* of the *sosyete* that initiated them.

Kanzo Initiation

The *Kanzo* initiation of Haitian Vodou's *asson* lineage is related ritually to the *Sèvis Tèt,* and it also creates *hounsi.* It is the only initiation in the *asson* lineage to create a priest of either rank (*si pwen* or *asogwe*). *Kanzo* is where the *mambos* and *houngans* of the *asson* lineage are made, and it is the only form of initiation in Haitian Vodou that produces *asogwe* priests, as there are no *asogwe* in the non-*asson* lineage.

Like *Sèvis Tèt,* a *Kanzo* initiation involves ritual seclusion in the *djevo,* and again, all of the things that occur inside the *djevo* are secrets that cannot be discussed publicly. I will share what I am permitted to discuss concerning initiation here. If you have additional questions, I strongly recommend you contact a *mambo* or *houngan* and talk to them personally. Different houses have different beliefs about how much of this material is oath-bound, and here I am erring on the side of caution; I have no desire to break any of my own vows.

Unlike *Sèvis Tèt,* a *Kanzo* takes a great deal longer to complete (anywhere from five to nine days of ritual seclusion, including days set aside before and after the seclusion for other rituals), requires a much larger number of people to perform (and thus incurs greater costs), and in most lineages, is not conducted outside of Haiti. A *Kanzo* initiation is a massive undertaking for a Haitian or a non-Haitian, involving at least two weeks of twenty-four-hour involvement at the ceremonies themselves, thousands of dollars, and a lifetime commitment to the vows taken as part of those ceremonies. In the case of a non-Haitian or a Haitian living outside Haiti, making *Kanzo* will also generally require having to go to Haiti for two to three weeks minimum at the time of the *Kanzo,* as well as many future trips. *Kanzo* is not something that many people do or need to do, though those who have gone through the *Kanzo* gain significant benefits and blessings from this experience.

As in *Sèvis Tèt,* ceremonies and dances are held before the candidates enter the *djevo* for ritual seclusion. The dances, called *bat gè* ("beating a war"), are designed to call all the spirits of a lineage to the *peristil* and let them know new people are coming to *Ginen* to meet their Lwa. A series of ritual baths is given to the candidates, and new *pwen* and *assons* are constructed and blessed for their use, as well as very long beaded necklaces called *kòlyes,* which the candidates will wear after *Kanzo* as a sign of their rank. A special ceremony is held for Ayizan, the Lwa of *Kanzo* initiation, and her sacred palm fronds are placed in the *djevo* to bless it. Eventually, the candidates are taken into the *djevo,* where they will be taught and consecrated as *hounsi* or *mambos* or *houngans* as their ranks require. All *Kanzo* initiates receive the same basic ceremonies; *mambos* and *houngans* also receive additional ceremonies and training, depending on their rank. Only other *mambos, houngans,* and *hounsi* who have been through *Kanzo* are permitted inside the *djevo* with the candidates. Often, *mambos* and *houngans* from other houses and lineages will be invited to visit a *djevo* to verify that it has been made correctly, so that they can vouch for that house and its candidates' ranks once *Kanzo* is over.

The night before the candidates are released from the *djevo* for baptism, a very special, moving ceremony is held in the *peristil.* Called *Brule Zin* (or *Boule Zin,* BROO-lay zin, "burning of pots"), this ceremony involves proving that the Lwa have accepted and blessed the *Kanzo* candidates by testing them with fire in front of the entire *sosyete* and any audience. The next morning, the candidates dress in new white clothes and veils and hats woven from Ayizan's palm fronds, come out ("rise up from the *Kanzo,*" or *leve Kanzo,* LAY-vay kon-ZO) to take their vows and be baptized with their Vodou names in front of the community, and a huge celebratory dance closes the *Kanzo* cycle. As in the *Sèvis Tèt,* there are temporary and permanent taboos following *Kanzo,* depending on each initiate's lineage and rank.

Se bezwen ou wè, mache ou wè
("What you need to see, go out and see")
—Brav Gede's instructions to me, July 2001

ELEVEN

<><><><><><><><><><><><><><><><><><><><><><><><><><><><><><><><><><><><><>

First Steps in Haitian Vodou

In October 2010, I was in New York preparing for the arrival of four of my *hounsi* and three potential house members for a *fèt* that would be held on Long Island the following night at the main temple of my Vodou lineage outside Haiti. A *fèt* (FETT, from French *fête*) sometimes also called a "party" as the word literally translates into English, is an amazing affair, including praying, singing, dancing, and the appearance of the Lwa in possession. For some of my guests and some of the other guests my mother had invited, this would be their very first *fèt*, and some of them weren't even familiar with Vodou yet. If I thought this was a tense situation, imagine what my *hounsi* thought—they were expected to perform songs and other ceremonial duties in front of the head of our lineage and around a hundred Haitians—or how anxious the people who'd never even seen Vodou before must have been!

It takes a certain amount of confidence to go out and find a group of strangers to talk to, no matter what you're talking to them about. It takes courage to ask those same strangers if you can have an invitation to a private family affair, especially if that affair is a religious or cultural event outside of your own experience. Getting involved in Haitian Vodou, if you are not Haitian or do not already know Haitians, is not easy at the beginning. You will have to be patient as well as diligent. It may require many phone calls or letters or e-mails before you even find a house willing to entertain the idea of permitting you to attend a *fèt*; and then, how you act and the impression you give will make or break your ability to be invited back again, or to join that house someday, should you decide you'd like to.

These are not easy things to do. Any person who goes through the steps to get an invitation to a *fèt* in the first place, let alone follow up and join Haitian Vodou from the outside, may get frustrated or overwhelmed by this process from time to time. It is a bit like pounding on random doors hoping someone will open, and then once you find a door that does open, convincing the people on the other side to let you come inside.

Obviously, if and when you get to the stage of being invited to a Vodou ceremony, or you are lucky enough to live in an area where a public ceremony is being given and you can attend, you will want to make a good impression. You will want to understand what it is going on and you don't want to embarrass yourself or offend anyone. What will you need to know?

Attending Your First Vodou Service

So you've managed to find a Vodou house willing to permit you to observe or even participate in a ceremony. Great! Before you go, you will want to ask a few questions, and you'll want to be prepared.

What to Ask Before You Go

Long before you get to the *peristil*, you want to know more than where the ceremony will be held and when. You will also want to ask the following questions and make sure you understand the answers, as it is unlikely the *mambo* or *houngan* will have time to talk to you about them on your arrival and before the ceremony begins.

1. *What spirit(s) will be honored at the party?*

   Every Vodou service is dedicated to various spirits. At different times of year, at different holidays, or because someone in the society owes a Lwa a ceremony, a party will be held in honor of a particular spirit or group of spirits. This is important to know, because which spirits are being honored at a particular party influences the answers to some of the other questions you should ask.

2. *What should I wear?*

   At a ceremony, different kinds and colors of clothing may be expected. For example, at a ceremony for Zaka, participants might wear blue denim, and for *Fèt Gede*, it is traditional to wear black and purple, the Gede's colors. Depending on the house, you may be asked to dress in a certain color or style, or, if you will only be observing, you may not be required to observe any dress code at all.

   No matter what a house's dress code is, ANYONE who attends a Vodou ceremony needs to wear clean, modest clothing in good condition. For example, it is never appropriate for a woman to have bare shoulders, a mini-skirt, or too much cleavage revealed by her dress or top. Some houses do not permit women to wear pants. Some of the same houses do not permit men to wear tank tops, shorts, or blue jeans. If you are at all uncertain about the dress code of a particular house, ask explicit questions ahead of time to make sure what you intend to wear will be appropriate. If you need to change into the clothes you intend to wear at the *fèt* once you arrive, most houses provide a place you can change. Do not be surprised if it is a communal space, like someone's bedroom or a spare room off the *peristil,* and you will very likely be changing clothes at the same time as other people who will also be changing their clothes. Remember that Vodou is a family-oriented practice from a country that has a smaller sense of personal privacy than most Western countries, and that standards of modesty and embarrassment might be quite different than you are accustomed to.

As far as the color of your clothes, be aware that black clothing, while stylish, is ONLY worn for Gede ceremonies, and even then, sometimes only for part of the ceremony. Some *mambos* and *houngans* do not permit anyone wearing black clothes, even observers, to enter their *peristil* if a ceremony is for Rada Lwa. Traditionally, white clothes are acceptable for Rada ceremonies and colored clothes (bright red or multicolored clothes are most common, but any color besides black or white should be acceptable) for Petro ones. Some houses, including my own, may permit men to wear pants of a light tan or beige or light blue color during the Rada ceremony in certain circumstances, as finding white pants is not always easy. (I recommend checking with kitchen supply companies for chef's pants, or surgical supply companies for white cotton "scrubs.")

If you will be participating versus merely observing, you will most likely be asked to cover your head with a kerchief, or *moushwa*, if you are female. Some houses ask male *hounsi* to do the same, and then tie the *moushwa* around the neck of *houngans* or non-initiate participants; others have all male participants drape their *moushwa* around the neck or shoulders. If you don't have a *moushwa* and can't get one or make one, ask the *mambo* or *houngan* if you can borrow one, or find out where you can purchase one inexpensively before the service. Depending on the nature of the service, you may need more than one, e.g., a white one for Rada and a red one for Petro.

Don't be embarrassed to ask these questions. You will not be very happy if you get all the way to the ceremony only to be turned away because your style of dress is inappropriate.

3. *Is there anything specific I can bring as an offering to the Lwa?*

You may be asked to bring something particular to a ceremony, such as a bottle of liquor, some food, candles, bottles of perfume, flowers, or other sundries. If you intend to speak with a Lwa or have work done for you by a Lwa during the ceremony, you may need to bring other things, which the *houngan* or *mambo* will explain to you.

No matter what you are asked to bring or not to bring, you should ALWAYS bring a small amount of money, in cash, enclosed in a plain envelope, with the name of the *mambo* or *houngan* written across the front. When you arrive at the house, or during a break in the service, locate the person who is "second in charge" (usually another *mambo* or *houngan)* and give them this envelope.

It costs a great deal of money put on a Vodou ceremony, especially in the United States. The drummers alone for an average ceremony can cost more than a thousand dollars; the cost to put on the entire party, including drummers, offerings, and other necessities, comes out of the pocket of the person throwing the party and the people of his or her house. In attending a ceremony, you've received the kindness of the *sosyete,* the attention of the Lwa, and free food and drink for a ceremony's duration, which is often more than eight hours. A donation to the hosts of $20 or $25 at minimum is a respectful gesture and will be very much appreciated by the people who invited you to observe. It will also send the message that you understand the effort and work put into serving Spirit, and that you thank the Lwa for encouraging the hosts to permit you to attend.

4. *Can I bring anyone with me? Can I bring my child(ren)?*

Unless it is a particularly important ceremony where there won't be room, or the *mambo* or *houngan* decides against it, most houses are happy for you to bring a guest. However, most houses also like to know who that person is beforehand, their interest (or not) in Vodou, and if they will be arriving with you or meeting you at the *peristil*. Since most Vodou parties in the United States are held in private homes, it is polite to make sure the *mambo* or *houngan* knows if you're coming alone or with someone else. Children are generally welcome at Vodou events, though as a parent, you will need to gauge how comfortable your own children will be at a long ceremony with strangers and loud drumming and singing in language(s) they may not understand, not to mention the appearance of spirits who are often delighted to talk to and visit with children.

5. *What time would you like me to arrive, and how long should I expect to stay?*

A Vodou ceremony often begins the morning or afternoon before the *Priyè Ginen* is begun and the dancing and singing for the Lwa actually starts. Generally, guests are not expected until right before the start of the formal *Priyè*, sometime in the evening. In most houses I have been exposed to inside and outside of Haiti, the public part of a ceremony kicks off with prayers in the late afternoon or evening, and will continue throughout the night until the following sunrise.

Depending on whether you are observing or participating, you may be asked to come early, come on time, leave early, or stay for the entire ceremony. Expect to be at the *fèt* for some time. Also expect that you may not be able to be interrupted during that time. You will want to turn off your cell phone and participate. If you are participating, you will be singing, dancing, and meeting with the spirits and the people of the house. A Vodou ceremony is a high social function in Haitian culture: a combination of church service, family gathering, and dance party. It can be a great amount of fun and a great amount of work at the same time. Above all, have an open mind and a smile, and enjoy yourself.

At the Ceremony

In most houses, someone will come and speak to you when you arrive at a *fèt*. Let them know who you are and who invited you. If you have brought guest(s) with you, introduce them and ask where you should sit. Change clothes if you need to at this time. You may ask if there is anything you can help with, but if you are unknown to the house, don't be offended if you are simply told to have a seat and wait. During a party is not a good time to ask questions, unless someone has been assigned to answer your questions during the event. If you are simply observing and everyone is busy, save your questions for the day after, or a later time when you can speak to the *mambo* or the *houngan* about what you saw and did.

Do not be surprised or offended if the ceremony seems to take longer to get going than you expect it to. Preparation for a Vodou ceremony looks like chaos from the outside, with *mambos* and *houngans* giving orders; *hounsi* running back and forth from the kitchen to the *peristil* with food, offerings, and chairs; last-minute changes and arrangements; and important guests arriving late or drummers getting caught in traffic between various *fèts* that evening. Don't worry; the ceremony will begin precisely when it is supposed to, and however long it took to get started will fade from your mind as the excitement at your first Vodou ceremony begins and the *sosyete* takes their seats before the altar for the *Priyè*.

Once you enter the *peristil*, if you are simply observing, go and sit where you are directed to sit. During the *Priyè*, you may bow your head or close your eyes if you want to. It is not required that you sing or pray, but it is required that you are respectful during the ceremony. Please turn your cell phone off, and try not to leave your seat. Should you arrive late for some reason, don't walk into the *peristil* in the midst of a song. Wait for a break in the singing and then quietly make your way to a seat.

If you have been invited to participate, be respectful. Do not touch anything without permission. This includes drums, chairs, and people, ESPECIALLY if those people are possessed. It is human nature to want to help if you see someone fall. However, every house has designated people to tend to the Lwa when they arrive; your help, however well meant, will simply end with you being in the way. Even if you have experience with possessions in other types of spiritual practices, it is considered respectful to only do what you are told to do by the people in charge. While some houses permit photographs of the *peristil*, the people in it, the ceremonies, and/or the Lwa, others do not permit any cameras during a ceremony. All houses have their own rules on photography and video recording. For your first *fèt*, I recommend you leave the camera at home and concentrate on participating. If you absolutely need photos of something later on, you can work that out with the house leadership.

You may be invited to salute or speak to a particular Lwa that has come to the ceremony, especially if the reason that you were invited was to meet that Lwa. Wait until you are directed to do so and then follow the directions of the people assisting the Lwa. Do not touch the Lwa without permission. Do not touch the Lwa's objects without permission. When a Lwa is done speaking to you, go back to your seat. You may have questions about what a Lwa has said to you. These are important to keep for future discussions with the *mambo* or *houngan*, which may occur after the ceremony is over and you have a chance to talk, or someone may come and speak to you about them during a break in the ceremony.

I recommend that you bring a notebook with you—not to take notes during the ceremony, which would be rude, but to write down your impressions and your experiences immediately afterward or during scheduled breaks. If you intend to continue investigating Haitian Vodou, this can be a very useful practice. If bringing a notebook is not practical, write down your experiences and questions in a notebook in the car or as soon as you get home.

Finding the Vodou House that Is Right For You

After you attend a Vodou ceremony (or a few), you will probably understand a great deal more about Haitian Vodou than you did before you began. Or, you may discover that you have even more questions, and you may end up attending more ceremonies or visiting different kinds of ceremonies or different *sosyetes* or houses. At some point in this experience, you may conclude that Vodou is not for you—that it is interesting but not interesting enough for more than an occasional *fèt*—or you may conclude that you would like to become a member of a Vodou house or *sosyete*.

Just like the long and sometimes frustrating process of finding a house willing to let you observe, finding a house willing to take you in as a potential family member (you are not and will never be "just a student"—Vodou is not a school, it is a way of life) is more of the same. It may take you a long time to find the house that you end up joining. You may have to knock on many doors, travel great distances, or even go to Haiti to find the place where your spirits tell you is the place you should stay. In my case, I had to go to Haiti twice and visit with several other Vodouisants in the United States before I found the place I was eventually to call home; the process took almost five years.

Know that if you are supposed to do something, the Lwa will make it happen, and, as the proverb says, *Si se Bondye ki voye ou, li peye fre ou:* "If it's God that sends you, He'll pay your expenses." Bondye willing, if the Lwa want you in Haitian Vodou, you *will* find your family if you keep your heart and your eyes and ears open, and your life will never be the same.

Notice that the title of this section is not "Finding the Right Vodou House." There is no such thing, really. What there is, is family, where you are "inside"—and there is everywhere else, where you are "outside." Since we are not all the same, we do not all have the same house or family. Just as there is no One True Religion in Haitian Vodou, there is no One True House, either. Nor is there One True Lineage or One True Initiation, no matter what any *mambo* or *houngan* tries to tell you to the contrary. Every house is its own entity; your job will be to find the one that fits you, and since there are many, many houses … this could take a while. Be patient and keep the faith.

That being said, there are things, such as the *règleman,* that all Vodou houses hold in common. If a house loudly advertises practices that don't seem to be done by ANY other house you've ever encountered or which directly contradict common sense or *règleman* you know about, consider that a red flag. More likely than not, it won't be one or two things that tell you a house is not for you or might not necessarily be legitimate, it will be a collection of things that make you uncomfortable or doubtful. This feeling should tell you to keep walking.

As an outsider, you may be taken advantage of (or marked as someone who could be taken advantage of) by less-than-scrupulous individuals. I would be lying if I said Haitian Vodou was somehow immune to con artists, frauds, or bigots. Sadly, every spiritual tradition has these kinds of people, and Vodou is no exception. Ask polite questions. If you don't understand something, or something seems confusing, ask again. Ask another house how it understands certain practices or performs certain ceremonies for comparison. Try not to word this as *"Houngan* Y does it THIS way…,*"* which can potentially lead either to a hard-sell approach ("Oh, we don't do it like *that* here!"), or the assumption by the *houngan* or *mambo* you are speaking to that you are either an opportunist or are seeking gossip about how some other house is "doing it wrong."

If it wasn't painfully apparent to you from reading the history chapter, some *mambos* and *houngans* inherently mistrust non-Haitians, no matter how sincere they may be. There are others who will permit non-Haitians to be members of their *sosyetes* but will never initiate them; still others will initiate only to certain ranks or do not permit non-Haitians in their houses at all. A minority few may attempt to sell you what is derisively called an "American *asson,"* a sham initiation that will earn you little more than an empty bank account. If you take your time and pay attention, your chances of being taken in by someone who would do such a thing to you are slim to none. If it looks like a shortcut, it's not likely to take you down a road you want to go. Anything worth doing is worth taking your time doing, and your Lwa will gladly wait for you to find the right door to *Ginen*.

Questions You Should Ask About a Potential House

Should you come to the place where you are looking for a Vodou *sosyete* to join, any or all of the following questions can be asked of the head of that house. Any *mambo* or *houngan* should be more than happy to answer these questions in detail, without sounding suspicious or insulted by them, if you ask them sincerely and politely. (Obviously, if you give the impression that you don't trust them to answer fully, you may get a less than warm response; after all, who'd want to join a house full of people you don't trust?) None of these questions requires oath-bound or otherwise-secret information to be revealed.

1. *How long have you been practicing Vodou? When did you become a* mambo/houngan? *Who initiated you?*

   Every *mambo* and *houngan* is proud of their lineage and should be happy to tell you when they were initiated, who initiated them, and what rank(s) they have received or taken. If you ask if you could talk to their initiator(s) as well, most *mambos* and *houngans* will provide contact information for their initiatory parent(s) to verify and vouch for their character. In the case of older clergy, or those who are in Haiti, you may need to make international calls and/or speak Kreyòl, and it is possible that their initiator(s) could be deceased. It may be important to you to know if someone was initiated in Haiti; most lineages still hold that all or some initiations need to be held on the island, while others are adapting to life in the wider world and initiating outside Haiti. If this is a concern for you, ask.

2. *How many people are in your house? How many people have you initiated personally? Would it be possible for me to talk to them?*

   If you would like to interview the initiatory siblings or children of a potential house leader, they will usually happily supply that information as well. In some cases—particularly if red flags come up in other portions of the interview process—you may opt to talk to former children of a house as well. Note that how long a person has been involved and/or initiated in Vodou is not necessarily an indication of quality, though it is unlikely that a new priest (initiated less than a year or two) will have all the knowledge necessary to run a successful house alone, and he or she will probably work with his or her initiatory parent(s) for a time in apprenticeship before going completely independent. They may also work in concert with those parent(s) on a permanent basis. Vodou is a community practice. A *mambo* or *houngan* with no initiatory children (if she is *asogwe*) or established house, or who actually claims to be a "solitary," would be instantly suspect in Haiti and should, at very least, be a cause of further questions for you. A house that has more former members than current ones or that seems to initiate many people who then don't stay very long is also a cause for concern and additional questions.

3. *What sorts of ceremonies and services does your house perform/ offer? (If you haven't already) Can I attend one? Where is your* peristil *located?*

Some houses are full-service houses, offering all the varied services of Haitian Vodou; others are satellite houses of larger lineages with headquarters in Haiti or somewhere else. Find out if you will have to travel to attend ceremonies, and if so, how far and how often. If the house is headquartered outside Haiti, does it do services in Haiti? Will you be able to go to Haiti to take part in them if you choose to or need to? Will you be required to attend a certain number of ceremonies, and if so, where and when?

4. *What is your expectation of people who would like to join your* sosyete?

This is an open-ended question that will tell the *mambo* or *houngan* that you understand the two-way nature of a family relationship, and that you understand that what you bring to a house is just as important as what it can give back to you. It will also give him or her an opportunity to elaborate on other questions or have a conversation with you about personal philosophy. Listen carefully to what she chooses to emphasize here. Is it all about "you can have this or that for

X amount of money/time"? Does it sound like Haitians and non-Haitians, and initiates and non-initiates, work together and are treated respectfully? Does he ask you questions too, and are they questions that make you feel more (or less) comfortable as the conversation goes on?

5. *Which Lwa is your house/lineage dedicated to?*

The answer to this question may help you choose a house, or it may not. While all houses and lineages, at least according to *règleman,* serve all the Lwa of *Ginen,* most have patron Lwa, or Lwa that show up constantly and are considered to be the "mama" or "papa" spirits of the house. The character of these Lwa is generally felt as a "flavor" throughout that entire *sosyete,* even if individual members do not serve those Lwa strongly. A house with heavy emphasis on Petro spirits might be a bad fit for someone who is very Rada-oriented, at least initially, and different lineages from different parts of Haiti serve different Lwa in different ways and depths. It is interesting to me that almost all of my potential *hounsi* so far have come to me initially with questions about the Lwa who are the patrons of our house—Lwa that I never advertised as our main Lwa before they asked. It was almost as if those spirits were sending those people to me to be part of the house ... or perhaps that's exactly what the Lwa intended.

Causes for Concern

Red flags that should definitely make you ask more questions, and/or consider looking elsewhere, include any combinations of the following, along with your "gut feeling" about a house. You will also want to add your own assessment of any advice or interviews you get from current and former members and other elders whose opinions you trust. Red flags include:

- Excessive emphasis on money, beyond a reasonable exchange for goods received. This could include extra costs for things already paid for; a philosophy that one can be initiated as soon as one has the cash, or at whatever rank one can afford; constant requests for cash; or divinations that start with small fees and quickly become "you are in serious trouble and the Lwa want you to do X and Y and Z, which will cost more." If a house tells you that you are cursed and MUST initiate, or must pay an exorbitant amount of money for spiritual protection or some special ceremony, definitely get more than that house's opinion before you sign any checks.

• Assertions that one's lineage or house is "orthodox" or "true" Vodou, that they are better than other houses, or that they are the only ones who do it "right," beyond simple statements one could attribute to the *règleman* or to pride in one's training. A *mambo* or *houngan* who has all kinds of time to trash the competition is evidently not busy enough with children and clients and serving the Lwa properly.

• A house filled with people who seem unstable, who move from misery to misery, or who don't seem particularly happy or satisfied with themselves. Even as hard as life in Haiti is, most Vodouisants derive comfort and happiness from serving the Lwa. The Lwa take care of those who serve them. A house that is constantly in crisis or filled with angry, unhappy people or nothing but drama is a sign that something is not right. Crises are often a sign from the Lwa that something has been neglected or is not being done properly.

• Too much complaining about or actually slandering former members. A busy, stable Vodou house doesn't have time to sit around complaining about how terrible this *hounsi* or that *mambo* is or was. Beyond simple statements of fact or answering direct questions, a house that spends its energy on denigrating a list of former members as "enemies" is not serving *Ginen*. Besides, should you decide to leave that house eventually for whatever reason, you know how you will be treated. Is that something you really want?

- Too much complaining about or actually slandering CURRENT members. Believe it or not, I have heard *houngans* badmouth their own children to me or to others. I have seen *mambos* complain to one of their children about how terrible another one is. This is not how a good family works. A Vodou family is a *Ginen* family. It does NOT have to be dysfunctional, and you do NOT have to accept a house where you can't even trust your own parents to love you. We all have disagreements and arguments, but how we deal with them says much about our character and about the kind of family we are.

- A house that deviates from the *règleman* in significant ways that don't seem to be supported by Vodou (or common sense) rationale. Most often, these houses are headed by non-Haitians or expatriate Haitians, but even outside Haiti, most of us observe the *règleman* to the best of our abilities. For example, houses that insist that their Lwa do not eat meat need to be honest with themselves, and say that THEIR Lwa do not eat meat because they personally choose not to feed it to them, not that the Lwa are universally vegetarian (only a rare few are). I know of houses that refuse to serve Petro, saying they are "devils" and that only *bokors* serve Petro, which is both ridiculous and utterly ahistorical. Some houses outside and inside Haiti claim to be creating "new" forms of Vodou. This is all well and good, and the Lwa may very well be drawing people to do these things; it is not mine to say or judge. However, these sorts of practices are not *Haitian* Vodou, and if the house doesn't seem to understand the difference—or worse, tries to tell you Haitians are doing it wrong or are unenlightened, or "we're in the modern world and we have changed and we don't have to do it that way anymore"—this should be a cause for further questions.

After you've amassed all the information, asked the questions, and taken part in the ceremonies, remember that it's still all in your hands, and no one can make these sorts of decisions about your spiritual journey except you. Listen to your heart. Get divinations, or do them yourself. Keep a dream journal and listen to the messages your ancestors and Lwa provide in those dreams. You will be led to *Ginen* if you are meant to get there, and I wish you all the best on your journey home, wherever home is, whether it's *Ginen* or somewhere else.

Appendices

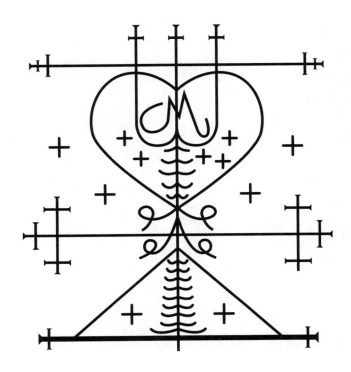

APPENDIX A

✧✧✧✧✧✧✧✧✧✧✧✧✧✧

Glossary

Kreyòl words are followed by alternate spellings in parentheses, French cognates (where known) in brackets, and then English translations in quotation marks. Note that Haitian Kreyòl follows the same pronunciation rules as French.

aksyon de gras [action de grâce]: A simple Vodou ceremony designed to give thanks to Bondye, the ancestors, and/or the Lwa. Not as involved as a full ceremony or *fèt.*

anba dlo [en bas de l'eau] "under the water": Idiom for saying a person has died. Vodou belief states that a person's soul rests *anba dlo* in Mèt Agwe's kingdom for a year after bodily death, and then can be retrieved via special ceremony. See *Dessounin, Kase-Kanari.*

anvwa mo (anvwaye mo) [envoy les morts] "sending the dead": A *travay* to send the spirit of an angry dead person to attack a living individual. Many Vodouisants refuse to do this kind of work, though *mambos* and *houngans* know how to protect against it.

asogwe: The highest rank of priesthood in Haitian Vodou's *asson* lineage. *Mambos* and *houngans asogwe* can serve all the Lwa of *Ginen,* and can initiate *hounsi* and all priesthood ranks.

asson (ason): A small, dried gourd (*kalbas kouran* in Kreyòl) wrapped in a net made of beads, snake vertebrae, and other items, connected to a small silver bell. The *asson,* which is related to similar instruments still used in Africa, is an instrument used by *mambos* and *houngans* of the *asson* lineage to call Rada Lwa. Because training in its use is limited to Kanzo priesthood, it is a symbol of Vodou priesthood and kingship in the *asson* lineage.

Ayiti "mountain land" or "mother land": The Taino name of the island Haiti is located on.

badji: A special room in a *peristil,* containing altars to various Lwa.

banda: A frantic dance performed by and on behalf of the Gede Lwa that mimics the motions of sexual intercourse; also the rolling and catchy drum beats that accompany this dance.

batem [baptisme]: The first ceremony given to an initiate who has risen from the *djevo,* either in *Sèvis Tèt* or *Kanzo* initiation. It is a full baptism, with holy water and prayers, in the same format as a Roman Catholic baptismal rite, and is often conducted by a Catholic priest.

blan [blanc] "white": Both the color and the term for a person of European heritage (and "white" skin). Before the Revolution, *blan* in Haiti were divided into *gwo blan [grands blancs]* ("big whites," European landowners and plantation owners) and *peti blan [petits blancs]* ("little whites," the plantation workers, lawyers, police, soldiers, merchants, immigrants, visitors, and other non-landowning whites on the island). Since the Revolution, the term *blan* is derisive, quite offensive, and has come to mean "anyone who is not Haitian," regardless of skin color.

bohique: A Taino priest or priestess of the *zemi.* This term is also probably the basis of the indigenous name for the island now called Puerto Rico (*Bohicua*). Some *bohiques* became *zemi,* and some of them are honored as Lwa in Haitian Vodou and/or Dominican Vodou.

bokor: A Vodouisant who runs a *peristil* or performs *travay* like a *mambo* or *houngan,* but who has never been initiated. Some use this term derisively to refer to anyone who performs negative *travay* or curses or other "evil" magic, a person said to "work with both hands," but it does not always have this connotation. In the Dominican Republic, the related term *Papa* (or *Mama*) *Boko* is a title in Dominican Vodou, in the same way *houngan* or *mambo* is used in Haitian Vodou.

Bondye [Bon Dieu] "(The) Good God": The deity responsible for the creation and maintenance of the universe. Sometimes equated with the Roman Catholic or Christian God. Sometimes called *Gran Mèt.* Bondye is served first in all Vodou ceremony.

boutèy [bouteille] "bottle": A bottle (usually an empty glass rum bottle) that has been decorated with bright-colored cloth, sequins, mirrors, and seed beads, among other items. *Boutèy* are kept on altars as a *repozwa* for a Lwa's favorite drinks and are used during salutes at Vodou ceremonies. Non-Haitians have been known to collect *boutèy* as Haitian folk art objects.

cacique: A Taino chief or king/queen. Some *caciques,* such as Queen Anacoana, are honored as Lwa within Haitian Vodou and/or Dominican Vodou.

Cacos: Haitians who fought against the majority government set up by the U.S. Marines during the first American occupation of Haiti (1915–1934). Named for frogs that made lots of noise at night, the *cacos* were expert at guerilla warfare.

chwal [cheval] "horse": A person whose body has been or is currently possessed by a Lwa, or who is capable of being possessed by Lwa.

Dessounin: A special Vodou ceremony held shortly after a Vodouisant's death, to permit their soul to be separated from their physical body. See *anba dlo, Kase-Kanari.*

djab [diable] "devil": A nickname for Lwa or other spirits that are angry, fierce, dangerous, or "hot," often used to describe Petro and Kongo spirits. A female *djab* is called a *djabla.*

djevo: A specially prepared room within a *peristil* where initiations are conducted. This may be a temporary or permanent space, and only initiates and candidates for initiation may enter.

drapo (dwapo) [drapeau] "flag": A large piece of cloth that has been intricately decorated with sequins, seed beads, and other items to depict various Lwa and their symbols. Drapo can be large or small, hung on altars or in *peristils,* or worn like capes across the shoulders of Vodouisants as they salute the Lwa. Like *boutèy, drapo* are purchased and collected by non-Haitians as folk art.

esko [escort]: A small "family" of Lwa. There are *esko* within the various nations of Lwa, and there are *esko* of Lwa that are served by Vodouisants individually, or by individual lineages.

fèt [fête] "party": A Vodou ceremony involving dancing, singing, drumming, and lots of food.

Fèt Gede "Gede Party/Festival": A special holiday for the Gede Lwa held November 1–3 annually (and/or the entire month of November, depending on lineage).

gad [garde] "guard": A form of *travay* that provides protection. *Gad* can be physical, involving anything from liquids to drink, to herbs rubbed into the skin, to talismans and intangible magic. The term is also used to describe spirits that are either Lwa-invoked strictly for protection services, or the "servants" of various Lwa who perform such services.

Gede: The nation of Lwa associated with the unnamed and unknown dead. Baron Samedi and Manman Brijit are the parents and leaders of the Gede nation.

gens de couleur "people of color": The French term for men of mixed-race backgrounds in the colony of Saint-Domingue. The *gens de couleur* changed sympathies from pro-European (pro-*blan*) to pro-slaves at several different times during, before, and after the Revolution. Their mixed-race, lighter-skinned descendants in Haiti today often consider themselves apart from darker-skinned Haitians, perpetuating a class disparity that has been going on since Haiti started.

Ginen (Ginè) [Guinea]: The mythical, ancestral Africa of Vodou philosophy and liturgy.

Gran Mèt [Grande Mâitre]: See *Bondye.*

houngan (ou(n)gan): A Haitian Vodou priest. The equivalent female rank is *mambo.*

hounfo (houmfor, houmfort): A Haitian Vodou temple and its supporting buildings.

hounsi: A male or female Haitian Vodou initiate who is not a priest. Two forms of initiation can create a *hounsi:* the *Sèvis Tèt* and the *Kanzo.* The term is sometimes also used generically for an uninitiated Vodouisant who has been accepted as a member of a Vodou *sosyete.*

Iliminasyon [illumination]: A Vodou ceremony involving lighting a lamp for a special purpose.

jete-dlo [jeter de l'eau] "throw(ing) water": Pouring ritual libations of water along with prayers. The number of times the water is poured and the words said while pouring differ from *sosyete* to *sosyete;* individual techniques are taught by lineage elders.

Kanzo: The initiation ceremony that creates *hounsi, mambos,* and *houngans* in the *asson* lineage of Haitian Vodou. Not all Vodou lineages perform *Kanzo.*

Kase-Kanari "breaking pots": A Vodou ceremony held a year after a person's death (see *Dessounin*), to release their soul from *anba dlo* and send it to the afterlife, as well as to ensure it has a welcome place in the *peristil,* if it should come to visit.

kivet [cuvette]: An enameled steel basin, used as a wash basin in Haiti. With the advent of plastics, many larger *kivet* are now made of plastic, but in Vodou we use enameled and/or plain metal *kivets* for many ritual purposes, as well as for a safe, fireproof place to burn candles.

kleren [clairin]: Raw sugarcane rum of exceptionally high proof (up to 180 proof is common). Nago Lwa and Petro Lwa are very fond of *kleren,* which they often drink or set on fire.

kòlye [collier]: Long ritual necklaces made of beads, snake vertebrae, and other objects, that are worn by *Kanzo* initiates. The style and weight of a *kòlye* indicate the initiate's rank; a *hounsi's kòlye* consists of a single strand of beads and other items up to four feet long, whereas *mambos* and *houngans* have much more elaborate *kòlye*.

Kongo: A subset of the Petro nation, the Kongo Lwa hail from areas of modern-day Benin, reaching eastward toward modern Congo. Some of these Lwa are served in other Kongo-derived rites in the Western Hemisphere, including Palo.

Kreyòl *[Creole]:* The official language of Haiti. Kreyòl is a mixture of French with various West African dialects, featuring French pronunciation and some West African vocabulary and grammar. There are other creole languages in the Antilles and even in other parts of the world, but in this book, *Kreyòl* denotes the language of Haitian Kreyòl.

lakou: A compound or walled structure, containing houses and other buildings that belong to one family unit or group. In Vodou, a *lakou* refers to the *peristil* and all its outbuildings, as well as the houses of *mambos* and *houngans* and *hounsi* who live on the property.

langaj [language]: Non-Kreyòl words of West African origin, sung or recited as part of Vodou ceremony or *travay*. While many of these words are taken from Fon, Bantu, Yoruba, Kikongo, or Bakongo, among other languages, a few of these words can no longer be translated.

leve [lever] "to rise": The phrase indicating the ceremonies of leaving the *djevo* and public baptism as a Vodou initiate.

Lwa *[Loa]:* The spirits of Haitian Vodou.

macoute (makout): A woven straw bag with a shoulder strap, used like a backpack or purse. Tonton Macoute, "Uncle Sack," is both a Haitian folklore bogeyman and the name for the secret police forces employed by Papa Doc and Baby Doc Duvalier.

mambo (manbo): A Haitian Vodou priestess. The equivalent male rank is *houngan*.

Manje-Lwa "feeding the Lwa": A ceremony where food is offered to a Lwa or group of Lwa.

manje-sèk [manger-sec] "dry food": Bloodless offerings that do not contain animal products.

manman-hounyo (mama hounyor): The *mambo* who oversees and takes care of initiation candidates while they are secluded in the *djevo*. The *manman-hounyo* is usually a different *mambo* than the initiatory mother, and she is treated like a second mother forever afterward.

maroon: Taino, African, or mixed-race slaves who ran away from their masters and hid in the mountains of Ayiti. The *maroon* resistance fueled and eventually caused the Haitian Revolution. The word derives from the Spanish word for "runaway," *cimarron.*

Maryaj-Lwa "Lwa marriage": A Vodou ceremony where a human being marries a Lwa.

mèt tèt [maître tête] "master of the head": The single Lwa that is one's personal Lwa, the personal guardian angel, and special protective spirit.

MINUSTAH: French acronym for the late-twentieth-century and early-twenty-first-century United Nations Stabilization Mission in Haiti.

moushwa [mouchoir]: A headscarf or kerchief worn during Vodou service. These are often made of satin or other shiny and beautiful material.

Nago: Both a tribal name and the nation of Lwa hailing from the Yoruba-speaking peoples of what is now Nigeria and Benin. The Nago nation in Haitian Vodou is considered a subset of the Rada nation. Outside Haiti, these Lwa are often called *orishas.*

nanchon [nation]: A larger grouping of Lwa and Lwa *esko*. The most common *nanchon* served in Vodou are Rada, Petro, Kongo, and Nago, though tradition says there are twenty-one *nanchons* total.

noiriste: A group of black-empowerment academics that sought control of Haiti during the early twentieth century. The most successful *noiriste* was President François "Papa Doc" Duvalier.

orisha (olisha): See *Nago.*

paket [pacquette]: A *pwen* made of various items, tied up in cloth to make a bag-like object.

paket Kongo: A special kind of *paket* made with cloth and other things such as ribbons, sequins, and feathers, and used by initiates. Like *drapo* and *boutèy,* non-functional *paket Kongo* replicas are often sold as art objects, and they represent one of the more beautiful forms of Vodou folk art.

peristil [peristyle]: A Vodou temple and all its rooms.

Petro (Petwo): A nation of Lwa comprised of spirits of the Haitian Revolution, Taino spirits, and spirits from the Kongo and non-Rada areas of Ginen. Petro spirits are hotter and fiercer than Rada spirits, and they are served with their own colors, songs, and drumbeats.

piman: A favorite drink of the Gede Lwa, made by marinating very hot peppers in *kleren.*

poto mitan [poteau Mitan] "Mitan pole": The central pillar in a Vodou *peristil.* Dances revolve around the *poto mitan,* and offerings and salutes are given at its base. The word *mitan* is most likely *langaj,* but it could be etymologically derived from French *matin,* "morning."

Priyè Ginen [prière Guinea] "African Prayer": The formal songs and prayers that begin Vodou ceremonies. The *Priyè* represents an oral history of Vodou and of the specific lineage leading the *Priyè.*

pwen [point]: A magical object designed to act as a repository *(repozwa)* for a Lwa or spirit.

pwen achte [point acheter] "bought point": A *pwen* constructed by a *bokor* or a *mambo* or *houngan,* with a spirit that has been compelled to reside inside, like the "genie" of Islamic magic. A *pwen achte,* as the name implies, can be sold for the use of another. Some *mambos* and *houngans* do not create *pwen achte,* citing ethical issues.

pwen cho [point chaud] "hot point": A pwen that traps a spirit considered strong or fierce or dangerous ("hot") and is more difficult to handle and control than a regular *pwen achte.* (*Pwen cho* can also be sold.) Some *mambos* and *houngans* do not create *pwen cho* for ethical reasons.

pwomès (promès) [promesse]: A formal arrangement that one will do something for a Lwa in return for a favor granted by that Lwa. For example, a person can make a *pwomès* to give a party for a Lwa in return for a job, a marriage, or recovery from illness.

Rada: The nation of Lwa associated with *Ginen,* containing all the *esko* of the various spirits of Dahomey and other African nations, as well as the Nago nation. Rada spirits are cooler and less fierce than Petro spirits, and they are served with their own colors, songs, and drumbeats.

rara: A Haitian cultural tradition engaged in mostly during Lent, where Vodouisants and other Haitians go from town to town singing, dancing, and performing instrumental folk music.

rasin [racine] "root(s)": The place where one's ancestors come from, or the ancestral spirits themselves.

règleman [règlement] "rule(s)": The agreed-upon regulations for how a Haitian Vodou ceremony is organized and conducted.

repozwa [reposoir] "resting place": A ritual object, place, or person designated as a sacred place or altar for a Lwa or other spirit to reside. From the French word for "altar."

Sanpwel *[Sans-Pouils]:* A secret society in Haitian culture, sometimes associated with Vodou, but actually separate of it. They are rumored to use *wanga* as punishment for severe crimes, for example, by creating a *zombi.*

sèviteur (Sèvite) [Serviteur]: A Vodouisant. One who serves (the Lwa).

Sèvis Tèt [Service Tête] "head ceremony": The initiation ceremony of the non-*asson* lineage of Haitian Vodou. Sometimes it is referred to as *Lave Tèt,* "head washing," but this is also a term for a non-initiatory *travay* where a person's head is washed in herbs for various purposes. Not all Vodou houses perform *Sèvis Tèt.*

si pwen [sûr point]: The first rank of priesthood in the *asson* lineage of Haitian Vodou. A *mambo* or *houngan si pwen* is permitted to serve his or her Lwa *esko,* the Lwa of his or her house, and to assist in almost all other ceremonies. A *si pwen* person cannot initiate Vodouisants.

sosyete [société]: An individual Vodou house and/or lineage.

tcha-tcha: A gourd rattle painted in bright colors used to call the Petro, Kongo, and Gede Lwa in the *asson* lineage; and to call all spirits in the non-*asson* lineage. A similar instrument was used in Taino ceremony, and is still used in parts of West Africa and in other African Diasporic traditions in the Western Hemisphere.

ti-mesh: Hand-twisted cotton wicks placed in ritual lamps.

tohossu: In Dahomey, a child born with congenital defects, born only to die at birth or before puberty, or said to be the child of a human being and a spirit, was called a *tohossu*. Some of our Lwa, including Bosou and Agassou, are *tohossu*.

travay [travaille] "work": A word used to describe magical practice in the abstract.

trêteman "treatment": Where a *bokor* or *mambo* or *houngan* diagnoses and offers treatments for medical or spiritual illnesses, or other problems.

veve: A symbol indicating a Lwa or *esko* of Lwa, drawn on the floor of the *peristil* before or during a ceremony using a special powder made from cornmeal and other ingredients. *Veve* are often incorporated into Vodou art, including *drapo* and *boutèy, peristil* paintings, and nonreligious folk art. The prevalence of and particular uses of *veve* differ from *sosyete* to *sosyete*.

wanga: A type of *travay* involving tangible objects. Also used to describe special herbal packets made in other African-derivative traditions in the Western Hemisphere (e.g., "wanga bag").

woulo "steamroller": Flash-mob demonstrations and riots of lowerclass Haitians, orchestrated by Haitian Presidents including Fignolé and Aristide.

zansèt-yo "the ancestors": All the blessed dead.

zanj (lezanj) [les anges] "the angels": Another word for Lwa.

zemi (cemi): Spirits and/or gods of the Taino people. Some *zemi* are now honored as Lwa.

zombi: A person rendered into a catatonic state by herbs, either as punishment (see *Sanpwel*) or other reasons; sometimes also a phrase to describe wandering dead (see the entry in Chapter 6 for Gede Plumaj about "astral *zombi*").

APPENDIX B

Timeline of Haitian History

Pre-1492: Arawak-speaking tribes live on an island called Ayiti

Dec. 1492: Christopher Columbus lands and renames the island Hispaniola

1496: Spain establishes a formal colony called Santo Domingo

1517: Spain signs a contract to import African slaves directly to Hispaniola

1697: Spain cedes the western third of Hispaniola (Saint-Domingue) to France via the Treaty of Ryswick

1751–1758: François Makandal leads *maroon* forces and slaves in rebellion against white slave owners

Aug. 26, 1789: The French Revolution changes legal status and relationships between white slave owners, white and mixed-race colonists, and African slaves

Oct. 1790–Feb. 6, 1791: *Gens de couleur* revolt by Vincent Ogé and his followers

May 1791: French government grants citizenship to the *gens de couleur*

Aug. 1791: The Vodou ceremony at Bwa Kayiman sparks the slave rebellion and the Haitian Revolution

1793: France executes King Louis XVI and declares war on Great Britain; Saint-Domingue's *grands blancs* appeal to Britain for help with the rebellion; Spain sends forces from Santo Domingo

Aug. 29, 1793: French forces free Saint-Domingue's African slaves and arm them to fight against the *blancs* and Spain; Spain is driven back into Santo Domingo

Dec. 1800: Toussaint L'Ouverture's forces defeat the Spanish in Santo Domingo

Jan. 3, 1801: L'Ouverture abolishes slavery across Hispaniola and declares himself its governor-general; Napoleon sends troops to restore French rule over Saint-Domingue

May 1802: France invites L'Ouverture to a parley; he agrees but is arrested and shipped to France

Nov. 1802: The cruel Vicomte de Rochambeau takes lead of the French forces; many French loyalists join Dessalines and Pétion in the rebel army

Apr. 1803: British naval blockade eats into French profits; France reduces troops in Saint-Domingue and sells Louisiana Territory to U.S.

Nov. 1803: Dessalines defeats Rochambeau and is elected Haiti's first undisputed leader; France abandons Saint-Domingue

Jan. 1, 1804: Dessalines declares himself governor-general for life; white slave owners are told to leave or be executed, and the Vatican orders clergy to leave Haiti

Sep. 22, 1804: Dessalines crowned Emperor Jacques I of Haiti

Oct. 17, 1806: Dessalines assassinated; Haiti divides in two: the northern State of Haiti under Henri Christophe, and the southern Republic of Haiti under Alexandre Pétion

Feb. 17, 1807: Christophe elected president and general of the State of Haiti

1810–1820: Thousands of Haitians are worked to death expanding Christophe's fortress

Apr. 1–Jun. 2, 1811: Henri Christophe coronated as King Henri I; the State of Haiti becomes the Kingdom of Haiti

1816: Pétion declares himself governor for life of the Republic of Haiti

1818: Pétion dissolves parliament in the Republic of Haiti

Mar. 29, 1818: Pétion dies of yellow fever and Jean-Pierre Boyer becomes president of the Republic of Haiti

Oct. 8, 1820: King Henri I commits suicide rather than be overthrown; Boyer assumes presidency of a reunited Haiti

1821–1822: Boyer invades Spanish Haiti (formerly Santo Domingo) and becomes president of the entire island of Hispaniola

1825: France offers to recognize Haiti—for a enormous restitution fee; Haiti agrees

1834: France establishes diplomatic relations with Haiti

1860: The Vatican restores ties to Haiti and clergy return; anti-Vodou campaigns begin

July 1861: Santo Domingo returns to Spanish control

1864: President Geffrard and the Vatican join forces to destroy Vodou temples, drums, and ritual objects after a young girl's murder; Vodouisants retreat to practice in secret

Jan. 20, 1875: Haiti and Santo Domingo (now the Dominican Republic) end border hostilities

1886: Sir Spenser Saint John's *Hayti or the Black Republic* is published, vilifying Vodou

Dec. 6, 1908: Francois C. Antoine Simon appointed president; his daughter is publicly known to be a Vodou priestess

Aug. 8, 1912: Haiti's National Palace destroyed by a suspicious explosion, killing President Cincinnatus Leconte

Jul. 27–28, 1915: President Jean Vilbrun Guillaume Sam executes political prisoners and is later killed by a mob; U.S. Marines seize the capital and the first U.S. occupation of Haiti begins

Oct.–Dec. 1929: U.S. dispatches a team to Haiti to discuss withdrawal and establishment of free elections

1934: President Sténio Vincent persuades U.S. to withdraw troops

Oct. 2–8, 1937: Dominican Republic President Rafael Trujillo orders the "Parsley Massacre" of twenty to thirty thousand Haitians living near the border

Oct. 11–12, 1954: Hurricane Hazel kills at least a thousand and causes widespread crop and economic damage

May 25, 1957: Daniel Fignolé named provisional president of Haiti but is quickly removed from power, sparking violent protests

Sep. 22, 1957: François "Papa Doc" Duvalier elected president

1958: Papa Doc creates his own Presidential Guard

1959: Papa Doc creates the National Security Volunteer Militia, or Tonton Macoutes

May 24, 1959: Papa Doc suffers a massive heart attack; upon his return to power, Papa Doc imprisons his interim leader, Clement Barbot

1961–1962: Papa Doc disbands his government and holds a rigged election; the U.S. suspends aid to Haiti and the Vatican excommunicates Papa Doc

Apr. 1963: Barbot attempts to kidnap Papa Doc's children and rumors claim Barbot has used Vodou to avoid being arrested; he is later caught and executed

Nov. 22, 1963: Papa Doc claims that JFK's assasination was the direct result of a *wanga* he made against the president for withdrawing foreign aid

Jun. 14, 1964: Papa Doc rigs a constitutional referendum to declare himself president for life

1966: The Roman Catholic Church readmits Papa Doc

Apr. 21, 1971: Papa Doc dies and the presidency is given to his son, Jean-Claude "Baby Doc" Duvalier

1978: U.S. Department of Agriculture demands the destruction of all Haitian wild pigs to stop the spread of swine fever

1980: AIDS rumors discourage Haitian tourism, further damaging the fragile economy

1983: Pope John Paul II visits Haiti and condemns its conditions and government, encouraging activism against the Baby Doc regime

1985: Catholic priest Jean-Bertrand Aristide gives anti-Baby Doc homilies in Haiti

Mid 1985–January 1986: Food riots paralyze cities and the U.S. pressures Baby Doc to leave

Feb. 7, 1986: Baby Doc exiled to France; General Henri Namphy becomes interim president and begins the bloody "Duvalierism without Duvalier" period

Sep. 11, 1988: Armed men attack Aristide's church, killing fifty and injuring more; Aristide escapes

Sep. 17, 1988: Namphy deposed by a coup led by General Prosper Avril, who declares martial law

Mar. 10, 1990: Avril forced into exile after public demonstrations; Lieutenant General Hérard Abraham sworn in as president

Mar. 13, 1990: President Abraham voluntarily gives power to Ertha Pascal-Trouillot, Haiti's first female president

Dec. 16, 1990: Acting President Pascal-Trouillot oversees the first set of free elections in Haiti; Aristide receives 67 percent of the vote

Jan. 6–7, 1991: Exiled Tonton Macoute Roger Lafontant takes Pascal-Trouillot hostage in an attempt to stop Aristide from taking office; citizens protest

Feb. 7, 1991: Aristide sworn in as Haiti's first democratically elected president; he arrests Pascal-Trouillot, but U.S. intervention moves her into exile

Feb.–Sep. 1991: Aristide enacts many positive reforms that irritate neighbors and allies and nominates René Préval as prime minister; world media characterizes Aristide as a dangerous dictator

Sep. 29, 1991: Aristide sent into exile with the assistance of U.S., French, and Venezuelan diplomacy; CIA support of the coup triggers U.S. Congressional hearings

1993: The Front for the Advancement and Progress of Haiti (FRAPH), a paramilitary death squad, targets Aristide's remaining allies; the UN enacts a trade embargo (which the U.S. largely ignores)

Jul. 31, 1994: The UN Security Council authorizes a multinational force to restore Aristide to power; U.S. orders Marines to Port-au-Prince once again

Sep. 18–Oct. 12, 1994: U.S. politician Bob Bennett asks Jimmy Carter and Colin Powell, among others, to negotiate for Aristide's return

Oct. 15, 1994: Aristide resumes his presidency, disbanding the army and creating a civilian police force

1994–1995: U.S. attempts to influence Aristide's policies through embargo exemptions and agricultural programs

1995: The Organization of the People ("Lavalas") party decides Prime Minister René Préval should run for president when Aristide's term ends; legislative elections set for June, and a presidential election for December

Mar. 31, 1995: Bill Clinton is the first U.S. president to visit Haiti; authority is transferred from Marines to the UN Mission in Haiti (MINUHA)

Dec. 1995: Préval wins presidential elections by a landslide, though turnout is low

1996: Aristide creates a new political party Fanmi Lavalas ("Lavalas Family"); years of disagreement between the two parties ensue

1999: Préval dissolves parliament and rules by decree

May 2000: Fanmi Lavalas wins legislative elections by order of the Provisional Election Commission (CEP) it controls

Dec. 2000: Aristide re-elected in an election boycotted by all opposition parties and protested by the U.S.

Early 2003: Aristide demands that France repay the restitution paid between 1825 and 1947

Sep. 2003–Feb. 2004: Buteur Metayer starts a rebellion and prepares to march on Port-au-Prince

Feb. 26, 2004: The Caribbean Community (CARICOM) requests UN peacekeeping forces for Haiti; the request is denied, partly due to France's objection

Feb. 28–29, 2004: Aristide resigns and enters a second exile in South Africa, claiming he was kidnapped and forced to resign by U.S. and other governments

2004: MINUSTAH, a new UN peacekeeping force, created and deployed to Haiti; Prime Minister Gerard Latortue withdraws Aristide's demand for French reparations

2005: Legislative and presidential elections are delayed and rescheduled four times

May 7, 2006: René Préval declared winner of the presidential election despite UN allegations of voter fraud

May 14, 2006: Préval is sworn into office, signs oil deals with Venezuela, and tours Cuba, France, and the United States

Apr. 2008: Food riots break out; Parliament dismisses Prime Minister Jacques-Édouard Alexis; Préval subsidizes food prices with foreign aid

2008: Four hurricanes batter Haiti, leaving hundreds dead and thousands homeless

Jan. 12, 2010: A magnitude 7.0 earthquake strikes near Léogâne, redtucing Port-au-Prince to rubble and killing more than 300,000; another 300,000 are injured and 1.5 million are left homeless

Jan. 12–22, 2010: First responders are thwarted by damaged infrastructure and strong aftershocks continue; despite this, violence and looting are minimal

Feb. 2010: Many nations promise long-term aid and vast amounts of money are raised; elections are postponed until November

Jul. 2010: Cleanup is remarkably slow or absent; more than 1.5 million Haitians are living in squalid tent cities

Aug. 7, 2010: Candidates file for the November 28 presidential election; CEP denies Aristide participation

Aug. 16, 2010: World leaders (unsuccessfully) pressure France to refund Haiti the money it paid France between 1825 and 1947 as part of their contribution to earthquake aid

Aug. 20, 2010: The CEP clears more than thirty candidates for the November 28 ballot

Oct. 2010: Cholera discovered in tent camps, caused by MINUSTAH neglect; thousands are infected and die

Nov. 28, 2010: Voter turnout is low (22 percent); initial results mandate a runoff between Mirlande Manigat and Jude Célestin

Nov.–Dec. 2010: Candidate Michel Joseph Martelly alleges election fraud; Préval asks the CEP for a recount

Dec. 10, 2010: The CEP releases a questionable recount

Jan. 2011: Parliament authorizes Préval to remain in office until May; the Organization of American States (OAS) releases a review of November's results and suggests Célestin be dropped from the runoff in favor of Martelly

Jan. 12, 2011: One year after the 7.0 earthquake, only 5 percent of rubble has been removed, and only 15 percent of housing rebuilt

Jan. 16, 2011: Runoff election postponed; exiled Baby Doc returns to Haiti and is arrested and released after questioning, and no trial date is set

Feb. 3, 2011: Martelly certified to replace Célestin on the runoff ballot

Mar. 2011: Cholera sweeps through Haiti

Mar. 19, 2011: Aristide returns to Haiti

Mar. 20, 2011: Martelly-Manigat runoff election held but many Haitians boycott

Apr. 21, 2011: The CEP certifies Martelly as the winner

May 14, 2011: Martelly sworn in as president of Haiti, though controversy over military and domestic affairs continues

Appendix C

Priyè Katolik ("Catholic Prayers" in English and French)

The Hail Mary (English)
Hail Mary,
Full of grace,
The Lord is with Thee.
Blessed art Thou amongst women,
And blessed is the fruit of Thy
    womb, Jesus.
Holy Mary,
Mother of God,
Pray for us sinners,
Now and at the hour of our death.
    Amen.

The Hail Mary (French)
Je vous salue, Marie,
Pleine de grâce,
Le Seigneur est avec vous.
Vous êtes bénie entre toutes les femmes,
Et Jésus, le fruit de vos entrailles,
    est béni.
Sainte Marie,
Mère de Dieu,
Priez pour nous, pauvres pécheurs,
Maintenant et à l'heure de notre mort.
    Amen.

The Apostles' Creed (English)

I believe in God, the Father Almighty,
Creator of heaven and earth.
I believe in Jesus Christ, His only son,
    our Lord.
Who was conceived by the power
    of the Holy Spirit
Born of the Virgin Mary.
Suffered under Pontius Pilate,
Was crucified, died,
And was buried.
He descended into Hell.
On the third day,
He rose again from the dead.
He ascended into heaven,
And is seated at the right hand of God,
    the Father Almighty.
From there he will come to judge
The living and the dead.
I believe in the Holy Spirit,
The holy catholic church,
The communion of saints,
The forgiveness of sins,
The resurrection of the body,
And life everlasting.
Amen.

The Apostles' Creed (French)

Je crois en Dieu, le Père tout-puissant,
Créateur du ciel et de la terre.
Et en Jésus-Christ, son Fils unique,
    notre Seigneur,
Qui a été conçu de
    Saint-Esprit
Et qui est né de la Vierge Marie.
Il a souffert sous Ponce Pilate,
Il a été crucifié, il est mort,
Il a été enseveli.
Il est descendu aux enfers.
Le troisième jour
Il est ressuscité des morts,
Il est monté aux cieux,
Il siège à la droite de Dieu,
    le Père tout-puissant.
Il viendra de là pour juger
Les vivants et les morts.
Je crois en l'Esprit-Saint.
Je crois la Sainte Eglise catholique,
La communion des saints,
La rémission des péchés,
La résurrection de la chair,
Et la vie éternelle.
Amen.

The Lord's Prayer (English)

Our Father, Who art in Heaven,
Hallowed be Thy name.
Thy kingdom come,
Thy will be done,
On earth as it is in heaven.
Give us this day our
    daily bread,
And forgive us our trespasses,
As we forgive those who trespass
    against us.
And lead us not into temptation,
But deliver us from evil.
For Thine is the kingdom,
    and the power,
And the glory, forever and ever.
Amen.

The Lord's Prayer (French)

Notre Père, qui es aux cieux,
Que ton nom soit sanctifié
Que ton règne vienne,
Que ton volonté soi faite
Sur la terre comme au ciel.
Donne-nous aujourd'hui notre
    pain de ce jour.
Pardonne-nous nos offences
Comme nous pardonnons aussi à ceux
    qui nous ont offenses.
Et ne nous soumets pas à la tentation,
Mais délivre-nous du mal,
Car c'est à toi qu'appartiennent la
    régne, la puissance
Et la gloire, aux siècles des siècles.
Amen.

Appendix D

Lwa Correspondences

I have included the most commonly-served Lwa in this Appendix, as a general reference. Specific information on how to serve these Lwa will vary from lineage to lineage, and you should always defer to your lineage elder(s) on any such information.

Note on days of the week: ALL Lwa may be served on Saturdays. No Lwa should be served on Sundays, at any time during Holy Week, or between Christmas and Epiphany.

Papa Legba

Nation: Rada

Saints: Lazarus, Anthony of Padua, sometimes Peter

Days of the Week: Mondays or Thursdays

Colors: red, white/red, or gold/brown/purple

Sample Offerings: rum, unsalted popcorn or toasted corn, a cane or crutch, a round straw bag, tobacco (and a pipe to smoke it in), strong black coffee, beans and rice, cornbread, cane syrup

Symbols: crossroads, cane

Concepts: road opening, enabling communication with Spirit

Danbala-Wedo

Nation: Rada

Saints: Moses with the Ten Commandments (north Haiti); Patrick (south Haiti)

Day of the Week: Thursdays

Colors: pure white (sometimes white and deep green)

Sample Offerings: an uncooked white egg resting on a bed of white flour on a white plate; milk; white foods such as *akasan,* white bread, rice, or coconut; almond syrup (orgeat); no alcohol or tobacco; *Lotion Pompeia* perfume

Symbols: snakes (pythons and other constrictors), eggs, Earth

Concepts: Earth, creation, purity, abundance, wealth, peace

Ayida-Wedo

Nation: Rada

Saint: Miraculous Mother (Our Lady of the Miraculous Medal)

Day of the Week: Thursdays

Colors: white or pastel rainbow colors

Sample Offerings: white foods such as milk, *akasan,* rice, white bread, coconut; no alcohol or tobacco

Symbols: rainbows, snakes, the sky

Concepts: coolness, purity, rainbows, peace

Met Agwe Tawoyo

Nation: Rada

Saints: Ulrich, Archangel Raphael (both holding fish)

Day of the Week: Thursdays

Colors: blue and white and gold, ocean colors

Sample Offerings: champagne, coffee with cream and sugar, rice boiled in sweet milk, melon, cakes with blue and white icing, whole fish, white roosters and white rams or goats

Symbols: a boat or ship (called *Imamou*), the ocean, an admiral's hat, oars and flags, anything related to the sea or fishing or boating, conch shells

Concepts: the ocean and all of its riches

Lasirèn

Nation: Rada

Saints: Diosa Del Mar ("Lady of the Sea") or Our Lady of Charity (*Caridad del Cobre* in Spanish)

Day of the Week: Thursdays

Colors: white, light blue, silver and gold, ocean colors

Sample Offerings: champagne, perfume, a mirror and comb, seashells or pearls, silver coins or jewelry, rice boiled in sweet milk, melon, cakes with blue and white icing, whole fish

Symbols: mermaid, whale, dolphin

Concepts: abundance, fertility, beauty, nurturing, wealth, water

Ezili Freda

Nation: Rada

Saint: Mater Dolorosa (Our Lady of Sorrows)

Day of the Week: Thursdays

Colors: white, soft pink, sometimes gold

Sample Offerings: perfume (especially Lotion Pompeia), mirrors, cosmetics, fine jewelry, luxury items, fine candies, fancy cookies, cakes with white or pink frosting, whole fish baked without hot spices, fine champagne, flowers (particularly red or pink roses)

Symbols: hearts, gold, jewelry

Concepts: love, desire, femininity

Azaka

Nation: Rada (Djouba)

Saint: Isadore of Seville

Day of the Week: Thursdays

Colors: denim blue, green, brown, yellow

Sample Offerings: popcorn, rice and beans, grilled meats and root
vegetables, manioc, cassava bread, *tchaka,* raw rum (*kleren*),
absinthe, tobacco and a pipe to smoke it in, a *makout* (a woven
straw bag) to keep his things in, a walking stick or machete, a
straw hat

Symbols: peasants, farmers, working-class men

Concepts: the hard-working Haitian country cousin, working
for one's living

Ogou Badagri

Nation: Rada (Nago)

Saint: George slaying the dragon

Days of the Week: Wednesdays or Thursdays

Colors: red, khaki, dark green

Sample Offerings: spiced rum, cigars, spicy meats, rice and beans,
a machete, red *moushwa* (headscarves), military uniforms or
medals, strong black coffee, metal (iron); in my lineage, Badagri
is a native American Lwa and also receives stylized images of
Indians, feathers, stone tools, squash, tobacco and other native-
appropriate foods and gifts in addition to the usual Ogou
offering—many Badagri are African and do not receive these
items (check with your lineage's elders)

Symbols: generals, military officers, swords

Concepts: diplomacy within war, controlled violence, protecting the innocent

Ogou Feray

Nation: Rada (Nago)

Saints: James the Greater, Santiago Matamoros (James on horseback)

Days of the Week: Wednesdays or Thursdays

Colors: red and royal blue

Sample Offerings: rum or *kleren* (and lots of it), cigars, spicy meats, rice and beans, a machete, red *moushwa* (headscarves), military uniforms or medals, strong black coffee, metal (iron)

Symbols: soldiers, freedom fighters, machetes, horses, generals, military officers

Concepts: fighting for what is right, protecting the innocent, masculine force, war and violence

Ogou Balindjo

Nation: Rada (Nago; also part of Met Agwe's *esko*)

Saint: Charles Borromeo (many lineages in Haiti and the Dominican Republic simply use the same image as for Feray)

Days of the Week: Wednesdays or Thursdays

Colors: red and teal or red and green

Sample Offerings: red wine or whiskey, cigars, military uniforms or medals, coffee with whiskey added to it, rice and beans, swords

Symbols: military officers (particularly merchant marines), sailors, sea captains, flags

Concepts: fighting for what is right, protecting the innocent, masculine force, healing through strength, military (and ethical) duty

Legba Petro

Nation: Petro

Saints: Peter (with keys and a rooster), Jude (with fire or a club)

Days of the Week: Mondays or Tuesdays

Colors: red and white or red and black

Sample Offerings: *kleren,* pipe tobacco, spicy bread, mango, rice and beans, red *moushwa* (headscarves), a walking stick or crutch, keys

Symbols: opening the crossroads to do magic

Concepts: as described in Rada Legba but oriented toward the Petro and Kongo spirits

Simbi-Dlo

Nation: Petro (Kongo)

Saints: John the Baptist as a child holding a lamb and a staff (north Haiti), Moses with the Ten Commandments (south Haiti)

Day of the Week: Tuesdays

Colors: white and green

Sample Offerings: cool, clear water; *kleren;* river rocks (smooth stones); grilled pork; images of snakes

Symbols: snakes, water

Concepts: water and the spiritual world, magic, protection

Ezili Danto

Nation: Petro

Saints: *Mater Salvatoris* ("Our Lady of Perpetual Help"); Our Lady of Czechostowa, any "black Virgin" holding a child

Day of the Week: Tuesdays

Colors: red and royal blue or royal blue and gold

Sample Offerings: kleren, pipe tobacco, spicy grilled pork, griot, chicharones (pork rinds), pineapple, mango, papaya, bright flowers, crème de cacao liqueur, strong black coffee or coffee with rum poured in it, black pigs, dolls—particularly baby dolls with dark skin

Symbols: a heart pierced by a dagger, daggers and machetes, the Madonna and Child

Concepts: motherhood, womanhood, the Haitian woman and the necessities of her life

Simbi-Andezo

Nation: Petro (Kongo)

Saints: John the Baptist baptizing Christ (north Haiti), Andrew (various parts of Haiti), Moses with the Ten Commandments (south Haiti)

Day of the Week: Tuesdays

Colors: green and red or teal and red

Sample Offerings: cool, clear water; *kleren;* river rocks (smooth stones); grilled pork; images of snakes; whiskey; ribbons and feathers; seawater

Symbols: snakes, water

Concepts: water and the spiritual world, magic, protection, the ability to be in two worlds at once

Baron Samedi

Nation: Gede

Saints: Gabriel, Expedite

Day of the Week: Fridays

Colors: black, purple, and white

Sample Offerings: *piman*, stale bread, strong black coffee, extremely spicy food, cigarettes, a top hat, sunglasses, an obviously phallic cane (often painted black with white stripes)

Symbols: cemetery crosses, skulls, coffins, bones, top hat, sunglasses, shovels, other grave-digging tools

Concepts: death and the dead, life and fertility, sexual regeneration, children as representatives of the future ("life goes on")

Brav Gede (and all other Gedes)

Nation: Gede

Saints: Gerard Majella, occasionally Martin De Porres

Day of the Week: Fridays

Colors: black, purple, and white

Sample Offerings: *piman*, stale bread, strong black coffee, extremely spicy food, cigarettes, a black or purple hat or a straw hat, sunglasses, an obviously phallic cane (often painted black with white stripes)

Symbols: cemetery crosses, skulls, coffins, bones, hats, sunglasses, shovels, other grave-digging tools

Concepts: death and the dead, life and fertility, sexual regeneration, children as representatives of the future ("life goes on")

Manman Brijit

Nation: Gede

Saints: Rosalia, Helen, Rita in some areas

Day of the Week: Fridays

Colors: black, purple, and white

Sample Offerings: *piman*, stale bread, strong black coffee, extremely spicy food, cigarettes, a hat or bonnet, sunglasses, dried flowers, mirrors

Symbols: cemetery crosses, skulls, coffins, bones, trees

Concepts: death and the dead, life and fertility, sexual regeneration, children as representatives of the future ("life goes on"), protection of one's business as a life-giving mechanism

ʇURTHER READING AND RESOURCES

Books and Print Resources

Haitian Culture and History

Arthur, Charles, and Michael Dash, eds. *Libète: A Haitian Anthology.* Princeton: Markus Wiener Publishers, 1999.

Courlander, Harold. *The Drum and the Hoe: Life and Lore of the Haitian People.* Berkeley, CA: University of California (Berkeley) Press, 1960.

Farmer, Paul. *The Uses of Haiti. Third Edition.* Monroe, ME: Common Courage Press, 2006.

James, C. L. R. *The Black Jacobins: Toussaint L'Ouverture and the San Domingo Revolution.* Second Revised Edition. New York: Vintage Books, 1989.

Jeanty, Edner A., and O. Carl Brown. *Parol Granmoun: 999 Haitian Proverbs in Creole and English.* Pétionville, Haiti: Editions Learning Center, 1996.

Haitian Vodou

Brown, Karen McCarthy. *Mama Lola: A Vodou Priestess in Brooklyn.* Berkeley, CA: University of California Press, 1991.

Cosentino, Donald J. *Sacred Arts of Haitian Vodou.* Los Angeles: UCLA Fowler Museum of Cultural History, 1995.

Davis, Wade. *The Serpent and the Rainbow.* New York: Touchstone, 1997.

———. *Passage of Darkness: The Ethnobiology of the Haitian Zombie.* Chapel Hill, NC: University of North Carolina Press, 1988.

Deren, Maya. *Divine Horsemen: The Living Gods of Haiti.* London: Thames and Hudson, 1953. (Reprinted in many times and forms with a companion film that is available on VHS and DVD.)

Desmangles, Leslie G. *The Faces of the Gods: Vodou and Roman Catholicism in Haiti.* Chapel Hill, NC: University of North Carolina Press, 1992.

Dunham, Katherine. *Island Possessed.* Chicago: University of Chicago Press, 1969.

Filan, Kenaz. *The Haitian Vodou Handbook: Protocols for Riding With the Lwa.* Rochester, VT: Destiny Books, 2007.

Galembo, Phyllis. *Vodou: Visions and Voices of Haiti.* Berkeley, CA: Ten Speed Press, 1998.

Hurbon, Laënnec. *Voodoo: Search for the Spirit.* Lory Frankel, trans. New York: H. N. Abrams, 1995.

Hurston, Zora Neale. *Tell My Horse: Voodoo and Life in Haiti and Jamaica.* New York: Perennial Library, 1990.

Marcelin, Milo. *Mythologie Vodou* (3 volumes, in French). Port-au-Prince: Les Éditions Haitiennes, 1949.

Métraux, Alfred. *Voodoo in Haiti.* New York: Shocken Books, 1972.

Olmos, Margarite Fernandez, and Lizabeth Paravasini-Gebert. *Creole Religions of the Caribbean: An Introduction from Vodou and Santeria to Obeah and Espiritismo.* New York: New York University Press, 2003.

Rigaud, Milo. *Secrets of Voodoo.* San Francisco: City Lights Books, 1985.

Turlington, Shannon. *The Complete Idiot's Guide to Voodoo.* New York: Alpha Books, 2001.

Related Practices

Awolalu, J. Omosade. *Yorùbá Beliefs & Sacrificial Rites.* Brooklyn, NY: Athelia Henrietta Press, 1996.

Filan, Kenaz, and Raven Kaldera. *Drawing Down the Spirits: The Traditions and Techniques of Spirit Possession.* Rochester, VT: Destiny Books, 2009.

Gandolfo, C.M. *Voodoo Ve-Ve's & Talismans and How to Use Them.* Booklet. New Orleans Historic Voodoo Museum, nd.

Glassman, Sallie Anne. *Vodou Visions.* New York: Villard Books, 2000.

González-Wippler, Migene. *Santería: the Religion.* St. Paul, MN: Llewellyn, 1989.

Lampe, H. U. *Famous Voodoo Rituals & Spells: A Voodoo Handbook.* Minneapolis, MN: Marlar Publishing Company, 1974.

Long, Carolyn Morrow. *Spiritual Merchants: Religion, Magic, and Commerce.* Knoxville, TN: University of Tennessee Press, 2001.

Malbrough, Ray. *Hoodoo Mysteries: Folk Magic, Mysticism and Rituals.* St. Paul, MN: Llewellyn, 2003.

Mbiti, John S. *Introduction to African Religion. Second Revised Edition.* 1991, Heineman Educational Books, Ibadan, Nigeria. (also available from Heineman Press, Oxford, England).

Mickaharic, Draja. *A Spiritual Worker's Spell Book.* Philadelphia: Xlibris, 2002.

Pinckney, Roger. *Blue Roots: African-American Folk Magic of the Gullah People.* St. Paul, MN: Llewellyn, 2000.

Riva, Anna. *Voodoo Handbook of Cult Secrets.* Los Angeles: International Imports, 1991.

Voeks, Robert A. *Sacred Leaves of Candomble: African Magic, Medicine, and Religion in Brazil.* Austin, TX: University of Texas Press, 1997.

Yronwode, Catherine. *Hoodoo Herb and Root Magic: A Materia Magica of African-American Conjure.* Forestville, CA: Lucky Mojo Curio Company, 2002.

Online Resources

All websites are provided as resources only. Internet addresses were correct at the time of this publication but may change over time. The author makes no endorsements or claims of ownerships for sites other than her own.

Vodou Practitioners and Clergy

http://www.imamou.org

Sosyete Fòs Fè Yo Wè—This is the official website of my own Vodou *sosyete*. Our name translates roughly as "It is (our) strength that will make them see," and is a line from a Vodou song about Ogou. On this site you will find links to a blog, forums, and other resources about Haitian Vodou and our family. We are a daughter temple of Sosyete La Fraîcheur Belle Fleur Guinea of Long Island, New York, and La Plaine, Haiti; and of its sister-temple Sosyete Sipote Ki Di of Port-au-Prince, Haiti.

http://www.freewebs.com/danbalawedo

Sosyete Danbala Wedo—Mambo Jennifer's website for her Indianapolis-based *sosyete*. Her *sosyete* is a daughter temple of Sosyete La Fraîcheur

Belle Fleur Guinea of Long Island, New York, and La Plaine, Haiti; and of its sister-temple Sosyete Sipote Ki Di of Port-au-Prince, Haiti.

http://www.ezilikonnen.com

Sosyete Gade Nou Leve—Houngan Hector is a *houngan asogwe* in Haitian Vodou, and also an initiate of Dominican Vodou (or "21 Divisiones"), and the *Sansé* and *Espiritismo* traditions of his native Puerto Rico. His website includes information on all of these traditions, as well as a store, and his house is located in southern New Jersey. His *sosyete* is a daughter temple of Sosyete La Fraîcheur Belle Fleur Guinea of Long Island, New York, and La Plaine, Haiti; and of its sister-temple Sosyete Sipote Ki Di of Port-au-Prince, Haiti.

http://blog.vodouboston.com

Houngan Matt's Vodou Blog—Houngan Matt (Houngan Bozanfè Daguimin Minfort) is a *houngan asogwe* with Sosyete Nago, a Jacmel-based Vodou *sosyete* with a satellite house in Boston. His relatively new blog contains thoughtful, well-written essays about Haitian Vodou and serving the Lwa.

http://www.kenazfilan.com

Houngan Coquille du Mer (Kenaz Filan)—Houngan Kenaz is the author of several books about Haitian Vodou and an initiated *houngan si pwen* in a Jacmel-based Vodou *sosyete* with a satellite house in New York.

http://www.kiwimojo.com

Kiwi Mojo (Hounfor du Racine Deesse Dereyal)—Kiwi Mojo is the official website of a Haitian Vodou *sosyete* in New Zealand, under the direction of *houngans asogwe* Liam (Pa Presse Soulage Minfo Edeyo) and Alistair (Pese Verance Soulage Minfo Edeyo). Hounfor du Racine Deesse Dereyal is a daughter house of the Sosyete La Belle Deesse listed below.

http://www.labelledeesse.com

Sosyete La Belle Deesse Dereale—The official website of Belle Deesse, headed by two *mambos* by the same name (mother and daughter) with *peristils* in Pétionville, Haiti, and Quebec, Canada.

http://being.publicradio.org/programs/vodou/index.shtml

Living Vodou/Vodou Brooklyn (Mambo Étoile Brilliante (Mambo Marie Carmel)—Journalist Stephanie Keith interviewed and then recorded Vodou ceremonies at the house of a Brooklyn-based Haitian *mambo* (not my initiatory mother, though they have similar names). In addition to a beautiful picture book of the ceremonies, this website provides podcast and video about what a Vodou ceremony is like, along with additional information about Haitian Vodou.

http://www.vodou.org

The Temple of Yehwe/Le Péristyle de Mariani (Houngan Max Beauvoir)—Currently the chief priest (*ati nasyonal*) of the National Confederation of Haitian Vodouisants (Konfederasyon Nasyonal Vodouizan Ayisien or KVNA) in Haiti, Houngan Max-G. Beauvoir founded his *peristil* near Mariani, Haiti, in 1974, and he is often interviewed for documentaries concerning Vodou in Haiti. The Mariani *peristil* also sponsors the Temple of Yehwe, a 501(c)(3) Vodou organization located in Washington, D.C. His Caribbean Herbalist link at *http://vodou. org/caribherbalist.htm* provides a taxonomy of Haitian herbs and their names in English, Spanish, Kreyòl, and French, along with drawings or photographs where available—this is an extremely useful resource.

http://www.vodoun.com

Vodoun Culture—The late Estelle Manuel (who went *anba dlo* in 2009) is an initiatory daughter of Houngan Max Beauvoir. Her website remains on the Internet as a memorial, and it is filled with information about *veves*, songs, drumbeats, and dances for hundreds of Lwa and their nations. Available in both English and French versions.

http://www.mypapillonvert.com/index.html

Voodoo For Real (Houngan Neite Decimus)—I don't know this Haitian *houngan* personally, but his website is well written, and he lives in Massachusetts. An included video links to an interview with Houngan Neite at *http://www.boldfacers.com/index.cfm?page=profile&profile_id=60.*

http://zantray.html

Zanfan Tradisyon Ayisyen (ZANTRAY, "Children of Haitian Tradition")—Like Houngan Max Beauvoir's KVNA network, ZANTRAY represents practitioners of a non-*asson* Vodou lineage called *Deka or Deka Vodou,* concentrated mostly in the area of Souvenance.

Haitian and Vodou Art

www.haitianart.com

Fine Caribbean Art—A website with gorgeous items created by Haitian painters and artists, both to look at and for sale.

http://www.indigoarts.com/gallery_haiti_main.html

Indigo Gallery: The Haitian Spirit—Gorgeous paintings, sculptures, and traditional sequined Vodou flags are on display on this extensive website from a gallery in Philadelphia.

http://www.amnh.org/exhibitions/vodou

Sacred Arts of Haitian Vodou—The 1988–1999 museum exhibition of the same name, created by the American Museum of Natural History and sent all over the United States in a traveling exhibition, is responsible for bringing many Americans into knowledge of Haitian Vodou and its art and symbolism. (While I was aware of Vodou before 1988, during this exhibit's stay in Chicago at the Field Museum of Natural History, a staff meeting where I met a Haitian drummer and *houngan* began my own journey into the tradition.) This site contains both basic information about Vodou and the items that were displayed during this important exhibition.

Haitian and Vodou Music

http://www.bookmanlit.com/songofthemonth.html

Bookmanlit's Song of the Month—This awesome website has a special page with essays and information on a different Vodou song every month.

http://www.boukmaneksperyans.com

Boukman Eksperyans—Named for Dutty Boukman, the *houngan* of Bwa Kayiman, this Haitian group has been nominated for a Grammy and they tour the United States, Haiti, and the Dominican Republic regularly.

http://www.twitter.com/#!/RAMHaiti

Ramhaiti Richard Morse (RAM)—Named for the abbreviation of Richard Morse's name, RAM is a "Vodou rock" band based in Port-au-Prince, where Richard and his wife own and operate the famous Hotel Oloffson. The band performs live at the Oloffson every Thursday and tours when possible. Richard's personal Twitter feed contains information about the band, as well as his musings about life in Haiti.

http://www.makandal.org

Houngan Frisner's drumming and dance troupe Troupe Makandal (Houngan Frisner Augustin)—Has performed Vodou music and ceremonies all over the world. I have been blessed to hear his drumming and singing at a number of ceremonies, and I can say that seeking out his troupe's recordings or going to see a performance or ceremony they attend is well worth your time. Check out his website for videos and information on a workshop or performance near you.

http://www.toutmizik.com

Tout Mizik ("All Music")—Video collections from Haitian pop artists.

Haitian and Vodou History and Culture

http://www.webster.edu/~corbetre/haiti/haiti.html

Bob Corbett's Haiti Pages—A portal to hundreds of documents and websites collecting information about Haiti and its culture and history, as well as Haitian Vodou. Bob has hosted a Haiti mailing list since 1999 and provides archives to more than 30,000 important conversations.

http://www.bookmanlit.com/home.html

Bookmanlit: Literature for the Bicentennial Generation—A spectacular site with material about Haiti and its history and culture, as well as Haitian Vodou, written by Haitians in the Diaspora.

http://www.hartford-hwp.com/archives/43a/index.html

Haines Brown's Haiti Archives—An extensive and useful collection of Haitian history links and resources.

http://davidco.tripod.com/#haiti

Links on Haiti (David Collesano)—Random links to all kinds of Haitian subjects.

http://www.travelinghaiti.com/history.asp

Traveling Haiti: The History of Haiti—This website contains various useful information about Haiti and Haitian history and culture.

http://windowsonhaiti.com

Windows on Haiti (Guy Antoine)—Forums, links, and information about Haitian art, music, history, and food.

Kreyòl Language Resources

http://www.microsofttranslator.com

Bing Translator—This handy translation tool lets you translate back and forth between Kreyòl and English or any other language. It will also enable you to translate websites or have multilingual chats via the MSN/Windows Live Messenger chat system.

http://www.byki.com/fls/free-haitian-software-download.html?l=haitian%20creole

Byki Flashcards for Haitian Kreyòl—This free download provides a dozen or more lessons in Haitian Kreyòl for Windows or Macintosh, Pocket-PC, or Palm platform computers in the form of cute little flashcards with video and recorded sounds. For a small fee, you can upgrade Byki Express to a deluxe version that includes even more lessons in

Kreyòl. A reasonable, and useful, alternative to expensive Pimsleur or Rosetta Stone programs or tapes.

http://translate.google.com

Google Translator—Another translator like the Bing translator, which permits translation within Gmail and Google itself as well as site translation.

http://www.haitisurf.com/dictionary.shtml

Haiti Surf's Kreyòl Wordlist—A useful and extensive listing of words from Kreyòl to English.

http://www.iadopt.info/kreyol

iAdopt's "Kreyòl Crash Course"—While I'm not sure what I think about the rest of this website (adopting a child from another culture is serious business), the Kreyòl "crash course" on this page is not bad at all.

http://www.kreyol.com/dictionary.html

Kreyol dot com Dictionary—This website has a frustrating interface but a fairly comprehensive English/Kreyòl dictionary and word list.

Vodou Supplies

http://www.legba.biz and *http://www.legbastore.com*

Legba's Crossroads (my website)—Two portals where I offer Vodou supplies and services such as readings and *wanga* to clients.

http://erzulies.com

Erzulie's Authentic Voudou—This New Orleans shop offers both New Orleans and Haitian Vodou products, and they recently released a free "Voodoo app" through their website and the iTunes App Store.

http://www.feyvodou.com/index1.html

Island of Salvation Botanica—Store and website for Mambo Sallie Ann Glassman, who is a *mambo* in Haitian Vodou as well as New Orleans Voodoo.

http://www.luckymojo.com

Lucky Mojo Curio Company—Though Cat Yronwode's store caters mostly to Hoodoo and Rootwork/Conjure workers and clients, some of the items we use in Vodou are also available here. Those who are interested in learning more about African influences in the United States, from Hoodoo to the blues, are encouraged to check out her essays or her herbal Hoodoo classes.

http://www.voodooshop.com

Voodoo Authentica—This shop, located in the New Orleans French Quarter, caters mostly to New Orleans Voodoo but also hosts Haitian Vodou events and provides some Vodou supplies.

Related/Useful Sites

http://www.facebook.com

Facebook—Believe it or not, Facebook is a great place to meet Vodouisants. Many Haitians and others who practice Vodou have taken to congregating on Facebook, using the "Groups" function. Some groups are public, some private, some by invitation only. If you'd like to find some links, consider friending me on Facebook at *http://www.facebook. com/chitatann*, and you'll be able to see a listing of some of the larger groups as part of my Info and Wall pages.

http://www.catholic-forum.com/saints/gallerys.htm

Image Galleries of the Saints—A massive collection of thousands of saints and their images from standard Catholic lithographs and medals. If you can't find a saint in your local Catholic supply store, you can always print one out from here, or just spend hours looking at the beautiful pictures.

http://www.lonelyplanet.com/maps/caribbean/haiti

Lonely Planet: Haiti—The famous travel guide has an interactive website with maps and other information about Haiti.

http://myhoodoospace.net

MyHoodooSpace—MyHoodooSpace is a social network space (powered by the Ning network) organized by Dr. Christos Kioni. It bills itself as "Juju Central for Rootworkers, Eclectic Conjurers, Spiritual Workers and You!" It includes extensive forums, a very busy chatroom, and other benefits. Having your own page on MyHoodooSpace is free.

http://blog.themysticcup.com

The Mystic Cup – a high-quality, thoughtful collection of blogs and resources for various native American and Afro-Caribbean religions, run by practitioners along with guest writers.

http://www.voodoomuseum.com

New Orleans Historic Voodoo Museum—The official museum of Voodoo in New Orleans, in the French Quarter since 1972, has a website complete with blog and store.

http://www.nganga.org

Nganga.org (Dr. Eoghan Ballard)—Tata Eoghan is an initiated priest of Palo, an African Diasporic tradition that comes from Bantu-speaking slaves who landed in Cuba and elsewhere in the Western Hemisphere, including Haiti. His website explains much about Kongo/Bantu traditions, which have tremendous influence on Haitian Vodou's Kongo and Petro rites.

http://www.americancatholic.org/Features/Saints/bydate.aspx

Saint of the Day Calendar—This entire website is useful for saint information, but the "Saint of the Day" comes in handy when planning offerings or ceremonies to the Lwa.

http://www.voodoospiritualtemple.org

Voodoo Spiritual Temple (Priestess Miriam)—The most famous New Orleans Voodoo Temple in the city, directed by Priestess Miriam Chamani. It has a sister house in Russia.

ÎNDEX

–Y–

Yocahu, 51

Yoruba people, 94, 104, 190

–Z–

Zaka (Kouzen Zaka, Azaka
Mede), 38, 53, 92, 103,
135, 142, 169

zemi, 52–53, 81, 88, 112,
186, 195

zetwal, 72

Zobop, 71

zombi/"zombies," 3, 51, 63,
71–74, 121, 124, 193, 195

GET MORE AT LLEWELLYN.COM

Visit us online to browse hundreds of our books and decks, plus sign up to receive our e-newsletters and exclusive online offers.

- • Free tarot readings • Spell-a-Day • Moon phases
- • Recipes, spells, and tips • Blogs • Encyclopedia
- • Author interviews, articles, and upcoming events

GET SOCIAL WITH LLEWELLYN

Find us on

www.Facebook.com/LlewellynBooks

GET BOOKS AT LLEWELLYN

LLEWELLYN ORDERING INFORMATION

 Order online: Visit our website at www.llewellyn.com to select your books and place an order on our secure server.

 Order by phone:
- • Call toll free within the U.S. at 1-877-NEW-WRLD (1-877-639-9753)
- • Call toll free within Canada at 1-866-NEW-WRLD (1-866-639-9753)
- • We accept VISA, MasterCard, American Express and Discover

Order by mail:
Send the full price of your order (MN residents add 6.875% sales tax) in U.S. funds, plus postage and handling to: Llewellyn Worldwide, 2143 Wooddale Drive Woodbury, MN 55125-2989

POSTAGE AND HANDLING

STANDARD (U.S. & Canada):
(Please allow 12 business days)
$30.00 and under, add $4.00.
$30.01 and over, FREE SHIPPING.

INTERNATIONAL ORDERS:
$16.00 for one book, plus $3.00 for each additional book.

Visit us online for more shipping options. Prices subject to change.

FREE CATALOG!

To order, call
1-877-NEW-WRLD
ext. 8236
or visit our website

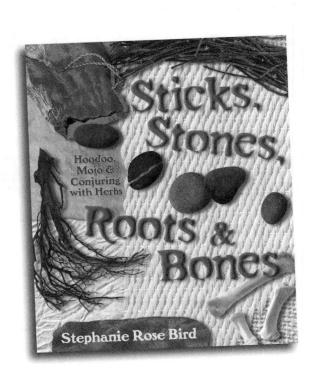

STICKS, STONES, ROOTS & BONES
Hoodoo, Mojo & Conjuring with Herbs
STEPHANIE ROSE BIRD

Learn the art of everyday rootwork in the twenty-first century. Hoodoo is an eclectic blend of African traditions, Native American herbalism, Judeo-Christian ritual, and magical healing. Tracing Hoodoo's magical roots back to West Africa, Stephanie Rose Bird provides a fascinating history of this nature-based healing tradition and gives practical advice for applying Hoodoo magic to everyday life. Learn how sticks, stones, roots, and bones—the basic ingredients in a Hoodoo mojo bag—can be used to bless the home, find a mate, invoke wealth, offer protection, and improve your health and happiness.

978-0-7387-0275-9, 288 pp., 7½ x 9⅛   **$19.99**

A Shaman's True
Story of Indigenous
Witchcraft, Devil's Weed,
and Trance Healing
in Aztec Brujería

the
flying
witches
of veracruz

The Flying Witches of Veracruz
A Shaman's True Story of Indigenous Witchcraft, Devil's Weed, and Trance Healing in Aztec Brujeria
JAMES ENDREDY

Waking up blind in a cave, nearly dead from an evil witch's attack, is merely the beginning of James Endredy's true and utterly gripping adventure with the witches of Veracruz, Mexico. As the apprentice of a powerful curandero (healer), Endredy learns the mystical arts of brujeria, a nearly extinct form of Aztec witchcraft. His perilous training—using dream trance to "fly" and invoking spirits of the underworld—is fraught with spiritual trials. Upon becoming a curandero himself, Endredy takes on real-life cases: battling malevolent witches, healing a young man possessed by an Aztec spirit, rescuing a teenage girl from a Mexican drug cartel, and hunting down a baby-killing vampire witch.

978-0-7387-2756-1, 240 pp., 5³⁄₁₆ x 8 **$14.95**

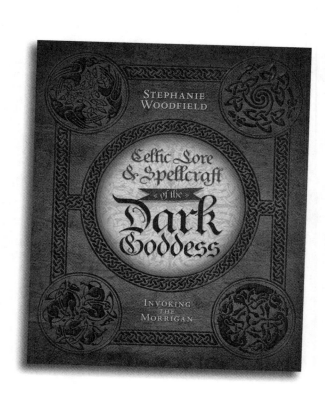

Celtic Lore & Spellcraft of the Dark Goddess
Invoking the Morrigan
Stephanie Woodfield

Experience the life-transforming beauty of Celtic Witchcraft by calling upon the Morrigan—the Celtic embodiment of the victory, strength, and power of the divine feminine.

In this comprehensive and hands-on guide, Stephanie Woodfield invites you to explore the Morrigan's history and origins, mythology, and magic. Discover the hidden lessons and spiritual mysteries of the Dark Goddess as you perform guided pathworkings, rituals, and spells. Draw on the unique energies of her many expressions—her three main aspects of Macha, Anu, and Badb; the legendary Morgan Le Fay; and her other powerful guises.

From shapeshifting and faery magic to summon-ing a lover and creating an Ogham oracle, the dynamic and multifaceted Dark Goddess will bring empowering wisdom and enchantment to your life and spiritual practice.

978-0-7387-2767-7, 432 pp., 7½ x 9⅛   **$21.99**

The Woman Magician
Revisioning Western Metaphysics from a Woman's Perspective and Experience
Brandy Williams

The Woman Magician is a thought-provoking and bold exploration of the Western magical tradition from a female perspective, celebrating the power of women's spirituality and their vital role in the magical community.

Drawing on thirty years of study and personal experience, Brandy Williams reframes magic around women, examining and challenging traditional Western notions of women's bodies, energies, and spiritual needs. She discusses women's roles throughout magic's history, gender issues, and honoring the voice within to live authentically as women and magicians.

Part two features personal and group initiatory rituals based on Egyptian cosmology, created by the Sisters of Seshat, the first all-female magical order since the French Revolution.

978-0-7387-2724-0, 384 pp., 6 x 9 $19.95

To order, call 1-877-NEW-WRLD
Prices subject to change without notice
Order at Llewellyn.com 24 hours a day, 7 days a week!